INSTITUTIONAL INEQUALITY AND THE MOBILIZATION OF THE FAMILY AND MEDICAL LEAVE ACT

How do the rights created by the Family and Medical Leave Act operate in practice in the courts and in the workplace? This empirical study examines how institutions and social practices transform the meaning of these rights to re-create inequality. Workplace rules and norms built around the family wage ideal, the assumption that disability and work are mutually exclusive, and management's historical control over time all constrain opportunities for social change. Yet workers can also mobilize rights as a cultural discourse to change the social meaning of family and medical leave.

Drawing on theoretical frameworks from social constructivism and new institutionalism, this study explains how institutions transform rights to re-create systems of power and inequality but at the same time also provide opportunities for law to change social structure. It provides a fresh look at the perennial debate about law and social change by examining how institutions shape the process of rights mobilization.

Catherine R. Albiston is Professor of Law at the University of California, Berkeley. She is active in the American Sociological Association and the Law and Society Association, serving in several capacities, including Trustee for the Law and Society Association. Her research has been supported by grants from the National Science Foundation and the American Bar Foundation, and she has published widely in peer-reviewed journals and law reviews, including *Law & Society Review* and *Annual Review of Law & Social Sciences*.

CAMBRIDGE STUDIES IN LAW AND SOCIETY

Cambridge Studies in Law and Society aims to publish the best scholarly work on legal discourse and practice in its social and institutional contexts, combining theoretical insights and empirical research.

The fields that it covers are: studies of law in action; the sociology of law; the anthropology of law; cultural studies of law, including the role of legal discourses in social formations; law and economics; law and politics; and studies of governance. The books consider all forms of legal discourse across societies, rather than being limited to lawyers' discourses alone.

The series editors come from a range of disciplines: academic law; socio-legal studies; sociology and anthropology. All have been actively involved in teaching and writing about law in context.

Series Editors

Chris Arup *Monash University, Victoria*

Martin Chanock *La Trobe University, Melbourne*

Pat O'Malley *University of Sydney*

Sally Engle Merry *New York University*

Susan Silbey *Massachusetts Institute of Technology*

Books in the Series

The World Trade Organization Knowledge Agreements
2nd Edition
Christopher Arup

Law and Nature
David Delaney

Constitutionalizing Economic Globalization: Investment Rules and Democracy's Promise
David Schneiderman

Law, Anthropology, and the Constitution of the Social: Making Persons and Things
Edited by Alain Pottage and Martha Mundy

Continued after Index

Institutional Inequality and the Mobilization of the Family and Medical Leave Act

RIGHTS ON LEAVE

Catherine R. Albiston

University of California, Berkeley

CAMBRIDGE UNIVERSITY PRESS
Cambridge, New York, Melbourne, Madrid, Cape Town, Singapore,
São Paulo, Delhi, Dubai, Tokyo, Mexico City

Cambridge University Press
32 Avenue of the Americas, New York, NY 10013-2473, USA

www.cambridge.org
Information on this title: www.cambridge.org/9780521878975

First published 2010

Printed in the United States of America

A catalog record for this publication is available from the British Library.

Library of Congress Cataloging in Publication data
Albiston, Catherine Ruth
 Institutional inequality and the mobilization of the Family and Medical
 Leave Act : rights on leave / Catherine R. Albiston.
  p. cm. – (Cambridge studies in law and society)
 ISBN 978-0-521-87897-5 (hardback)
 1. Parental leave – Law and legislation – United States. 2. Maternity leave –
 Law and legislation – United States. 3. Sick leave – Law and legislation –
 United States. 4. Leave of absence – Law and legislation – United States.
 I. Title. II. Series.
 [DNLM: 1. United States. Family and Medical Leave Act of 1993.]
 KF3531.A95 2010
 344.7301′25763–dc22   2010019218

ISBN 978-0-521-87897-5 Hardback

Contents

Preface

For many years the United States was virtually the only major industrialized country without a family and medical leave policy. Employers could legally fire a worker who needed time off to care for a seriously ill child, parent, or spouse. Employers had wide latitude to fire workers temporarily unable to work because of illnesses or injuries. Employers could legally fire women who needed time off for pregnancy and childbirth if they also denied time off to nonpregnant employees who were unable to work. And, although some employers provided parental leave after the birth of a new child, this discretionary leave was primarily available to professional or management employees and not to the rank and file (Kamerman et al. 1983). In short, national employment policy left many serious family and medical needs unaddressed.

By the end of the twentieth century, significant social changes made difficult choices about managing work, family, and illness more visible and compelling. Stagnating wages and changing gender roles meant more women with children entered the workforce, contributing to a time squeeze for many families (Epstein & Kalleberg 2004; Gornick & Meyers 2003; Jacobs & Gerson 2004; Presser 2003). Increasing divorce rates also left many working women as the sole source of support for their families (Reskin & Padavic 1994). As medical care improved and legal reforms required education for children with disabilities, there were more potential workers with disabilities (Shapiro 1993). As a result, the many ways in which the structure of work conflicted with caring for others or with living with disabilities became more apparent. Research about how workers handled this conflict revealed the ways in which social institutions construct the relationships among work, family, and disability (Hochschild 1989, 1997; Stone 1984). It also documented how the state, by failing to provide for family or medical leave, effectively defined the problem as a private dilemma.

Family policy in the United States has begun to change, however. Since 1993 the federal Family and Medical Leave Act (FMLA) has provided some workers with a legal right of up to 12 weeks of unpaid, job-protected leave for family or medical crises.[1] Both men and women may take leave to care for a sick child, parent, or spouse. Workers may also use FMLA leave for pregnancy disability, and both men and women may take parental leave after the birth of a new child.[2] The statute protects workers who take leave from retaliatory harassment, termination, and discrimination.[3] Perhaps most importantly, FMLA leave is an entitlement for workers; the statute requires employers to provide FMLA leave even if they do not allow time off for any other reason. In other words, the statute leaves employers no discretion to deny qualified workers job-protected leave.

The FMLA represents a significant shift in American employment policy, and it challenges implicit, fundamental assumptions about the nature of work. It rejects unbroken attendance as the measure of a good worker and it takes away some of employers' unilateral control over the schedule of work. It changes the often-gendered division between the public life of employment and the private life of family by forcing work to accommodate family needs on a gender-neutral basis. And by protecting

---

[1] 29 U.S.C. § 2612. Not all workers are covered by the FMLA. Workers who have worked for their employers for less than one year are not eligible for FMLA leave, nor are workers who work for companies with fewer than fifty employees. 29 U.S.C. § 2611.

[2] 29 U.S.C. § 2612.

[3] 29 U.S.C. § 2614, 2615.

the jobs of workers who are temporarily too sick to work, it undermines cultural conceptions of disability and work as mutually exclusive categories. In short, the FMLA not only creates a new benefit for workers, it also challenges entrenched conceptions of what being a good worker means. By attempting to change taken-for-granted workplace practices and norms, the law reconceptualizes the relationships among work, gender, and disability, and creates an opportunity for social change.

But what will this new law mean in practice? FMLA rights are not self-enforcing; to enjoy their benefits, individual rights holders must actively claim or "mobilize" them in the workplace and in the courts. Understanding what FMLA rights will mean requires examining how workers come to comprehend and claim their rights, especially when they encounter conflict over taking leave. In addition, workers do not mobilize their rights in a cultural vacuum. FMLA rights remain embedded within existing power relations, institutions, and culture, including deeply entrenched beliefs and practices associated with work, gender, and disability. Although the FMLA creates an opportunity for restructuring the workplace, what these new rights will mean in practice depends on the ways in which social institutions affect the rights mobilization process.

The existing empirical research paints a complicated and conflicting picture of rights to family and medical leave. Some empirical research indicates that the FMLA has significantly increased unpaid leave coverage for American workers (Han & Waldfogel 2003; Waldfogel 1999a, 2001), although class differences in leave coverage remain because low-wage workers tend to work for smaller employers who are not covered by the Act (Cantor et al. 2001; Gornick & Meyers 2003). Many employers who provided family and medical leave before the FMLA became effective substantially expanded benefits to bring their policies into compliance with the Act (Cantor et al. 2001). More organizations are adopting family-friendly policies in response to legal mandates and growing pressure from their organizational environments (Davis & Kalleberg 2006; Glass & Fujimoto 1995; Goodstein 1994; Guthrie & Roth 1999; Osterman

1995). The vast majority of employers report that leave requirements have not been difficult to implement and have had little or no impact on productivity, profitability, or growth (Cantor et al. 2001; Waldfogel 2001). The available evidence also indicates that employers have not shifted the costs, if any, of leave mandates to women in the form of lower wages or less employment (Baum 2003; Ruhm 1997, 1998; Waldfogel 1999b). In short, most large-scale, policy-oriented studies indicate that the FMLA has substantially increased access to leave with little downside for either employers or employees.

Sociological research about the dynamics of family and medical leave in the context of the workplace, however, tells a somewhat different story. Both experimental and observational research indicate that workers who take leave or use family-friendly policies suffer penalties at work (Allen & Russell 1999; Glass 2004; Hochschild 1997; Jacobsen & Levin 1995; Judiesch & Lyness 1999; Wayne & Cordeiro 2003). Indeed, in a post-FMLA survey, 32 percent of eligible workers who chose not to take leave reported that they opted against taking leave because they feared they might lose their jobs (Cantor et al. 2001). Empirical research regarding disability leaves indicates that employers often deny accommodations in the form of schedule changes even when their own policy and/or the law requires such accommodations (Harlan & Robert 1998). Research also indicates that more powerful workers within organizations, in terms of pay or status, have more family and medical leave options and are more likely to use the options they have (Blair-Loy & Wharton 2002; Harlan & Robert 1998). In addition, managers retain significant control over how these policies are implemented, and in some instances implement them as discretionary benefits rather than as legal mandates (Edelman et al. 1993; Kelly & Kalev 2006).

The research makes clear that cultural norms about gender, work, and family also continue to matter. Despite gender-neutral legal reforms, men are generally less likely than women to take leave (Armenia & Gerstel 2006; Gerstel & McGonagle 1999). Although this pattern may reflect gendered preferences, employers also expect gendered behavior from their employees in terms of taking leave and often resist leaves of more than a few days for male employees (Haas & Hwang 1995; Malin 1993–94; Pleck 1993). Experimental research also indicates that men who took parental leave are perceived to be less likely to help their coworkers, be punctual, work overtime, or have good attendance than men who did not take parental leave, even when performance was held constant (Wayne & Cordeiro 2003). Clearly the social meaning of taking leave is not the same as the entitlement created by the statute. Gendered cultural norms about the appropriate way to manage work and family continue to shape perceptions of leave, and may actively discourage some workers from taking leave.

The research suggests that although the FMLA mandates certain family and medical leave benefits for eligible workers, the reality on the ground may be quite different from the formal policies articulated by the law and by work organizations. Although organizations are adopting family leave policies, it remains an open question whether these policies are merely symbolic or whether they produce substantial changes in workplace practices (Edelman 1992; Meyer & Rowan 1977). Indeed, studies that examine whether workers actually use family-friendly policies suggest that gendered corporate culture, concern about losing a job, and fear of retaliation often discourage workers from mobilizing their rights to leave (Cantor et al. 2001; Fried 1998; Hochschild 1997). This research raises important questions about how systems of power and meaning in the workplace affect whether workers exercise their leave rights.

Questions of power and meaning are particularly salient to the process through which workers mobilize their rights. Like most employment discrimination statutes, the FMLA is enforced primarily through a private right of action that is mobilized by individuals. Of course, the government does litigate some claims, but the vast majority of employment rights claims – in some estimates more than 90 percent – are brought by individual plaintiffs (Burstein & Monaghan 1986). This book draws on interviews with workers who negotiated leaves in the workplace and on content analysis of federal court decisions to analyze what happens when workers attempt to mobilize legal rights that conflict with established practices and expectations about taking time off for family or medical reasons. Although this study focuses on FMLA rights, the larger question is this: Given that individuals attempt to mobilize their rights in some way, how do social institutions affect mobilization and the potential for law to bring about social change?

Understanding how legal reform can enable or constrain social change requires a close examination of legal mobilization in a variety of social contexts. This study does not privilege formal court claims over informal negotiations in the workplace, but instead examines legal mobilization in both locations. The chapters in this volume present a combination of quantitative and qualitative data, as well as a more traditional analysis of judicial reasoning. They draw on interpretive methodological traditions in the social sciences that emphasize the construction of meaning in social interactions. For example, they consider how cultural frameworks that arise from law and other social institutions influence individuals' preferences and perceptions when they decide whether to mobilize their rights. They examine how these same cultural frameworks influence judicial interpretations of FMLA rights. The analysis also considers the ways in which courts' procedural rules shape judicial interpretations of the FMLA that can facilitate or inhibit rights mobilization in the future. Finally, this study addresses how individual mobilization might produce collective results, including how legal rights can help workers connect with one another in the workplace and collectively resist their employers' reluctance to recognize FMLA rights.

The analysis in the chapters that follow explains how deeply ingrained social practices associated with work transform the meaning of FMLA rights and, ironically, help re-create the very inequalities that the FMLA aims to change. Chapter 2 sets the stage with a genealogy of work that highlights how entrenched work norms and practices incorporate, and help reinforce, systems of power and domination. It traces the historical origins of workplace standards regarding time and leave, focusing on how modern time norms embody not only historical struggles for management control of workers, but also social inequalities based on gender and disability. It also examines how social changes in the family and the workforce have eroded the social conditions on which institutionalized work practices rest, even as these practices remain largely the same.

To examine how work as an institution shapes the meaning of employment law, Chapter 3 analyzes how federal courts have interpreted civil rights laws related to work, gender, and disability, including the Americans with Disabilities Act, Title VII, and the FMLA. This analysis pays close attention to the ways in which courts deal with attempts to modify standard work schedules to accommodate pregnancy and disability. Courts rely on established cultural meanings of work and time, rather than on statutory mandates, to resist enforcing changes to institutionalized time standards that disadvantage women and people with disabilities. By relying on cultural, rather than statutory, definitions of work and leave, courts interpret legal rights narrowly and incorporate institutionalized understandings of work into these statutory reforms.

Chapter 4 presents data from in-depth, qualitative interviews with workers who negotiated contested leaves in the workplace but did not take their claims to court. It examines how cultural conceptions of work, gender, and disability inform the attitudes and actions of workers and employers, including how workers decide whether to mobilize their rights and how they understand conflict over leave. The interview data indicate that the meaning of FMLA rights in the workplace varies with both the gender identity of the worker and the reason for taking leave. This variation tracks cultural understandings of women as caretakers and men as breadwinners, and cultural assumptions that disability and work are mutually exclusive. Moreover, these cultural understandings reflect the same institutionalized conceptions of work and time that appear in judicial interpretations of these rights. At the same time, however, these rights provide a framework of meaning within which workers recognize their collective grievances and gain solidarity with one another around issues related to family leave.

Chapter 5 examines mobilization of FMLA rights in the courts, drawing on a content analysis of all FMLA opinions in federal courts that were published in the first five years after the statute was enacted. This analysis focuses on how institutionalized rule-making opportunities in the litigation process restrict opportunities for advocates to create judicial interpretations of the FMLA that are favorable to workers, skewing judicial interpretations of the Act in favor of employers. Despite the theoretical promise of litigation-based strategies for change, these data suggest that formal litigation offers only limited opportunities to generate expansive interpretations of rights.

The final chapter discusses the implications of this study for the American system of enforcing civil rights through private rights of action. It articulates a new institutional framework that focuses on how institutions affect mobilization across both court and noncourt settings. The book concludes by suggesting how the process of rights mobilization, if insufficiently insulated from these institutional influences, can allow deeply entrenched social practices, traditional conceptions of status based on gender and disability, and power to transform legal rights. It also examines how individual rights mobilization in all its forms creates unexpected opportunities for social change.

Acknowledgments

Although this book bears my name as author, it is the product of a long collaborative process with colleagues around the country who have given generously of their time and energy to read drafts, make suggestions, and challenge the ideas developed in this project. It has been my great fortune to participate in several wonderful working groups, all of which contributed immensely to this project. Many thanks to the members of the informal working group organized by Kristin Luker at University of California, Berkeley, all of whom read many very rough drafts of this manuscript. I drafted Chapter 4 while I was a Fellow at the Center for Working Families at Berkeley, and I owe a special debt to the group of scholars there, especially Arlie Hochschild and Barrie Thorne, for their support of this project. Many, many thanks to the members of the Junior Faculty Working Ideas Group (better known as "JWIG") at Berkeley Law for all of your insightful comments, moral support, and terrific suggestions for a title.

This book benefited enormously from numerous discussions with my colleagues at the University of California, Berkeley, and the University of Wisconsin, Madison. I am deeply indebted to Kathy Abrams, Marrianne Constable, Lauren Edelman, Malcolm Feeley, Rosann Greenspan, Angela Harris, Herma Hill Kay, Joan Hollinger, Amy Kapczynski, Linda Krieger, David Lieberman, Goodwin Liu, Kristin Luker, Ali Miller, Melissa Murray, Sarah Song, Eleanor Swift, and Jan Vetter for reading various drafts and providing detailed and insightful comments. Thanks to Chris Edley for providing time and resources to work on this manuscript and for suggesting to me that book projects are never finished, only abandoned. I also owe a debt of gratitude to my colleagues during my time in Madison, including Tonya Brito, Alta

Charo, Jane Collins, Howard Erlanger, Myra Marx Ferree, Bert Kritzer, Stewart Macaulay, Jane Schacter, and Mark Suchman, for their generosity, support, and mentorship.

I have been privileged to discuss this project with law and society scholars around the country, including Shelley Correll, Scott Eliason, Tristin Green, Kaaryn Gustafson, Erin Kelly, Kay Levine, Ann Lucas, Cal Morrill, Robert Nelson, Laura Beth Nielsen, Deborah Rhode, Vicki Schultz, Reva Siegel, Susan Silbey, Robyn Stryker, and Joan Williams. A special thanks to Noah Zatz, who went out of his way to read hundreds of pages of the draft of this manuscript and to give me brilliant comments and suggestions. Thanks also to the anonymous reviewers at Cambridge University Press for their helpful comments, and to my editor, John Berger, for his patience.

A heartfelt thanks to my respondents for their willingness to talk with me and to entrust me with their experiences. I am grateful to them for remembering and sharing with me a difficult time in their lives. My thinking and research about rights and social change also reflect lessons I learned as a public interest attorney. My clients taught me how much strength and courage it takes to claim rights, and how fragile and malleable legal rights can be. I owe them thanks for inspiring this project.

I am grateful for the generous financial support of the National Science Foundation (#SES-0001905) and the Sloan Foundation, which funded my fellowship at the Center for Working Families. Thanks also to Justin Reinheimer and Sandy Levitsky for their excellent research assistance on this project, and to Jane Cavolina for her meticulous copy-editing. Many, many thanks to Anna Lee Allen for her friendship and logistical support.

Finally, I thank my family for their constant support and encouragement while I conducted this research and wrote this book. Many years have passed since I began this project, but throughout them all my husband Marc Melnick has offered his unfailing kindness, support, and encouragement, not to mention countless loads of laundry, dinners, and hours of entertaining children who wondered when mom's book would finally be done. Without him, this project would not have been possible.

1 Institutions, Inequality, and the Mobilization of Rights

FOR THE PAST ONE-HALF CENTURY, INEQUALITY IN EMPLOYMENT has been addressed through antidiscrimination laws that prohibit discrimination on the basis of certain protected categories. These statutes conceive of inequality as the product of individual animus toward traditionally subordinated groups, including those defined by race, gender, and disability. Individual animus is clearly unacceptable, and workplace policies or rules that disproportionately disadvantage workers within a protected class are subject to challenge in some limited circumstances. Courts have also allowed challenges to workplace practices such as subjective decision making that allow animus to operate freely. Institutions, however, are at most marginal concerns for these statutes. In evaluating claims of discrimination, courts examine actions and rules within specific workplaces on a case-by-case basis; they do not consider the industry-wide practices, such as time norms, attendance requirements, or workplace schedules, which largely define work in our culture. Until recently, basic institutional arrangements that make up what we understand to be work have been largely insulated from any meaningful substantive legal reform.

A few laws enacted toward the end of the twentieth-century attempt to address work institutions directly. For example, the Americans with Disabilities Act (ADA) requires workplaces to provide reasonable accommodations to workers with disabilities, including changes to workplace structures and practices. The Family and Medical Leave Act

(FMLA), which is the subject of this study, requires specific modifications of time standards and the schedule of work to allow workers time off for their own illnesses, to care for ill or injured family members, for pregnancy and childbirth, or to care for a new child in the family. These statutes move away from the individual animus model toward an institutional-reform approach to ameliorating inequality. Like their antidiscrimination predecessors, however, these laws tend to treat institutions as structures within a single workplace, focusing on whether a particular employer's attendance policies, schedule requirements, and the like impermissibly affect workers protected by these statutes.

A different way to think about institutions is to view them as cross-workplace, culturally determined beliefs, norms, values, and practices that are self-perpetuating and reinforcing. In this view, institutions are so taken for granted that we rarely view them as changeable choices; instead, they seem to be natural and inevitable background features of our everyday lives. For example, time standards and attendance policies in a particular workplace also connect to broader cultural understandings of work as a full-time, year-round endeavor. In this sense, workplace practices that the ADA and the FMLA attempt to change, such as time norms and attendance requirements, are not just the rules of a particular employer, but instead are a social institution that is reinforced by collective values and beliefs that legitimize and naturalize those practices. In the context of inequality, this self-perpetuating aspect of institutions can create resistance to laws designed to change problematic practices, particularly in a legal regime in which rights are enforced primarily through a private right of action.

The thesis of this book is that, although rights are embedded within social institutions that often constrain social change, rights also operate as social institutions to create unexpected opportunities for change. New legal rights such as the FMLA do not change entrenched practices and meanings overnight. Workers who claim rights to time off must contend with established social practices and norms regarding work, gender, and disability that are antithetical to FMLA rights. These include workplace cultures that presume that women, but not men, prioritize family over work, that disability and work are mutually exclusive, and that any deviation from a standard year-round, full-time work schedule justifies penalties at work. But these cultural systems of meaning are not confined to just one workplace, nor do they affect only the actions of employers who are resistant to new rights. These workplace cultures also affect how workers, families, and friends understand FMLA rights, and they shape how judges interpret FMLA rights when workers mobilize those rights in court. As a result, rights like the FMLA that challenge institutionalized practices regarding work face resistance on multiple fronts: from skeptical courts, from resistant employers, and even from workers themselves, all of whose cognitions and behavior are subtly shaped by the institutions the FMLA was intended to change.

One strand of sociolegal theory suggests that, despite initial resistance from entrenched practices and norms, successful rights mobilization in the courts will eventually legitimize FMLA rights and help change cultural expectations about work and leave. Indeed, law can have an expressive, symbolic effect such that authoritative statements of legal requirements change individuals' normative beliefs and behaviors (Berkowitz & Walker 1967; Galanter 1983; Suchman 1997; Sunstein 1996). But institutional factors come into play here as well. Even when workers go to court, formal procedural rules determine which cases reach adjudication and produce decisions that become precedent. As this study will show, these institutional rules effectively screen out the cases most likely to lead to expansive interpretations of FMLA rights, and in this way constrain the symbolic impact of law.

That legal rights do not translate directly into social change is a long-standing theme in law and society literature. The fact that the law on the books and the law in action are different – and often contradictory – is a familiar story. This study builds on that simple premise by analyzing in detail the process by which institutions play a role in hindering, but also sometimes facilitating, social change through law. It examines not only how legal rights can be weakened, expanded, or even nullified in particular social contexts, but also the ways in which that transformation is connected to larger social institutions. It also contributes to this literature by documenting the process through which interactions in particular social contexts can remake the meaning of institutions from the ground up. It thus speaks to broader questions about the conditions under which legal rights matter, and how cultures of power and inequality reproduce themselves when law operates in particular social settings.

This study lies at the intersection of several areas of law and society scholarship, including the debate about the utility of rights, research about rights mobilization and dispute resolution, and the literature regarding law's relationship to other normative systems. The remainder of this chapter briefly sets out how this project fits within and contributes to these theoretical traditions. A short historical background of the FMLA as a social policy is followed by a discussion locating this study within the ongoing debate about the utility of rights for social change. This discussion also lays out in more detail the institutional context of rights mobilization, by which I mean the entrenched workplace practices and accompanying expectations about law and inequality within which individuals come to understand and claim their rights.

The FMLA and American Family and Disability Policy

The cultural norms, expectations, and institutional arrangements within which FMLA rights are embedded draw their meaning in part from how American social policy historically has dealt with maternity, family, and disability. Although the FMLA is the first American policy dealing with family and medical leave, it is by no means the first maternity policy, nor is it the first disability policy. The FMLA must be understood against the backdrop of earlier policies, which incorporated assumptions about the nature of gender and disability. Accordingly, a brief history of the social policies and civil rights laws that led to the FMLA is useful, particularly considering how these policies construct the meaning of work, gender, and disability.

Historically, family and disability policies have focused on women and people with disabilities as nonworkers rather than as workers, and have presumed that women and people with disabilities should not or could not work. This approach set up a mutually constitutive dichotomy between work on the one hand, and gender and disability on the other. Over time, this dichotomy gave meaning not only to social welfare provision but also to work itself, and constructed cultural understandings of work that implicitly excluded women and people with disabilities.

With regard to gender, that model of work and social life had at its center the family wage ideal, which presumes that the most common and most desirable family configuration is the male breadwinner/stay-at-home housewife model. Family wage ideology treats work as secondary to a woman's primary roles as mother and wife. Work in this rubric is a way for women to pass the time between childhood and marriage, or a means of earning a little "extra" income, but not a lifelong endeavor (Frank & Lipner 1988). Work practices reflected this presumption. Historically, women were commonly fired when they married or became pregnant, and employers justified paying women less than men by pointing to the male breadwinner ideal (Smith 1987). Even though many of these practices are now illegal, the cultural beliefs that support them remain: Women who become mothers still consistently find themselves devalued as workers (Budig & England 2001; Hochschild 1997; Williams 2000). In addition, modern work arrangements are still constructed around an ideal worker/marginalized caregiver model that allocates less desirable and less secure work to those, still primarily women, who meet family obligations (Kalleberg 1995; Kalleberg et al. 2000; Williams 2000).

Family wage ideology permeates the history of American social welfare policy directed toward women, much of which has assumed, and in some instances enforced, the breadwinner/homemaker model. For example, early maternity policy, such as mother's pensions and the Sheppard–Towner Act, focused on supporting women in their roles as mothers, not in their roles as workers (Frank & Lipner 1988; Skocpol 1992). Similarly, early twentieth-century protective labor legislation relied on women's roles as mothers and wives to justify limiting their working hours and banning them from certain occupations (Frank & Lipner 1988; Kessler-Harris 1982). The Depression Era Economy Act enforced the family wage model by requiring married persons to be the first to be discharged from federal employment if their spouses were also government employees, recognizing only one person per couple as a "breadwinner" (Frank & Lipner 1988). Before portions of the Social Security Act were ruled unconstitutional in the 1970s, a wife, but not a husband, could collect survivor benefits upon the death of her working spouse because it was unthinkable that a wife might have provided the primary support for the family.[1] Even modern, facially neutral Social Security provisions still provide greater benefits to a family consisting of a single earner with a stay-at-home spouse than to a dual-earner family, even if the earnings of these two families are exactly the same (Liu 1999). Similarly, nominally gender-neutral New Deal policies tended to direct benefits toward long-term, full-time wage workers and their dependents (Mettler 1998), effectively excluding many women who worked part time, part of the year, or interrupted their work for childbirth and family responsibilities, while benefiting families that conformed to the breadwinner/homemaker ideal. Thus, American social welfare policies reflect and incorporate a deep ambivalence about whether mothers should work outside the home, and this historical ambivalence has helped constitute contemporary cultural frameworks for understanding the relationship between work and gender.

The story with regard to disability, although driven by different social dynamics, is much the same. American social policy has long incorporated a model of work and social life that constructs the meaning of disability in opposition to labor, and assumes that people with disabilities should be excluded from public life. By the twentieth century, it had become taken for granted that people with disabilities were not and

---

[1] See Califano v. Goldfarb, 430 U.S. 199 (1977).

should not be active participants in public life, including work (Stone 1984). Social policies tended to focus on residential homes and special schools that segregated people with disabilities from society, allowing the structure of the public world to develop without accommodating a range of abilities (Finkelstein 1980). Typically, social policies either institutionalized people with disabilities or provided for support outside of employment; these policies rarely aimed to remove barriers to participation in public life or work (Oliver 1990). Indeed, the very concept of "disability" evolved in part as an attempt to enforce participation in the labor market by identifying (and narrowly defining) the category of persons legitimately unable to work (Stone 1984); the inability to work continues to define eligibility for disability benefits today. In short, both work practices and disability policies developed around the assumption that disability and work were mutually exclusive.

Although their experiences differ, women and people with disabilities share a common historical relationship to the institution of work and its influence on the provision of social welfare benefits, and as a result, both gender and disability draw their meaning from a particular, historically contingent conception of work that was structured to exclude women and people with disabilities. Institutions such as work draw their power in part from how their assumptions and practices come to be naturalized and accepted as just the way things are, as unchangeable reality. Once these work structures and practices came to seem natural and inevitable, barriers to work for women who care for families and for people with disabilities appear to arise from their personal circumstances, rather than from the structure of work. For example, needing time off to care for sick family members becomes a "private" problem, and accommodations for disabilities become "special treatment." Consequently, statutes like the FMLA that change the structure of work run up against deeply entrenched beliefs about who can and should work, about which features of work are necessary, and about what it would mean to adjust workplaces to make them more accessible to a broader range of potential workers.

Of course, the FMLA is not the first attempt to challenge the notion that it is natural and normal that women and people with disabilities not work. Both the women's movement and the disabilities movement of the 1970s and 1980s attempted to debunk assumptions that the gendered and able-bodied structure of work was natural and inevitable. Feminist advocates brought successful constitutional challenges to social policies that presumed that women were never the family breadwinner and always the dependent spouse. They also undermined assumptions that women, but not men, were responsible for caring for children and the home. Similarly, disability activists argued against a medical model of disability that located impairment solely within the individual. Instead, they articulated a civil rights model of disability that focused on removing environmental constraints that create barriers for some individuals, and therefore socially construct them as disabled (Drimmer 1993). Partly in response to these social movements, Congress enacted legislation protecting both women and people with disabilities in their roles as workers, including Title VII of the Civil Rights Act of 1964, Title I of the ADA, and most recently the FMLA.

Although these statutes explicitly recognize the status of women and people with disabilities as workers, Title VII and the ADA provide employment protections on the basis of identities – gender and disability – which historically have been constructed in opposition to work. Rights claimants under these statutes have struggled to prove that they were excluded from work because of their identity, rather than for neutral reasons justified by taken-for-granted work structures, especially when accommodations based on time are at issue. For example, courts have held that although employers may not fire a woman simply because she becomes pregnant, Title VII does not require employers to restructure work to provide time off for pregnancy and childbirth. Title I of the ADA requires workplaces to provide reasonable accommodations to disabilities, and it has produced some changes in workplace structures, most notably removing physical barriers such as the lack of ramps or inaccessible bathrooms (Engel & Munger 1996; Harlan & Robert 1998).

Despite this accommodation mandate, however, ADA claimants have had little success obtaining changes to the schedule of work to allow for absences because of illnesses or medical treatment, even though schedule adjustments are far less expensive than changes to physical structures (Harlan & Robert 1998). Work's institutionalized time norms have remained largely impervious to legal challenge because, although these statutes now formally require protections based on these identities, the social meaning of these identities, particularly in relation to work, remain the same.

The FMLA followed these legal attempts to challenge work practices that exclude women and people with disability, and can be seen as part of the civil rights attempt to denaturalize the implicit relationships among work, gender, and disability. But the FMLA also marks a sea change in American family and disability policy because it is the first such legislation to focus primarily on the features of work itself rather than on the identity of the workers it protects. By modifying work's structure directly, the FMLA does more than simply regulate work practices; it disrupts assumptions that disability and work are mutually exclusive, and that the normative worker is an always-healthy, always-ready individual free from any caretaking responsibilities for others. For this reason, the Act promises to make explicit the web of mutually constitutive meanings among work, gender, and disability, and to bring about reform. Yet, compared to the voluminous literature on both Title VII and the ADA, relatively little analysis addresses the courts' interpretations of the FMLA's structural reforms or how these reforms operate in practice.

Although the FMLA offers a new paradigm for restructuring work, there is some question whether this legislation can successfully restructure the deeply entrenched social relationships between work and family (Dowd 1989; Kittay 1995). For example, the FMLA requires workers to work at least twenty-five hours per week to qualify for its benefits.[2] Ironically, given the perception that the FMLA is primarily directed at

---

[2] 29 U.S.C. § 2611(2).

women, this requirement disproportionately excludes women because they often work part time to accommodate their caretaking responsibilities (Williams 2000). Also, because men generally earn more than women, unpaid leave creates an incentive for women rather than men to take time off to minimize the families' loss of income, at least in two-parent families. This dynamic reinforces traditional arrangements in which responsibility for care falls primarily on women (Dowd 1989).

Inequalities based on class and disability also affect the FMLA's practical meaning. For example, the FMLA applies only to workplaces with fifty or more employees; this excludes half the workforce (Kittay 1995).[3] The fifty-employee threshold excludes seasonal laborers and workers who cannot find full-time work, as well as workers with physical or mental impairments that prevent them from working full time. It also excludes most domestic workers, home health care providers, and child-care workers, all positions typically held by low-wage working women. Although the FMLA does protect low-wage workers' jobs when leave is unavoidable, that leave is unpaid. Accordingly, some feminists argue the FMLA disproportionately benefits wealthier families that can afford unpaid leave (Kittay 1995).

These are significant limitations, but it is important not to lose sight of how the FMLA challenges institutionalized oppositions between work and gender or disability on a cultural as well as practical level. The FMLA's gender-neutral parental leave provisions help undermine the traditional division of labor in the family by allowing both men and women to take parental leave. The Act challenges the ideal of the always-healthy, always-ready worker because it allows temporarily ill or injured workers to take job-protected leave. In legal terms, the FMLA is important because it brings together two disparate standards of legal theory, one addressing maternity leave and pregnancy, and a second addressing the relationship between work and disability. To these it adds a third dimension, the recognition for the first time that workers need to

---

[3] 29 U.S.C. § 2611(4).

care for their family members in times of crisis. What remains to be seen is how these rights play out as workers mobilize them in the courts and in the workplace.

Rights Mobilization and Social Change

Although these new rights to leave seem to change the relationships among work, gender, and disability, can statutory rights like the FMLA change social practices and beliefs? This is an important question in light of research that indicates that legislative and judicial reforms have produced little lasting improvement in the social and economic circumstances of the disadvantaged (Rosenberg 1991). Answering this question requires some conception of the processes involved in social change through rights, the obstacles to change, and the opportunities for change that legal reforms present. Empirical research in this area documents some limits to rights-based reforms, but it also offers sophisticated accounts of how law produces change when it interacts with other systems of meaning.

Much of the research in this area focuses on rights mobilization, which has been defined in many ways. For example, Black (1973) defines mobilization narrowly as "the process by which a legal system acquires its cases," but this definition is too limited. Courts provide an obvious forum for legal mobilization, but individuals can mobilize law by referencing legal rules and norms in more informal ways. Lempert (1976) offers a broader definition of mobilization as "the process by which legal norms are involved to regulate behavior," a useful definition that can encompass more informal venues for claiming rights. Building on this definition, for purposes of this study the process of invoking legal norms includes the subjective framing of social events as legal disputes – "naming, blaming, and claiming" – including recognizing that one has legal rights as well as formally asserting those rights in a dispute (Felstiner, Abel, & Sarat 1981). Legal mobilization can also take place outside the context of a dispute when, for example, a worker takes protected leave under the FMLA without incident. Finally, mobilization includes invoking legal norms as categories of meaning to shape perceptions and social interactions (Ewick & Silbey 1998, 2003).

This broader definition of mobilization extends beyond court actions and remedies as the primary measures of the effects of law to include subtle changes in social meaning that may result from mobilization (Burstein 1991; Burstein & Monaghan 1986; Rosenberg 1991). In the American legal system, instrumental mechanisms of social change such as imposing sanctions on violators, providing remedies to wronged parties, and using the threat of penalties to induce compliance are important. These mechanisms of change, however, do not fully capture how rights mobilization in its broad, constitutive sense delegitimizes conduct previously accepted as normal and natural, undermines institutionalized understandings of social life, and names new roles and statuses (Engel 1993; Engel & Munger 1996; McCann 2006; Sarat & Kearns 1993; Williams 1991). Of course constitutive processes are constrained by the categories of social meaning available for interpretation, many of which are constructed by law (Bumiller 1987, 1988). Nevertheless, social actors retain some agency to make use of legal discourse in creative ways (Sewell 1992). Actors can deploy legal concepts and meanings to shape behavior, frame expectations, name previously unrecognized harms, and articulate alternative interpretations of social events (Lempert 1998). Along these lines, Galanter (1983) describes social change as an "enculturation" process in which law "affects us primarily through communication of symbols – by providing threats, promises, models, persuasion, legitimacy, stigma, and so on." In this view, rights can be mobilized, or "evoked to affect behavior," to construct social meaning as well as to impose sanctions.

Even within this more nuanced understanding of mobilization and social change, there are competing perspectives about the utility of rights as a social change strategy. What is often termed the "myth of rights" approach tends to be skeptical of the value of rights. In this view, although rights litigation allows individuals to influence policy without the need for coalition building, individual litigation also undermines collective action by narrowing issues and atomizing collective grievances (McCann 1986; Scheingold 1974). Critics also contend that courts lack the institutional authority to implement radical reform (Chayes 1976; Rosenberg 1991; Scheingold 1974). They note that legal victories can easily be dismantled without a sustained and coordinated effort toward reform (Handler 1978), and that relying on rights may merely reinforce and legitimize a legal system that masks inequality (Freeman 1982, 1998; Tushnet 1984). Critics also argue that opponents of rights claimants retain strategic advantages even within a formally neutral legal system (Galanter 1974). These perspectives raise serious questions about any direct connection between rights mobilization and meaningful social change.

A second perspective, which I call the "symbolic/strategic" perspective, offers a more optimistic evaluation of rights mobilization and social change (McCann 1994; Scheingold 1974). In this view, rights mobilization can change social meanings and understandings even when litigation strategies do not result in favorable legal rulings. For example, McCann's (1994) study of the equal pay movement finds that advocates mobilize law to attract media attention, to create an issue around which to organize a movement, and to publicly embarrass employers into changing pay scales. Other scholars note that even apart from collective action, rights provide individuals with symbolic recognition of personhood and dignity, and that rights shape how we understand our identities and the social interactions of everyday life (Engel 1993; Engel & Munger 1996, 2003; Williams 1991). These studies, which track the interpretive turn in social science, focus on how law affects the way individuals understand particular behaviors and institutions (Hiley et al. 1991; Scheppele 1994).

One should not make too much of the differences between these perspectives; many scholars recognize both views by acknowledging the advantages and disadvantages of rights strategies (see, e.g., Scheingold 1974). More generally, the rights debate is not so much about whether

Table 1.1. *A Typology of Rights Mobilization Research*

	Forum	
Agent	Court	Noncourt
Collective	Landmark impact litigation	Social movements
Individual	Individual legal actions	Informal mobilization and everyday life

rights matter, but in what ways and under what conditions rights mobilization might bring about social change (Table 1.1). Although the empirical research on these questions varies across level of analysis, organizational context, and doctrinal area of law, it can be roughly organized within a two-fold typology. One dimension of this typology differentiates between collective action and individual claims, while the other dimension distinguishes between court and noncourt forums for mobilizing rights.

Many important studies of rights mobilization focus on litigation, official legal institutions and actors, and collective action (Burstein 1991; Burstein & Monaghan 1986; McCann 1986, 1994; Rosenberg 1991). These studies vary in their conclusions about the utility of rights strategies and the conditions under which they are effective. Rosenberg (1991) concludes that rights litigation strategies are seldom successful without support from other actors and institutions, and that these strategies drain resources from potentially more effective political strategies. In contrast, Burstein (1991) finds that individual plaintiffs gain some form of success in a significant percentage of employment actions in court, and that public interest and government participation in those claims improved the likelihood of success. McCann (1994) finds that court litigation can lead to significant out-of-court benefits for social movements, including media attention, leverage in negotiations, and a symbolic cause to draw participants to the movement, even when the underlying legal action is ultimately unsuccessful. Although these studies offer nuanced understandings of what Galanter calls "the radiating effects of courts," for the most part they do not examine in detail how social institutions influence the construction of social meaning by the courts, instead focusing on how actors respond to and make use of court rulings and litigation more generally.

Other studies focus on extra-legal, nonsocial movement contexts for mobilization and social change, reflecting a growing interest in decentering law and legality to study law in everyday locations such as workplaces, neighborhoods, and schools (Ellickson 1986, 1991; Engel & Munger 1996, 2003; Ewick & Silbey 1992, 1995, 1998, 2003; Marshall 1998, 2003; McCann 2006; Nielsen 2000, 2004; Quinn 2000). Studies in this vein, which fit into the individual, noncourt section of the above typology, often posit that individual, microlevel mobilization creates opportunities to change the meaning of social relationships and identities (Engel & Munger 1996, 2003; Minow 1987; Williams 1991). Research on framing and mobilization suggests that in some instances, even informal rights mobilization can become a catalyst for collective action by putting in motion a framing process that reinterprets individual problems as part of a larger system of power and control (Snow et al. 1986). Studying the process of naming, blaming, and claiming in informal settings also yields some insight into why so few people who have potential grievances choose to mobilize their rights (Bumiller 1987. 1988; Felstiner et al. 1981; Miller & Sarat 1981; Tucker 1993). Along these lines, researchers are increasingly attentive to the ways in which rights and other social frameworks structure social discourse and interactions, sometimes in unintended and unexpected ways.

Findings from studies in this line of research vary in their optimism about whether legal rights can produce social change (Bumiller 1987, 1988; Engel & Munger 1996, 2003; Ewick & Silbey 1998, 2003; Marshall 2003, 2005; Morgan 1999; Quinn 2000). Engle & Munger (1996, 2003) found that law operates as a social discourse to change social perceptions and behavior – even absent any overt conflict – by changing the meaning of disability in the workplace and in society more generally.

In contrast, Bumiller (1988) found that some potential civil rights claimants choose not to pursue rights claims because they do not want to take on a victim identity, indicating that antidiscrimination laws create social meanings that suppress mobilization. Still other studies indicate that local norms against claiming can discourage mobilization and displace rights (Macaulay 1963; Ellickson 1986, 1991; Quinn 2000), and that organizational processes can deflect potential rights claims in the workplace (Edelman et al. 1993; Marshall 2005).

Although they break new ground in understanding microlevel interactions that relate to rights mobilization, these studies leave many questions unanswered. How do social frameworks of meaning operate across different levels of analysis in the rights mobilization process? To what extent are local forms of resistance to rights connected to broader institutions? What are the mechanisms through which law influences how actors understand their experiences and evaluate their options for acting? When law is not the only normative system influencing this process, how do rights interact with these other normative frameworks? Although researchers in this area acknowledge that legal rights are only part of a larger cultural "'tool kit' of symbols, stories, rituals and world views" that people use to make sense of the social world and to solve different kinds of problems (Swidler 1986:273), often law and other norms are treated as an either/or proposition: Either social relationships are organized according to law, or there is "order without law" (Ellickson 1991; see also Macaulay 1963). Less is known about how legal and other frameworks for social ordering interact with and construct one another in an ongoing dialog, even though this process may be a prime location for the incubation of social change (Sewell 1992).

This last point raises interesting questions about how everyday attempts to mobilize rights connect to larger structures of social organization, power, and inequality. Existing microlevel interpretive studies suggest that systems of meaning other than legal discourse can suppress mobilization or transform the meaning of rights in particular social settings (Ellickson 1991; Macaulay 1963; Edelman et al. 1993; Morgan

1999; Quinn 2000). For the most part, however, these studies do not connect local, contingent practices and norms to larger social institutions. Few scholars have examined how the process of meaning creation in the courts relates to (or differs from) the construction of meaning in more informal settings, or how these settings reinforce one another. Treating meaning as merely locally produced and context dependent, however, may overlook how broader systems of power and control reproduce themselves in the everyday interactions that frame the meaning of rights.

The Institutional Context of Rights Mobilization

To connect the diverse methods and locations for rights mobilization to larger patterns of social organization, this study develops the concept of *institutional inequality*, and relates that concept to rights mobilization and social change. By institutional inequality, I mean the ways in which institutions incorporate and perpetuate historically contingent social practices that define certain identities as subordinate to others. This concept takes into account how the objects of legal reforms designed to address these inequalities also influence the process of social change through law.

Institutional inequality is not the same as the more familiar concept of institutional discrimination. The latter term describes how structural conditions in workplaces facilitate conduct and decision making driven by bias against protected groups (Bagenstos 2006). Institutional discrimination perspectives focus on how workplace structures can be changed to guard against subtle or unconscious bias (Green 2003; Lawrence 1987; Sturm 2001), and these perspectives investigate which workplace practices and structures best alleviate persistent inequalities at work (Kalev et al. 2006). These approaches assume that individual animus or unconscious bias persists and must be guarded against, but they generally pay little attention to the origins of those biases.

Institutional inequality is also different from perspectives that view some workplace structures as gendered or able bodied (Acker 1990;

MacKinnon 1987). These approaches often argue that to eradicate inequality, laws must require that workplace structures accommodate the needs of certain protected groups. Examples include arguments that workplaces should accommodate workers with disabilities, or that workplaces should accommodate normal pregnancies by providing time off for childbirth and recovery. Although these approaches are closer to the concept of institutional inequality than are theories of individual animus, they nevertheless tend to reify the meaning of protected identities and to invite objections that the law should not require special treatment of some groups. These perspectives generally do not consider how workplace structures subtly construct the meaning of protected identities in ways that reflect historical patterns of inequality long since rejected as illegitimate.

In contrast, the concept of institutional inequality operates at a more societal and socially constructed level of analysis than these other perspectives. Institutional inequality posits that taken-for-granted workplace practices produce inequality because they recreate the social conditions that reinforce particular, historically contingent conceptions of gender or disability, even in the absence of individual animus. This approach draws on an historical analysis of institutionalization to explain how workplace practices came to be taken for granted, and the ways in which the contemporary meaning of those practices reflects the social conditions that accompanied their historical development (Jepperson 1991). In this view, institutions are important foci of study, not because they encourage or limit the operation of unconscious bias, but because they generate subtle social processes that perpetuate the subordination of historically disadvantaged groups and create resistance to legal reforms that were designed to benefit those groups.

Institutional inequality lies at the intersection of social constructionism and new institutionalist theories in sociology and sociolegal studies. Social constructionism focuses on uncovering the ways in which individuals participate in the collective construction of their perceived reality, emphasizing the reciprocal relation of structure and agency in social life

(Giddens 1984; Sewell 1992). In this view, social structure is the institutionalized outcome of past actions – rules or schemas that develop as the product of social behavior and also the medium through which social action occurs (Scott 1995; Sewell 1992). Social structure consists of the routine daily practices of social agents and the collective meaning we give to those practices that leads us to recognize them as legitimate and to conform our behavior to them (Giddens 1984; Krieger 2000; Lopez 1999–2000). Social constructivism contends that the social structure we perceive to be natural, objective, and external is generated through an ongoing, dynamic process in which people act on shared interpretations of the social world and does not exist apart from those interactions (Berger & Luckman 1967). Institutions are a major focus of study for social constructivism, which seeks to understand how social phenomenon come into being and become institutionalized or taken for granted.

By building on social constructivism, the concept of institutional inequality also offers a theory of social change. Social constructivist theorists argue that social transformation can occur through innovative use of cultural schemas to reinterpret meanings and to enact social practices in new ways (Sewell 1992; Swidler 1986). Opportunities for transformation arise as agents respond to conflicting and overlapping interpretations of social events, sometimes transposing systems of meaning developed in one context to another (Sewell 1992). Change is possible because although these webs of meaning shape behavior, they do not absolutely determine human action; actors retain the agency to make creative use of the meaning systems that shape and recreate social life (Sewell 1992). Because institutions actively construct the meaning of identities such as gender or disability on an ongoing basis, reforming institutions can change not only workplace practices, but also the social meaning of those identities.

New institutionalism builds on social constructionist ideas by examining how institutions affect organizational behavior. Neo-institutional perspectives emphasize the role of symbolic systems, cultural scripts, and cognitive frameworks in shaping organizational structures like workplace policies and practices. They posit that organizational features reflect not only technical demands and resource dependencies, but also rules, beliefs, and conventions operating in the social and political environment, whether or not those environmental factors produce organizational practices that are practical or efficient (Powell 2007; Powell & DiMaggio 1991). Rather than viewing structures and practices as organization-specific decisions, these theories see structures as the product of the wider social environment.

In contrast to rational choice theories, which tend to focus on individual choices and preferences, new institutionalism views human behavior as shaped and channeled by institutions. In this conception, institutions are much more than a particular hospital, workplace, or university; they are interorganizational cognitive and normative frameworks that both structure and give meaning to human interaction (Scott 1995). Institutionalization is a historical, path-dependent process such that choices made early in the existence of an institution tend to continue throughout the institution's development and reflect the social context of the institution at the time of its origin (Powell 2007). Once established, institutions encourage and reinforce behaviors consistent with themselves, which can also mean reinforcing behavior that reflects a now by-gone social era.

Studies of institutionalization, or the process through which social patterns become taken for granted, examine the mechanisms that reinforce the prevailing social order. These include coercive forces, such as law, as well as more diffuse normative processes that affect what practices and behaviors are understood to be morally authorized or obligatory and cognitive processes that involve shared interpretive frames through which the meaning of those practices is understood (Powell 2007). Some of these studies also examine how cross-cutting institutional pressures relate to the process of institutional and organizational change (Powell 2007). Recent work along these lines emphasizes the role of political opportunities and cultural frames, which are forms of power that shape the ways in which ideas and interpretations come to be accepted or rejected (Schneiberg & Soule 2005).

Drawing on social constructivist and new institutionalist theories, institutional inequality posits that workplace inequality results in part from how workplace policies and practices reflect and recreate the social relations that existed at their origin. Several important principles flow from this conception. First, inequality can be the product of impersonal institutional forces as well as individual animus. Second, structural context is no longer a neutral background to workplace interactions but instead an active part of the perpetuation of inequality. Third, social constructionism suggests that the identities protected by antidiscrimination law and the institutions the law attempts to reform, both of which appear to be objective components of the social world, in fact are constructed through ongoing social interactions and determined in part by each other. This last point helps bring into focus the relationship between protected identities and institutions, including the ways in which institutions give meaning to those identities, and, in the process, help perpetuate inequality.

This study examines the role of law, and, in particular, the mobilization of law in our civil rights society in overcoming institutional inequality in the workplace. It asks how social institutions shape the rights mobilization process across a range of social locations including both the courts and the workplace. How does rights mobilization operate within a set of institutionalized practices and beliefs that create and constrain opportunities for social change? How might institutions influence the social construction of meaning in nonlegal settings to displace or transform rights? How do institutions shape actors' interpretations of their experiences, as well as their preferences about claiming their rights? How do the overlapping and sometimes conflicting institutions of law and the workplace create opportunities for social change?

New institutionalist perspectives offer different ways to theorize how institutions shape the process of rights mobilization. Some perspectives focus on how the cognitive and normative frameworks that make up institutions can also reshape the meaning of law in particular social settings (Edelman et al. 1993; Heimer 1999; Nelson & Bridges 1999). In this view, institutions are important for understanding rights mobilization because they give rise to cognitive frameworks that actors use to interpret and respond to social events, including events that are potentially legally actionable. Institutions provide ready-made templates for categorizing and understanding social behavior in the workplace as natural and normal, or problematic and illegal, and thus affect whether individuals name wrongs, blame responsible parties, or claim their legal rights. Often legally mandated changes to formal structures can have difficulty penetrating these relationships and expectations. To the extent that established practices and norms embody relationships of inequality and power, as they often do, institutions also help legitimize and maintain those systems of domination even in the face of legal reforms (Bourdieu 1977; Foucault 1979; Sewell 1992).

Multiple normative and cognitive institutions operate in the context of the FMLA, including established conventions and beliefs associated with work, notions of traditional family relationships and responsibilities, and cultural conceptions of disability. The cognitive and normative frameworks that make up workplace time norms lie at the center of these three institutions. For example, full-time, year-round work schedules organize productive activities around an always-ready worker free from conflicting responsibilities. As a result, workers who deviate from that standard schedule seem at first blush to be problematic: "shirking" when workers use more than a few days of sick leave, or "not committed" when parents miss work to care for sick children. Although these interpretations seem to be about how good workers should behave, those normative judgments reflect deeply entrenched beliefs about the mutually exclusive nature of work and disability, and the appropriate roles of men and women in the family. This study examines how these institutions shape the way courts, employers, and workers understand the meaning of family and medical leave when these rights are mobilized in the courts and in the workplace. In some instances, these taken-for-granted work conventions around time norms create resistance to FMLA rights. At the same time, rights to leave time provide an alternative interpretive framework in which time off for family or medical reasons is legitimate. In this way, rights institutionalize new schemas for interpreting the meaning of time off from work, and workers create opportunities for destabilizing social structures when they draw on law to make sense of their workplace experiences.

A second strand of new institutionalist theory focuses on how formal rules or institutional arrangements (such as political structures or market conventions) shape processes and policy outcomes (see Scott 1995). To the extent that courts transform social understandings through symbolic and expressive transmission of social meaning, it is important to understand how the institutional processes that give rise to formal judicial interpretations of rights shape the substance of those interpretations. This study examines how formal institutions in the legal system, such as precedent, stare decisis, and adversarial control of the litigation process shape rule-making opportunities in employment litigation to affect how courts define the meaning of the FMLA. Drawing on analysis of the universe of federal court opinions interpreting the FMLA in the five years after its enactment, this study show that courts' formal institutional rules shape judicial interpretations of the FMLA in ways that limit the potential for social change.

Of course, informal negotiations in the workplace and formal court decisions are not unrelated. Workers may be able to mobilize rights discourse to their advantage in creative ways, but legal interpretations and legislative enactments constrain the discourse available for mobilization. Although not every legal victory requires a formal lawsuit, benefits obtained through informal workplace negotiations are largely invisible to courts and litigants in future cases. In addition, the same social institutions that shape workplace experiences – such as conventions about work, traditional family relationships, and cultural conceptions of disability – also shape how courts understand and interpret the FMLA.

For these reasons, understanding how the FMLA operates in both the courts and the workplace provides a much richer and complete picture of rights mobilization and social change. The conclusion of this book analyzes how these different processes of mobilization are related and discusses the implications of institutions for the processes of social change that operate at these diverse levels.

2 The Social Institution of Work

THE FAMILY AND MEDICAL LEAVE ACT (FMLA) REPRESENTS a significant change in family and disability policies, but these rights do not operate in a social vacuum. FMLA rights interact with informal norms, expectations, and practices that comprise modern workplaces. Some of these practices have become so taken-for-granted that it is hard for employers, courts, and even workers to imagine work being organized in any other way. Civil rights laws like the FMLA that set out to change established work practices often face resistance from the customs and informal expectations that constitute work. Even recognizing this resistance can be difficult because existing arrangements seem so natural, normal, and inevitable that they appear to be unchangeable reality, rather than workplace conventions.

A brief genealogy of work as a social institution can make the source of this resistance more visible and understandable (Dreyfus & Rabinow 1983; Foucault 1979). The purpose of genealogy is to investigate social categories such as work to uncover the historical struggles and events that give them shape and meaning (Dreyfus & Rabinow 1983). This analysis focuses on uncovering the relations of power embodied in the social practices and expectations that comprise work, especially on how standardized work practices relate to particular conceptions of gender and disability. Genealogy reveals that work, gender, and disability are not ahistorical or unchanging categories. It exposes how these concepts are socially constructed and give meaning to one another. In particular, historically contingent conceptions of disability and motherhood inform entrenched work practices, such as rigid full-time schedules and stingy leave policies, which the FMLA is intended to change. Modern work forms reflect how disability came to be defined in reference to wage labor as the inability to work, rather than as the presence of a particular impairment. In addition, modern work forms derived structure and meaning from ideologies about women's traditional roles as caretakers and homemakers as well as from men's status as independent breadwinners with primary authority within the family.

The social conditions that gave rise to standard work practices and expectations have begun to change, but work as an institution tends to persist and endure. Institutionalize work standards persist because constituencies have developed a stake in existing arrangements and because social life has been structured around these arrangements, which have become the invisible and uninterrogated background guidelines for everyday interactions. More generally, institutions mediate what rights mean in particular social settings. For example, courts often interpret civil rights laws so that they are consistent with institutionalized work practices even when those laws were specifically intended to reform those practices. In addition, informal practices and beliefs institutionalized in modern workplaces shape the pragmatic meaning of FMLA rights by influencing how employers respond to requests for leave and how workers think about mobilizing their rights to leave.

The FMLA undermines workplace practices regarding time off by making leave an entitlement rather than a management prerogative. It restructures the current boundary between work and private life by mandating time off for childbirth, family care responsibilities, and illness or injury. Yet legal reforms may have little effect on the ground because they have difficulty penetrating the practices and beliefs that constitute work as an institution. Existing workplace practices and the beliefs that support them are not merely local customs or the products of a specific workplace culture. Resistance to change, both in the courts and in the workplace, is linked to broader social institutions and dynamics of power that reflect historically contingent understandings of disability, gender, and work. Documenting these sources of resistance can help us to understand the subtle power dynamics in these situations, and to identify potential mechanisms of change.

Work as a Social Institution

In sociological terms, an institution is more than just a hospital, firm, or university. It is a set of complementary social practices and meanings that form taken-for-granted background rules that shape social life (Berger & Luckman 1967; Jepperson 1991; Krieger 2000; Lopez 1999–2000). Philip Selznick (1967: 44), one of the earliest institutionalist sociologists, defines the concept "institution" in this way:

> In sociology the term "institution" may refer to a group or a social practice, to the Republican party or to the secret ballot. This ambiguity is more apparent than real. Whether it be a group or practice, a social form becomes institutionalized as, through a process of social growth and adaptation, it takes on a distinctive character, competence, or function and becomes charged with meaning as a vehicle of group identity or a receptacle of vested interests.

An institution need not have a brick and mortar manifestation, and can be as varied as marriage, wage labor, the vacation, the 40-hour work week, or even Tuesday (Jepperson 1991).

New institutionalist perspectives in sociology draw on social constructivist theories of social organization to elaborate the concept of institution (Scott 1995; Suchman & Edelman 1996). In this view, institutions have a number of distinctive characteristics. First, institutions can be both normative and cognitive (Jepperson 1991; Scott 1995; Suchman & Edelman 1996). They are normative in the sense that they not only describe the way various social activities are typically done, but also how they come to be seen as the accepted way things should be done. People come to believe that institutionalized practices are correct, fair, and appropriate – in short, normal (Suchman 1997). Institutions can also be cognitive, in the sense that choices shaped by institutions cease to be a matter of conscious thought. For example, Tuesday is a socially constructed institution rather than a natural phenomenon, but we do not ordinarily consciously decide each day whether we should act as if it is Tuesday (or Friday or Sunday). Institutions consist of tacitly agreed-upon practices, routines, and scripts – such as Tuesday – that shape behavior and give meaning to social life such that compliance with these background rules is largely unconscious and routine (Suchman 1997; Suchman & Edelman 1996; Zucker 1991).[1] These mental templates cut down on conscious decisions, which facilitates cognitive efficiency but also implicitly constrains the available choices.[2]

Second, new institutionalists contend that institutions are the product of a social process over time through which human beings construct patterns of conduct and interaction (Berger & Luckman 1967):

> Institutions further imply historicity and control. Reciprocal typifications of actions are built up in the course of a shared history. They cannot be created instantaneously. Institutions always have a history, of which they are the products. It is impossible to understand an institution adequately without an understanding of the historical process in which it was produced. Institutions also, by the very fact of their existence, control human conduct by setting up predefined patterns of conduct, which channel it in one direction as against the many other directions that would be theoretically possible. (Berger and Luckman 1967: 54–55)

---

[1] Some understandings of institutions, primarily economic ones, posit that they are maintained and reinforced through a subtle system of rewards and punishments meted out for compliance with or violation of informal norms (see Scott 1992). In contrast, sociological theories tend to adopt more normative or cognitive explanations (Scott 1992; Suchman & Edelman 1996). Even those institutional accounts that focus on coercive factors, however, often emphasize how legitimacy is one of the many rewards organizations seek (Suchman & Edelman 1996).

[2] Jepperson (1991: 146) rightly points out that "[i]nstitutions are not just constraint structures; all institutions simultaneously empower and control." They facilitate social interaction and arguably coordination by making behavior predictable,

Institutionalization is an historical process through which these patterns come to be perceived as objective features of the external world and recede into the background of everyday life. What were once emerging patterns of conduct, initially viewed by participants as nothing more than an ad hoc consensus, become expected behavior and seem natural and inevitable.

Berger and Luckman are careful to distinguish institutional control from rational action in response to specific rewards or punishments. They note that "this controlling character is inherent in institutionalization as such, prior to or apart from any mechanisms of sanctions specifically set up to support an institution" (Berger & Luckman 1967: 55). Actors no longer perceive these patterns to be a conscious and changeable agreement, but simply the way things are, and, therefore, compliance with these patterns is automatic, rather than a calculated response to reward or punishment. Institutions come to be just "how these things are done," and "[a]ll institutions appear in the same way, as given, unalterable and self-evident" (Berger & Luckman 1967: 59).

> An institutional world, then, is experienced as an objective reality. It has a history that antedates the individual's birth and is not accessible to his biographical recollection. It was there before he was born, and it will be there after his death. This history itself, as the tradition of the existing institutions, has the character of objectivity. (Berger & Luckman 1967: 60)

In this way, social practices become objectified; they seem to exist apart from their human participants and they shape human actors' understanding of themselves and of the social world.

Third, new institutionalists view institutions as both social and socially constructed. Institutions consist of shared social understandings that cut across organizational and group boundaries. They are "both

patterned, and routine. This structure comes at a cost, however, because it also constrains the forms of social organization or behavior that are theoretically possible. Also, because power plays a role in which behavioral patterns become institutionalized, those constraints may benefit some groups within society more than others.

supraorganizational patterns of activity through which humans conduct their material life in time and space, and symbolic systems through which they categorize that activity and infuse it with meaning."[3] Social actors must recognize and comply with institutions to get along in the social world, as others expect them to behave in a manner consistent with shared social understandings. For example, one cannot very well act as if Tuesday did not exist because the rest of the social world will continue to assume that it does, attending work and school, refusing to deliver the Sunday paper, and the like. Once institutions become taken-for-granted, they invisibly structure social life in ways that reinforce and recreate themselves (Berger & Luckman 1967; Jepperson 1991). Everyday social interactions that conform to institutions generate regular patterns of behavior that support the existing social structure. As Sewell (1993: 3) notes, in this perspective, social structure means "the tendency of patterns of relations to be reproduced, even when actors engaging in the relations are unaware of the patterns or do not desire their reproduction." Although institutions may seem real, objective, and autonomous, they do not exist apart from these social interactions that continually recreate them. An institution's socially constructed nature is largely invisible, however, because the social practices associated with it have become routine, rationalized, and taken-for-granted.

This is not to say that social institutions absolutely determine social behavior. Social institutions can be more or less institutionalized, and more or less taken-for-granted or infused with values (Jepperson 1991; Selznick 1969; Zucker 1991). A social practice can be institutionalized even if some people do not follow that social practice. Deviations from institutionalized practices generally require conscious action and explanation, whereas institutionalized practices are taken-for-granted (Jepperson 1991), and deviations often are perceived as a threat to the institution (Knight & Ensminger 1998).

---

[3] Roger Friedland & Robert R. Alford. *Bringing Society Back In: Symbols, Practices and Institutional Contradictions, in* THE NEW INSTITUTIONALISM IN ORGANIZATIONAL ANALYSIS 232, 232 (Walter W. Powell & Paul J. DiMaggio eds., 1991).

It can be difficult to imagine how social change comes about once social practices become institutionalized. Yet institutions are variable and changeable (Jepperson 1991; Sewell 1992). When the social conditions that gave rise to and supported those institutions start to erode, institutions can be destabilized and vulnerable to challenge. If underlying social conditions change, institutions can develop contradictions with their environments, with other institutions, or with underlying social behavior (Jepperson 1991). Institutions then become ineffective or even dysfunctional, and, as a result, the contradictions between institutionalized assumptions and existing social conditions become more visible (Berger & Luckman 1967; Jepperson 1991). Some theorists contend that when these contradictions become apparent, human agents "can (or are forced to) improvise or innovate in structurally shaped ways that significantly reconfigure the very structures that constituted them" (Sewell 1992: 5). In this way, the dialectic between individual agency and the social patterns that help to (re)create those institutions becomes a mechanism through which institutions, and therefore society, can be transformed (Giddens 1984; Sewell 1992). Human action thus has the potential to change institutions, even when agency is constrained and shaped by those institutions.

Work can be understood as a social institution within this theoretical framework. The concept of work includes both taken-for-granted social practices and a web of social meanings, norms, and implicit expectancies about objective reality that form a background template for everyday life (Krieger 2000). Work incorporates standardized patterns of conduct through which productive activities take place. These routines channel work practices in a particular direction compared to other theoretically possible ways of organizing productive activities. The institution of work embodies normative judgments about how production should be organized and about the social meaning of working (and of not working). These social practices and the belief systems that underlie them constrain individuals' choices; by acting within those constraints, individuals reinforce and reproduce work as a social institution. Nevertheless, what we understand as work is not an objective reality, but was created through an historical process and is maintained by ongoing social interaction. Consequently, the social processes that continually recreate work may also provide a mechanism through which work can be transformed.

Inequality and the Characteristics of the Social Institution of Work

Many of the characteristics of work that seem natural, normal, and inevitable involve practices regarding time and employer control. For example, if we are asked to imagine work, our mental image is likely to include certain features such as permanent, uninterrupted year-round labor, or a standard 40-hour work week on a five-day schedule. We usually expect employers to control work schedules and to control the way productive activities are organized and performed. Many jobs deviate from this standard, but we mark those deviations by referencing (and thus reinforcing) the institutional norm. We speak of "part-time" work, "night shifts," or "working for oneself." Indeed, some forms of labor outside this rubric are not considered work at all, such as unpaid labor in the home. Employers that offer jobs that conform to implicit work standards need not specify that they do, but advertisements for positions that deviate from these standards usually state so explicitly, such as part-time or weekend work.

Institutionalized work practices embody normative judgments about how production should be organized and about the social meaning of working (and of not working). In American society, work lies at the intersection of ideologies about the capitalist economy and market, meritocracy, and economic independence as a safeguard against political tyranny (Fraser & Gordon 1994; Lipset 1996; Reich 1964; Weber 1930). These interlocking systems of meaning reinforce and justify existing work conventions. Because work is considered central to social and civic life, departures from the institutionalized features of work can provoke normative backlash, reflecting the social meanings of working and non-working. For example, workers are considered "productive members of society" and nonworkers are viewed as "slackers." Normative judgments may also follow distinctions between standard work that fits institutionalized expectations and nonstandard work that does not. For example, potential employers view intermittent work histories as a troubling lack of commitment to work, and women who work in the home (as opposed to at home) are devalued as "just housewives."

Although a variety of work patterns are possible, workers who depart from institutionalized time norms pay a stiff price (Epstein et al. 1998; Ferber & Waldfogel May 1998; Gornick & Meyers 2003; Kalleberg 1995; Kalleberg et al. 2000). For example, part-time workers, defined as those who work less than 35 hours per week, receive far less compensation than full-time workers, even on a pro-rata basis (Gornick & Meyers 2003; Kalleberg 1995) – part-time workers earn only about 60 percent of what full-time workers make among workers paid on an hourly basis (Kalleberg 1995; Kalleberg et al. 2000). Annually, part-time workers make much less than full-time workers on a pro-rata basis, even controlling for age, education, race, organizational size, occupational prestige, tenure with the organization, and whether the worker holds a supervisory position (Kalleberg 1995). In addition, these workers are often laid off before full-time workers regardless of seniority (Williams 2000).

Workers with nonstandard jobs forfeit other benefits as well. The degree to which work is associated with notions of citizenship in American society is evident in the way many social welfare benefits, which T. H. Marshall calls social citizenship rights, are attached to work (Marshall 1965). In the United States, many of these benefits are provided though private employment, rather than by the state, and they most often accompany employment that conforms to work's standard institutionalized features. For example, part-time workers are significantly less likely to receive fringe benefits such as medical insurance, dental care, life insurance, and paid sick leave (Kalleberg 1995; Kalleberg et al. 2000). They are also less likely to receive benefits such as flexible hours, private retirement or pension plans, and alternative forms of compensation such as stock or cash bonuses (Kalleberg 1995; Kalleberg et al. 2000). Even to the extent that the American state does provide social citizenship rights such as pensions or unemployment insurance, the beneficiaries of those rights tend to be long-term, full-time wage earners or their dependents (Mettler 1998; Nelson 1990).

Like many social institutions, work reflects and reinforces existing relations of inequality, subtly allocating social citizenship rights as well as social recognition along gendered and able-bodied dimensions. Feminist scholars have long recognized how work's institutionalized time norms assume an implicitly gendered worker. Year-round, full-time labor away from home without interruption is difficult to combine with childbirth, childcare, or care of elderly or ill family members, all of which are responsibilities that traditionally fall to women (Fineman 1994; Hochschild 1997; MacKinnon 1987, 1989; Okin 1989; Williams 2000). Women often work part time to accommodate these caretaking responsibilities, and disproportionately bear the losses that flow from deviating from standard work practices. Institutionalized work schedules are built for independent workers without family care responsibilities, and assume that full-time workers with children will be partnered with full-time caretakers for those children (Okin 1989; Pateman 1988). As a result, work-time norms implicitly incorporate women's traditional family roles in a way that shapes gender by encouraging – indeed, producing – a gendered division of labor within the family.

Disability scholars also have recognized how the institutionalized features of work segregate people with disabilities into nonstandard – and, therefore, often less secure – forms of work (Finkelstein 1980; Oliver 1990). Recent social models of disability note that institutionalized work schedules presume that workers can work full time without periodic interruption. Devaluing nonstandard labor also tends to disadvantage workers who have disabilities that limit when and how much they can work. Social models of disability reject how individualistic, medical models locate barriers to work within the individual, rather than in the socially constructed features of their environment (Oliver 1990). Instead, the social models of disability that underlie civil rights legislation focus on

how the interplay between impairments and the social context marginal-
izes people with impairments in the labor force (Drimmer 1993; United
States Commission on Civil Rights September 1983). From this perspective, blind individuals are disabled not because they cannot see, but
because their environment does not provide Braille signs, audible cues
for crossing the street, or easily navigated, hazard-free environments.

No matter how socially constructed they may be, conventional work
practices have significant consequences for the economic and social
status of women and people with disabilities. Although, theoretically,
work could be organized in many ways, most desirable and well-paid
jobs incorporate dominant time norms around full-time, uninterrupted
labor. Those who cannot meet this standard, like women with childcare
responsibilities or people whose disabilities limit their work schedules,
have diminished employment options. Moreover, because social citizenship rights, independence, merit, and cultural status are all associated with long-term, full-time wage labor, marginalization in the labor
market often means social marginalization as well. Because a particular standard of work has become pervasive, differential treatment of
nonstandard workers seems unproblematic, natural, and fair. Taken-for-
granted work practices and the beliefs that support them thus become a
means for legitimizing institutionalized inequality.

A Genealogy of the Institution of Work: Modernity
and Transformation

The social institution of work is both a product and an embodiment of
history. The features of work are not only determined by the inherent
requirements of production, but also reflect work's historical development. In the American context, this history includes the transition to
modern production and a capitalist economy, the bureaucratization of
work practices, and the role of the state in these social transformations.
Work also reflects the cultural ideologies that shaped these periods of
transformation, particularly the ways in which wage labor came to be

defined in opposition to motherhood and disability. A genealogy of work that focuses on these themes reveals the historically contingent nature of work practices, and shows how those practices incorporate complex relationships of power and inequality that are built around particular conceptions of gender and disability. This genealogical approach to the historical development of work departs from typical histories in that it focuses on the development of social categories and meanings, rather than the chronological unfolding of events. As a result, the following historical analysis is organized thematically, rather than chronologically, to reveal the historical sources of meaning for modern social institutions.

A vast historical literature explores the transition from preindustrial to industrial production in England and the United States from the eighteenth through the early twentieth centuries. Details of this shift, such as when and how much of a transformation took place, are highly contested, but broad generalizations are possible about two key themes: First, this historical period produced a fundamental reorganization of productive activities as society moved away from household economies toward entrepreneurial enterprises and centralized industrial production based on wage labor; second, this transformation was accompanied by a gendered division of labor, in which men performed wage labor outside the home and women performed the "residual" tasks of childcare and housekeeping in the home without pay.

In addition to discussing these material changes, most accounts document how cultural ideologies shaped the way this transformation was understood, noting how these same ideologies continue to give meaning to work practices today. For example, the time discipline of standardize wage labor in industrial settings came to define not only what work was, but also what work should be to justify workers' claims to independence and citizenship (Fraser & Gordon 1994). Similarly, modern expectations about management prerogatives, such as unilateral employer control over timing of work and the production process, are the result of historical struggles between capitalists and workers to define what work means (Edwards 1979; Jacoby 1985; Montgomery 1976; 1987). The origins of time norms and employer control are buried in this history, yet are essential to understanding modern conflicts over time, work, and leave.

The Reorganization of Production

Typically, historical interpretations of the eighteenth- and nineteenth-century reorganization of production emphasize the displacement of work from the household to the workplace, as well as the increasing rationalization, centralization, and specialization of work. In these accounts, preindustrial productive activities occurred within a self-contained household economy. Work, household upkeep, and childcare were all part of an undifferentiated process that took place primarily within the home. Work patterns in the household economy followed the production of goods and services for family consumption, and reflected natural rhythms, determined by the seasons, weather, or the worker's inclination. Accordingly, work could proceed in fits and starts, be interwoven with childcare responsibilities, and be performed at any pace (Cott 1977; Thompson 1967).

In these interpretations, industrialization moved productive activities from the household to a workplace based on a wage-labor system. This shift created two separate spheres of activity: the workplace, which was seen as economic in nature, and the home, which was viewed as noneconomic (Boydston 1990; Skocpol 1992). Wage labor outside the home became more visible and more important with the rise of cash markets, land scarcity, and modern work practices (Boydston 1990; Cott 1977). Although women performed significant wage labor by doing piecework in the home or even by working in factory settings, nonwage labor such as cooking, cleaning, and childcare continued to consume married women's time and to disadvantage them in the labor market (Hareven 1982; Kessler-Harris 1982). Although many women worked because of economic necessity, their labor force participation was constrained by segregated labor markets, protective legislation that limited their ability to work, and social norms that situated women's primary responsibilities in the home rather than the workplace (Kessler-Harris 1982). Over time, the (noneconomic) home sphere was perceived to be the primary location of women's labor, while men's labor came to be located in the (economic) workplace.

The distinction between work and home gradually deepened with industrialization, because household activities continued to be task oriented in sharp contrast to the time discipline of the factory clock (Cott 1977; Thompson 1967). For example, E. P. Thompson (1967), in his classic article on time and work, argued that a preindustrial task orientation toward work focused on the task to be performed, not the pace of performance. Task-oriented work made less of a distinction between activities of work and life, and followed natural rhythms dictated by the characteristics of tasks, like ploughing, which fluctuated with the season or weather. Thompson notes that preindustrial work typically proceeded in irregular patterns, such as alternating bouts of intense labor and idleness. Irregular working patterns also incorporated many traditional holidays and fairs, including a tradition of idleness on St. Monday.

In contrast, time became currency within the industrial wage system. Workers began to make sharp distinctions between time belonging to their employer and their own time, and employers used the regular rhythms of machinery, the time sheet, and time keepers to enforce time discipline. Some workers (particularly skilled workers who were in demand) resisted the time discipline of machine-driven factory production by frequently quitting and changing jobs, in this way approximating task orientation in a time-oriented industry controlled by employers (Jacoby 1985). But Thompson argues that, although workers initially resisted time-discipline and wage systems, over time they came to contest only the amount of time required for work. Through the wholesale reorganization of productive activities, time discipline came to be institutionalized.

The first generation of factory workers were taught by their masters the importance of time; the second generation formed their short-time committees in the ten-hour movement; the third generation struck for overtime or time-and-a-half. They had accepted the categories of their employers and learned to fight back within them. They had learned their lesson, that time is money, only too well. (Thompson 1967: 86)

Thus, as productive activities moved into rationalized workplaces based on regular work patterns controlled by the clock, time, and not task, came to define work.

Nevertheless, the transition to modern work practices was neither easy nor uniform and the move toward time discipline was uneven (Hareven 1982; Montgomery 1976; Whipp 1987). Even at the end of the nineteenth century, other ways of organizing work continued to exist alongside time-disciplined, employer-controlled labor. For example, as late as the 1920s, work hours for potters in the British ceramics industry varied so widely that there was no standard working day (Whipp 1987). In other instances, manufacturers simply provided raw materials and agreed to a price for the finished product; the workers collectively decided who to hire, how to train them, and how to pay themselves (Jacoby 1985; Montgomery 1976).

Standardization did not come without conflict, and several historical accounts focus on how the transition to modern forms of production created problems of coordination and control for employers (Edwards 1979; Jacoby 1985; Montgomery 1976). Most accounts trace the origin of the 8-hour day and employers' authority over the organization of work, as well as other institutionalized work practices, back to this early struggle for control (Edwards 1979; Jacoby 1985; Kessler-Harris 1982; Montgomery 1976). During this period, employers tried various strategies to extract the most labor power from workers, many of which focused on standardizing work, thereby narrowing the diversity of work practices that persisted after industrialization (Edwards 1979; Gordon et al. 1982; Jacoby 1985). Employers also used machines and scientific management techniques such as time standards, which removed workers' control over how long particular tasks took, to speed up production and solidify employer control (Edwards 1979; Gordon et al. 1982).

In this way, the decisions about the pace and structure of the labor process slowly came to be management prerogatives rather than decisions made by workers, and time standards came to define the production process.

The distinction between time discipline and task orientation is closely related to a second theme in this literature, the increasing division of labor between the sexes. The separation of home and work, time discipline, and the introduction of factory production set work and recreation in opposition to one another (Smith-Rosenberg 1985). Women became associated with private space in the home rather than the public industrial workplace, with task-oriented rather than time-discipline labor, and, increasingly, with domesticity (Smith-Rosenberg 1985; Welter 1966). As many scholars have noted, however, this conception of domesticity was not so much an accurate description of emerging patterns of gendered labor, but was touted as a morally appropriate arrangement that flowed from the nature of women and men (Skocpol 1992; Welter 1966). In fact, many women worked for wages during this transition, and single women as well as men transitioned from work at home to work in factories, for example, as factory girls in textile mills (Hareven 1982; Kessler-Harris 1982). Women, however, generally filled unskilled jobs, were paid very low wages, and received little help from labor unions, who viewed them as competition for scarce work for their predominantly male members (Hareven 1982; Kessler-Harris 1982). As the cult of domesticity took hold in the broader culture, work for women was increasingly seen not as a career or a vocation, but as a temporary interlude before marriage and motherhood, or as an unfortunate necessity resulting from poverty or the death of a spouse (Kessler-Harris 1982). Through practice and meaning, the division of labor based on gender became institutionalized in a new structure of a family wage for men and, at best, low wage, unskilled, temporary labor for women if they worked outside the home at all (Kessler-Harris 1982).

Ideologies regarding citizenship also shaped the transition from preindustrial to industrial economies and became entwined with this gendered division of labor. For example, early American ideals of democratic citizenship emphasized ownership of property to bolster economic self-reliance as a defense against tyranny (Fraser & Gordon 1994; Reich 1964). But as working-class men began to demand electoral and civil rights based on their wages rather than on property, wage labor became associated with independence and citizenship, and exclusion from wage labor came to imply dependency (Fraser & Gordon 1994). As social meanings became attached to industrial ways of organizing work, particularly long-term, full-time wage labor outside the home, working at home and part-time wage labor, once central to the idea of self-sufficiency, became devalued (Valenze 1995).

Modern time norms have their roots deep in the reorganization of production in the transition to modernity. During this social transformation, these norms helped to privilege certain ways of organizing work and to devalue others, even when multiple forms of productive labor took place side by side. Norms of standardized, full-time wage labor outside the home eventually came to define work itself. In this way, the transition to modernity not only constructed new forms of working, but also attached new meanings to full-time wage labor that eclipsed work done in other forms and in other places. Even today, this valorization of full-time wage labor outside the home reinforces existing work practices and evokes deep commitments to those practices.

The Legal Construction of Time Standards and Employer Control

How did law contribute to the transformation of work? During this historical transition, conceptions of employment as a free contract between employer and worker replaced customary means of regulating working conditions, and the legal relationship of contract, rather than ascriptive status or relationships, became the center of social organization (Horwitz 1977; Maine 1986). The contours of the employment relationship did not spring fully formed from the transition to industrial production, however; courts interpreted what these new relationships would mean (Orren 1991; Steinfeld 1991). Courts did more than enforce employment contracts in a new economy; they also constructed and gave meaning to the new social relationship of wage labor.

Courts generally enforced contractual bargains in favor of employers' interests and solidified control over the production process (Horwitz 1977; Orren 1991; Sellers 1992; Tomlins 1993). Over time, courts resolved initial ambiguities regarding employer control and employer discretion by ruling that the contractual exchange of a wage for work included not only the worker's labor power, but also his submission to the employer's authority (Tomlins 1993). Courts relied upon traditional class-based doctrines of master/servant to require submission, consistently recognizing employers' unilateral power to change the conditions of employment and rejecting workers' attempts to change or control their working environment (Orren 1991; Tomlins 1993). In this way, courts reinforced free contract as the ideology of wage labor while simultaneously interpreting the employment relationship to include relationships of authority and control that previously had been part of the traditional, class-based, master/servant relationship (Orren 1991; Tomlins 1993).

By enforcing the authority of employers in all employment relationships rather than only those traditionally associated with servitude, the law remade the meaning of work.

> These changes underwrote an employer's right and capacity, *simply as an employer contracting for the performance of services*, to exert the magisterial power of management, discipline, and control over others. During the first half of the nineteenth century, indeed, the exercise of power became decisive in determining whether relations of employment between two parties existed. To the courts, exerting power over another became a routine feature of what they recognized employment to mean as a legal relationship. (Tomlins 1993: 230–31)

These meanings underpin current work practices, including management prerogatives to control the timing and structure of production (Tomlins 1993). Once again, what was once a hotly contested question of the nature of the employment relationship has now become simply the ways things are.

Later legal developments also helped to install the 40-hour, five-day work week as the standard for wage labor. After making little progress in negotiations for shorter hours for anyone other than skilled workers, labor and reformers turned to legislative strategies to limit working hours, but met opposition in the courts, which consistently overturned regulation of working hours by relying on free contract principles (Hunnicutt 1988; Kessler-Harris 1982; Roediger & Foner 1989; Sellers 1992; Skocpol 1992; Whaples 1990). The paradigmatic example is *Lochner v. New York*, in which the Supreme Court struck down a New York law that limited bakers' hours to ten per day as "an illegal interference with the rights of individuals to make contracts."[4] Although three years later the Court upheld an Oregon law limiting the hours of working women in *Muller v. Oregon*,[5] it distinguished *Lochner* by relying on women's dependent status and roles within the family, setting women apart from wage laborers even when the Court considered them in their status as workers (Fraser & Gordon 1994). The famous Brandeis brief in *Muller* justified state regulation of working hours by focusing on women's traditional childbearing and childrearing roles, as well as their frailty (Kessler-Harris 1982; Skocpol 1992). The successful reformers in *Muller* used these gender-specific arguments to undercut free contract ideology, but in the process, full-time work became even more closely associated with men. In this way, the law constructed women as dependent wives and mothers even when they worked, a pattern that persisted well into the twentieth century.

The battle over time continued as shorter-hours legislation at the state level spread rapidly after *Muller* (Skocpol 1992). By 1933, in the early years of the Great Depression, national legislation limiting the work week to 30 hours seemed almost certain to be enacted as a temporary work-sharing provision to combat unemployment (Hunnicutt 1988). Faced with stiff and growing opposition from business interests that feared that

---

[4] Lochner v. New York, 198 U.S. 45, 61–62 (1905).
[5] Muller v. Oregon, 208 U.S. 412 (1908).

these restrictions would become permanent, President Roosevelt fought off this legislation with alternative proposals to decrease unemployment, including production limits, massive public works programs, and measures to promote consumption (Hunnicutt 1988). To undermine calls for shorter-hours legislation, businesses adopted their own time standards through industry-negotiated codes under the National Recovery Act. Hunnicutt (1988: 178) notes that "[o]ver 90 percent of NRA codes set hours at 40 a week or longer at a time when the actual average workweek in American industry was well under 36 hours." In the end, the Fair Labor Standards Act eventually set a much weaker federal standard work week of 40 hours that was riddled with exceptions and that allowed longer hours if overtime was paid (Hunnicutt 1988).

These historical developments teach that what now seems natural and inevitable were at one time contested elements of the employment relationship. The transition to a wage-labor economy, during which the scope of management prerogatives and the meaning of employment might have been reimagined, instead saw courts interpret the employment relationship to include the traditional privileges of control and authority associated with servitude. Even the later institutionalization of the 40-hour work week – an apparent victory for labor – staved off what had been a steady decline in weekly hours over decades and avoided restrictive legislation that would have limited work schedules even more (Hunnicutt 1988).

Institutionalizing Inequality

This brief genealogy of work suggests how institutionalized work practices embody the outcome of a series of protracted struggles over time, control, and the very meaning of work. This genealogy is incomplete, however. Although conventional historical accounts trace the transition to modern forms of production, they give insufficient attention to how implicit conceptions of gender and disability became embedded in work practices and the meaning of work. Alternative interpretations suggest that work practices and the beliefs that support them developed in opposition to historically and socially contingent conceptions of gender and disability, and incorporated the social inequalities that attach to these categories.

Gender

Conventional historical interpretations argue that gendered work practices and a gendered division of labor within the family are by-products of moving work from home to industrialized settings. In this view, modern work structures conform to male life patterns because, after industrialization, men performed work – meaning wage labor – and women performed "residual," nonwork life activities such as caring for children in the home. Accordingly, because work no longer took place in the household, women no longer worked in addition to their residual household tasks.[6] But this interpretation accepts modern understandings of work as given, and then applies them to historical analysis without interrogating how the meaning of work itself has changed over time. It takes for granted that work consists only of those activities that moved from the home to industrial workplaces, and assumes that the tasks left behind were residual or supplementary nonwork. As other historical accounts have shown, understandings of labor performed in the home as "residual" or "supplementary" are themselves historically and socially contingent, constructed by social and political responses to changing production patterns (Boydston 1990; Deacon 1985; Folbre 1991; Siegel 1994; Valenze 1995).

In contrast to approaches that claim that industrialization caused all work to leave the home, alternative interpretations describe how

---

[6] Alternatively, industrialization could be seen as forcing a division of labor between the sexes – where both women and men had previously performed productive labor and housework, now men would exclusively perform "work" while women exclusively performed homemaking. This interpretation is also suspect, as recent historical accounts make clear that a gendered division of labor predated industrialization (Boydston 1990; Valenze 1995).

industrialization redefined the meaning of work as a social category. In particular, accounts that focus on gender examine how women's labor, which was previously considered productive work, became defined through economic and legal changes as nonwork (Boydston 1990; Deacon 1985; Folbre 1991; Siegel 1994; Valenze 1995). As a first step, these interpretations posit that a gendered division of labor predated, rather than flowed from, industrialization. Although prior to industrialization women and men traditionally performed different tasks, culturally both men and women's labor were recognized as valuable contributions to the family's survival (Boydston 1990).[7] Preindustrial productive activities, however, were viewed in terms of specific tasks rather than in terms of work and nonwork. Indeed, the concept of work evolved as an abstract category in part in response to industrialization:

> [This period was] a critical point of transition in the history of work, when ideas about productivity and productive processes themselves underwent significant transformations. ... At this juncture, an "idea of work in general" emerged, "that is, work considered separately from all of its particular forms in agriculture, manufacturing or commerce." The abstraction was implicated in important determinations taking place in the late eighteenth and early nineteenth century: the assignment of tasks to individuals according to age and sex, the correct level of wages, the notion of worker incentive, and the designation of wage earning according to gender. (Valenze 1995: 6)

Not only the location but also the meaning of work changed with industrialization, and preexisting gendered patterns of labor helped give meaning to new conceptions of work. Rather than being caused by

---

[7] Boydston (1990) describes in detail how in colonial America, women and men performed different tasks, consistent with Protestant beliefs that women were the keepers of the home and helpmates to men. Women generally performed sewing, spinning, caring for children, cooking, cleaning, tending the kitchen garden as well as cows and chickens, and manufacturing products for the household such as soap, bedding, and clothing. Men cleared and cultivated the land, constructed household buildings, practiced a trade or craft such as shoemaking or weaving, managed household finances, and performed heavy labor.

industrialization's technological developments, existing gendered patterns of labor were an integral part of industrialization's technological and social changes (Berg 1985; Boydston 1990; Valenze 1995).

Economic, legal, and ideological factors helped infuse gender into the meaning of work that developed during this time. A confluence of social changes including urbanization, the scarcity of land for agriculture, and the decline of trades made wage labor an increasingly important source of family support (Boydston 1990). In addition, the decline of early American barter economies that relied on textiles, cheese, or butter as media of exchange made the products of women's labor less visible as direct contributions to household survival. Although both men and women continued to contribute labor toward their family's sustenance, the changing economic structure emphasized men's contributions and obscured the less market-oriented contributions of women (Boydston 1990).

At the same time, the meaning of work as a social category was becoming more closely associated with the time-disciplined labor of industrial factory settings. It was primarily men who moved toward more rationalized, time-disciplined work patterns, however. Women continued to perform task-oriented work at home, including caring for children and housekeeping, as well as piecework for the market, but by modern industrial standards women's work at home came to appear less efficient and less essential than time-disciplined labor. As a result, the differences between wage labor and household labor became more clearly drawn (Boydston 1990; Cott 1977).

Prevailing legal interpretations also obscured the contributions of women's productive labor by recognizing and valuing only market contributions to family survival, which were primarily made by men, while framing women's contributions in the home as gratuitous and obligatory labor in the private sphere (Boydston 1990; Siegel 1994). For example, courts and lawmakers drew on gender roles to grant wives the right to earnings only from their labor outside the home, defining other forms of labor performed in the home as marital service to a woman's husband (Siegel 1994). Similarly, over the course of the nineteenth century,

British and American censuses moved from defining women performing labor in the home as productive workers to classifying the same women performing the same work as nonproductive dependents, along with children and disabled individuals (Deacon 1985; Folbre 1991). Thus, law and the state contributed to the process through which women's labor gradually came to be disassociated from, and even set in opposition to, the evolving concept of work.[8]

Cultural ideologies about the appropriate gendered division of labor also contributed to work's emerging meaning. At least three interlocking ideologies contributed to this process: separate spheres ideology, the pastoralization of the home, and the family wage ideal. Separate spheres ideology emphasized women's cultural and moral authority as keepers of the home and caretakers and teachers of young children (Welter 1966), and contrasted sharply with the sources of cultural authority for men, namely their status as workers, breadwinners, and participants in civic activities. It associated women's labor with a sphere separate not only from men, but also from work. It taught that work outside the home not only contravened women's natural roles in life, but also threatened to undermine the social order by distracting women from their responsibilities and talents as wives, mothers, and homemakers (Welter 1966). In this view, women's inherent compassion, nurturing natures, and superior morality made them unfit for the competitive marketplace of wage labor (Kessler-Harris 1982).

A second, related ideological theme was the pastoralization of housework and the valorization of the home as a safe haven of peace

---

[8] In an even more extreme example, Valenze (1995) notes that during the enclosure movement in England, many traditional activities of women that historically had been performed on the common, such as gathering wood and tending cattle, became not only no longer possible but also criminalized. The criminalization of these activities transformed women's labor from a valued source of survival to punishable and reprehensible behavior. In addition, women who protested the prohibitions against their customary labor were cast as backward and ignorant opponents of the social progress of industrialization. This history shows one subtle way in which women's traditional forms of labor came to be devalued.

and rest from the demanding commercial activities of the marketplace. During the industrial transition, popular literature portrayed the home as a place of refuge and repose, drawing a sharp distinction between the tranquil home and the restive economic activities of the marketplace. Contemporary accounts portrayed basic household requirements, such as bread or meals, as bounty from nature rather than the products of women's traditional labor. Pastoralization helped make women's labor in the home less visible, as both women and the home ceased to be identified with work (Boydston 1990).

Third, family wage ideology, or the idea that the normative worker is a male breadwinner with a stay-at-home wife, contributed to this interlocking system of meaning. The family wage ideal was, in part, a gendered response to the changing economic system brought about by industrialization and the upheavals that threatened male exclusive competence and authority in the economic realm (Fraser & Gordon 1994). With industrialization, working-class women moved into factory work and other forms of wage labor out of economic necessity. They began to compete with men for wages at the same time that prior opportunities for economic support, such as land ownership and agricultural labor, or independently practicing a craft or skilled trade, began to diminish (Boydston 1990; Kessler-Harris 1982; Valenze 1995). Valenze (1995: 102) notes the connection between reduced opportunities for nonwage forms of support and male working-class hostility toward wage-earning women in England:

> The antipathy that working-class men felt toward wage-earning women had its roots, at least in part, in changes in the status of male workers during this period. Women became necessary and important wage-earners within the working-class family at precisely the point at which displaced skilled workingmen "found themselves pushed into an unfamiliar dependence on wife (and child) earnings" because of the decline of their trades. By the 1830s and 1840s, "the wage-earning wife," once seen as the norm in every working-class household, had become a symptom and symbol of masculine degradation.

Displaced artisans and craftsmen responded to these changes by organizing and negotiating skilled classifications for certain jobs, pushing
women into lower-paid, less-desirable wage labor or into unpaid labor
in the home (Boydston 1990; Kessler-Harris 2001; Valenze 1995).
Excluding women from many forms of wage labor also helped to rees-
tablish a material basis on which to rest patriarchal claims to authority
and independence (Boydston 1990; Fraser & Gordon 1994).

As opportunities to own property or survive through practicing a
trade became limited, family wage ideology offered a way to reimagine
the social basis of independence, citizenship, and patriarchal authority
in terms of wage labor. When male workers demanded a family wage
based on the image of a breadwinner who makes enough to remove his
dependent wife and children from wage labor, they simultaneously rees-
tablished their authority as independent citizens and implicitly defined
women as nonworkers (Boydston 1990; Fraser & Gordon 1994). Thus,
wage labor came to be an important indicator of manhood, authority,
and citizenship even as it was constructed in opposition to women.

Of course the family wage arrangement historically was a white,
middle-class ideal more than it was a universal reality. Women, particularly immigrant women, poor women, and women of color, have always
worked outside the home for wages despite the pervasive ideology of the
family wage (Boris 1993; Collins 1991; Lerner 1972). The gendered division between wage labor and household tasks was thus not a universal
pattern driven by the technological advances of industrialization, but
instead a cultural frame for interpreting (and, arguably, enforcing) modern labor patterns in terms of gender, and a particular classed perspective on gender at that. Family wage ideology also exacerbated class and
race distinctions. The cult of domesticity helped draw class lines more
clearly by glorifying middle-class women who could afford not to work
and condemning working-class women, often immigrants or women of
color, who worked to support their families (May 1987). Family wage
ideology also set class and gender interests in opposition by simultaneously bolstering the working class's arguments for higher wages while

justifying less pay for women or excluding them from work altogether (May 1987; Smith 1987). Employers who provided a family wage could also undermine unionization and appropriate unpaid women's labor in the home for capitalist production (May 1987). Although class and race were part of the story, nevertheless it is the relationship between gender and work that forms the common thread among these intertwined dimensions of social inequality.

Family wage ideology was a legal, as well as cultural, phenomenon because law referenced the family wage norm to justify restricting women's work. In the nineteenth century the Supreme Court upheld closing certain professions to women, relying in part on gendered rhetoric about their responsibilities as wives and mothers.[9] Similarly, early-twentieth-century statutes restricting women's working hours were passed by state legislatures and upheld in the courts based on women's special status as present or future mothers (Skocpol 1992). Some interpretations argue that unions supported this legislation to exclude women from certain occupations, creating less competition for their primarily male members (Kessler-Harris 1982; Skocpol 1992). Indeed, the National Congress of Mothers expressed concern that valorizing motherhood to justify protective legislation would enforce women's secondary position in the wage-labor market when employers found it cheaper to employ men than to comply with restrictions on women's wage labor (Skocpol 1992).

Perhaps because they recognized this danger, women reformers changed their arguments significantly between *Muller* in 1908 and their brief in *Adkins v. Children's Hospital*[10] in 1923, which also defended protective legislation. The *Muller* brief essentially advocated for a secondary labor-market position for women, a position consistent with maintaining the family wage model and women's traditional role in the home. In contrast, the *Adkins* brief argued for the need for government intervention to create gender equity *because* of women's

[9] Bradwell v. Illinois, 83 U.S. 442 (1873).
[10] Adkins v. Children's Hospital, 261 U.S. 525 (1923).

weaker position in the labor market. Reformers had begun to realize
that protective legislation structured around maintaining the family
wage system constrained work opportunities for women. Culturally,
however, the rhetorical battles regarding protective legislation had
already constructed work and motherhood in opposition to one another
(Lipschultz 1989).

Reformers promoting protective labor regulations used one cultural category, motherhood, against another, the free contract conception of work, to justify protection for some workers. By focusing
on women's roles as wives and mothers, however, they helped to reify
gender and work as oppositional social categories, to promote perceptions that women were less committed than men to work, and to foster
beliefs that women worked only sporadically and temporarily – for pin
money or to fill the gap between school and marriage. Indeed, even
into the second half of the twentieth century, it was still common to
fire working women when they married, or at the latest when they had
their first child (Smith 1987). Women's status as mothers and wives,
and not their abilities and worth as workers, continued to define their
roles both at work and at home. Law, therefore, helped to construct
work and, implicitly, the meaning of gender such that wage labor came
to mean different things for women and men. Work came to be seen
as a fundamental element of male identity, whereas for women, work
was assumed to be at most a short transition period from childhood to
marriage (Frank & Lipner 1988).

Even modern employment policies reflect these gendered assumptions. Although time norms around full-time labor remain strong,
the legal response to violations of these time norms varies with the
reason for the violation in gendered ways.[11] Unemployment insurance
provides support for interruptions in work related to economic down-
turns, but also is a routine source of periodic support for auto workers
and workers in the construction trades where irregular work patterns

---

[11] My thanks to Noah Zatz for suggesting this point to me.

are common and workers are predominantly male. For the most part, however, unemployment insurance is not available to workers who lose their jobs due to temporary disabilities or childcare difficulties. In addition, the law provides for job-protected leave for jury duty or military service, both historically associated with masculine citizenship, but the law only recently provided limited job-protected leave for childbearing and caring for newborns, and this leave applies to only a fraction of employees.

Conceptions of work and gender were also deeply tied to welfare policy, which continued to reference wage labor to set the boundaries of who was legitimately entitled to aid. American welfare policies have consistently resolved the tension between the norm of the autonomous, self-sufficient worker and the need to care for families in ways that reinforced and recreated the family wage ideal. For example, Skocpol (1992) notes that early twentieth-century mothers' pensions were premised on the idea that mothers, by definition, were not workers. Advocates justified mothers' pensions by citing women's traditional roles as the caretakers of children, which helped neutralize objections to their nonparticipation in the labor market and reduced the moral hazard of social support. Generally limited to widowed mothers who were in marital relationships until their husbands' deaths, these pensions did little to undermine the family wage ideal. The pensions also shored up the wages of male breadwinners. Labor organizations supported mothers' pensions specifically because widowed mothers would otherwise enter the labor market and work for less than others, which could undermine employment opportunities for men (Skocpol 1992).

Later New Deal policies continued to reinforce women's traditional roles. The most generous policies accrued to long-term, full-time workers, so that the part-time, intermittent work commonly done by women was seldom sufficient to make women eligible for substantial support (Mettler 1998). Explicit gendered exclusions also operated. For example, the Social Security Act of 1935 initially provided financial benefits to widows, but not to widowers, presuming that only the work of male breadwinners, and not the labor of wives, contributed to the support of their families.[12] Similarly, the Act provided aid to families whose dependent children were needy because of the death, incapacity, or absence of a parent. By excluding two-parent families from social welfare provision, the state both recognized and reinforced a particular, usually gendered, organization of labor at work and at home – one parent to provide care and the other to provide financial support (Law 1983). Even when benefits became available to two-parent families, married women with children were excluded from the program's work requirements, but single women with children were not (Law 1983). Thus, the state looked not only to motherhood but also to dependency in traditional family roles to justify eligibility for support outside the wage labor system.[13]

Much research argues that the gendered assumptions of these programs construct the meaning of welfare in terms of gender and race (Gordon 1990; Nelson 1990; Quadagno 1994). These programs also, however, construct the meaning of work. Economically and politically, support for these social programs was justified as protection for only legitimate and appropriate nonworkers. Thus, to the extent that motherhood rendered one a legitimate nonworker, work and motherhood come to be understood as mutually exclusive. By defining mothers as appropriately outside the wage-labor system, the state reinforced cultural expectations that women stay home and care for children without pay. It also facilitated structuring work around the assumption that workers are male breadwinners who have wives at home (Law 1983). The dichotomy between work and motherhood had, by this time, been fully institutionalized in practices like the 40-hour work week, which were incompatible with care responsibilities.

---

[12] This gender-specific standard fell to a legal challenge in 1977 with Califano v. Goldfarb, 430 U.S. 199 (1977).

[13] Of course, with recent welfare reforms, mothers on the least generous track of these welfare programs are now required to work, even though similar requirements do not apply to widows receiving Social Security benefits.

By the time women, especially mothers, began to enter the workforce in earnest in the last half of the twentieth century, both the full-time, year-round time norms of work and the implicit gendered meanings associated with wage labor were firmly in place. Antidiscrimination legislation, such as Title VII of the Civil Rights Act of 1964, made changes on the margin by prohibiting employers from assuming women had care responsibilities that conflicted with work, and by prohibiting employers from refusing to hire or promote women because of their gender. Nevertheless, the standard 40-hour work week, mandatory overtime, travel and relocation expectations, and lack of leave for parenting responsibilities continued to be common features of many jobs. Even after the law came to prohibit formal exclusion of women from the workplace, the historically determined structure of work continued to create significant barriers to employment, particularly for women who were also mothers.

Disability

Just as the meaning of work incorporates historically contingent concepts of gender, institutionalized work practices and norms also incorporate similar conceptions of disability. Although less has been written about the history of disability and the transition to modernity, a growing literature traces how the change to industrial production constructed the meaning of disability and work (Borsay 1998; Finkelstein 1980; Gleeson 1997; Oliver 1990; Russell 1998, 2001, 2002; Stone 1984). Although these accounts differ in focus, they agree that industrialization had the effect of economically and socially marginalizing people with disabilities. Most of the literature touches on three important themes: First, industrialization changed production in ways that decreased the flexibility of work and excluded impaired individuals from the production process. Second, the rise of the medical profession helped produce a medical model of disability that located disability in the individual rather than in the social environment. Third, the political economy of disability changed when the state began to enforce participation in developing capitalist labor markets by defining disability to include only individuals who were completely unable to work.

The first of these themes focuses on how the industrial transition from home production to factory work drastically diminished employment opportunities for people with disabilities. Finkelstein (1980) notes that preindustrial agriculture and home production could often accommodate disabilities because many productive activities could be performed at home in whatever increments were possible. For example, the elderly, the ill, and even children performed spinning or piecework when these activities were less time-oriented, less standardized, and less machine-focused (Finkelstein 1980; Oliver 1990; Valenze 1995). The transition to large-scale industry, however, removed many forms of productive labor from the home and reorganized them around time discipline and production norms. This transition excluded many people with impairments from employment, or relegated them to poorly paid jobs (Finkelstein 1980; Oliver 1990; Russell 2001).[14] Along these lines, historical materialist accounts emphasize how capitalist production methods pushed disabled workers to the bottom of the economic ladder, leaving them disproportionately represented in the reserve army of labor (Gleeson 1997; Russell 1998, 2001, 2002). Over time, the routines and even the architectural settings of work became standardized around nondisabled workers, institutionalizing an able-bodied worker norm (Hahn 1997). In addition, as Robert (2003: 137) points out, "the worth of individuals became tethered to new capitalist work roles." As wage labor became increasing associated with ideas of independence, individualism, and citizenship, those who were structurally excluded from work came to

---

[14] Although Oliver (1990) notes how the meaning of disability varies with modes of production, he cautions against a romantic interpretation of preindustrial times as unproblematic for people with impairments. He notes that social prejudice against physically or mentally impaired people predated industrialization, as they were sometimes viewed as possessed or evil. The transition to modernity, in which they became viewed as dependent and helpless, may have simply substituted one prejudice for another.

be viewed as dependent and not full participants in civic life (Fraser & Gordon 1994). As a result, capitalist production patterns deprived individuals with disabilities of the moral legitimacy that came to be associated with work.

The increasing separation between work and home made it more difficult for families to combine work and caring for disabled family members, and consequently helped segregate people with disabilities into separate institutions (Oliver 1990). Indeed, the transition to modernity coincided with the rise of institutions that were in part a response to the disintegration of once stable social relationships that were giving way to a new social order (Rothman 1971). Families struggling to work outside the home and to care for disabled relatives increasingly came to rely on asylums, which removed people with disabilities from public life (Oliver 1990). Institutions were more than practical solutions to the administrative problems of capitalist production, however; they also were a means of social control in the contested shift to a capitalist economy (Rothman 1971). For example, nineteenth-century English Poor Laws used incarceration and segregation to control members of the community who were unable (or unwilling) to engage in wage labor, including individuals with disabilities (Stone 1984). In this way, placement in an institution became a common consequence to failure to engage in wage labor, even if that failure was due to the incompatibility of an individual's physical abilities and the structure of industrial production.

A second theme in this literature focuses on the rise of the medical profession during the transition to modernity, and the role that the emerging medical profession played in defining, categorizing, and institutionalizing disability. Ideologies of individualism and the increasing influence of the medical profession helped create what many scholars label a medical model of disability (Oliver 1990; Robert 2003; Thomas 2002). The medical model constructs disability as an individual pathology, locating the problem within the individual, rather than in assumptions about normal (or abnormal) abilities and the social environment that creates these expectations. In this way, an individual's difference from the emerging able-bodied norm in industrial wage labor became not only a barrier but also pathology. These ideas of disease and dependency justified the social segregation of people with disabilities either in institutional settings or in homes that were now separate from workplaces (Borsay 1998; Oliver 1990).

The third theme of these historical accounts examines the political economy of disability by showing that the boundaries of the category of disability are not naturally occurring, but are politically defined (Russell 1998, 2001, 2002; Stone 1984). Over time, disability has come to be defined not only in terms of medical impairment, but explicitly with reference to the developing wage-labor market (Russell 2001; Stone 1984). For example, Stone (1984) argues that in the nineteenth century, the need to force workers into the labor market encouraged states to define disability narrowly in terms of residual work capacity. At the time of industrial transition, the category disability had been poorly defined and was unstable. Feigned illness or impairment, however, threatened to undermine the new wage-labor market by allowing potential workers to rely on charity rather than wages. Stone (1984) traces how nineteenth-century English poor relief statutes narrowly construed who qualified as disabled to close off means of support (i.e., charity) other than wage labor.

This analysis reveals how understandings of disability in both the American and the English systems "arose out of the need to ... distinguish between workers and non-workers within the new capitalist order," to draw the line between appropriate workers and nonworkers (Oliver 1990: 52). Medical professionals became the mechanism for identifying those with illnesses or impairments that fit the disability category created by the state (Borsay 1998; Stone (1984). Nevertheless, Stone (1984) shows through comparative analysis that the boundaries between those "able to work" and those who were deemed sufficiently "disabled" to be eligible for relief remained a political decision that varied across social and political contexts.

English-speaking countries generally defined disability as the inability to work. By referencing wage labor, rather than physical impairments, to set the boundaries of disability, these countries set the categories of work and disability in opposition to one another. The American social welfare system, which is based in part on the English poor relief system, adopted this approach. For example, the Social Security Act defines disability narrowly for the purposes of supplemental income replacement:

> [A]n individual shall be determined to be under a disability only if his physical or mental impairment or impairments are of such severity that he is not only unable to do his previous work but cannot, considering his age, education, and work experience, engage in any other kind of substantial gainful work which exists in the national economy, regardless of whether such work exists in the immediate area in which he lives, or whether a specific job vacancy exists for him, or whether he would be hired if he applied for work.[15]

A physical or mental impairment alone is insufficient to show disability; inability to work and the lack of any residual work capacity are also required. Disability and work thus become mutually exclusive categories.

Alternative approaches to defining disability that create a less rigid division between work and disability are possible. Sweden, for example, subsidizes the wages of people with disabilities entering the workforce to create an incentive for employers to hire them (Ruggie 1984). Historically, Germany's social security system has considered not only individuals' physical or mental condition, but also the availability of work in the definition of disability (Stone 1984). In the American system, however, disabilities are presumed to arise from the inherent limits of individuals rather than from the larger social context. Those who fall outside the state's definition of disability are, by definition, objectively able to work, and therefore either a worker or a shirker. In this way,

---

[15] 42 U.S.C. § 1382c(a)(3).

the politically determined definition of disability converts a range of abilities into a dichotomous division between work and disability that obscures and reinforces the socially constructed relationship between the two.

This historical analysis reveals that disability is a social construction that varies with political, economic, and social contexts (Gleeson 1997; Kudlick 2003). Drawing on this insight, public policy and academic conceptions of disability have moved from medical models toward more rights-based or social models of disability that locate disability in the interaction of the individual with the social environment (Drimmer 1993; Finkelstein 1980; Hahn 1997; Oliver 1990; Robert 2003; Russell 1998, 2001, 2002; Scotch 1984). These approaches often draw an important distinction between impairments, such as a missing limb, and disability, which is a social status ascribed to individuals who have impairments. From this perspective, there is no necessary or natural connection between impairment and disability (Gleeson 1997; Oliver 1990). The connection, if any, is created by the social environment, which is historically contingent.

The late twentieth century gave rise to rights-based campaigns premised on the social model of disability that focused on removing environmental features that create barriers for impaired individuals. These approaches have encountered significant backlash and resistance, however (Krieger 2000), reflecting the degree to which the mutually dependent meanings of work and disability have become normalized, taken-for-granted, and thus invisible. As the relationship between work and disability became institutionalized in work practices and social policy, the barriers people with impairments face at work appeared to arise from their personal circumstances, rather than from workplace practices and the physical environment. Thus, backlash results because employers and nonimpaired workers perceive changes in established work practices to be illegitimate, special treatment of a particular group, rather than recognition of how existing work practices implicitly incorporate an historically determined able-bodied ideal. In this way, the role that workplace practices, such as time standards, play in recreating inequality becomes

invisible, and penalties for failing to meet those standards become naturalized as just the way things are.

The Social Meaning of Work, Gender, and Disability

This brief genealogy of work documents that, as time standards became
normalized, nonstandard patterns of productive labor came to be devalued or not recognized as work at all, and institutionalized work practices came to incorporate and reinforce inequality based on gender and
disability. Historically, women and people with disabilities shared the
common experience of exclusion or marginalization in the labor market.
For women, this exclusion flowed from their traditional responsibility for
caregiving and from ideologies that held that women are unfit to compete
in the marketplace and belong in the home. For people with disabilities,
exclusion resulted from the increasing inflexibility and standardization
of work, which created environmental barriers to full participation in
public life. To be sure, there are normative differences between them: It is
thought that people with disabilities by definition *cannot* work, whereas
mothers with small children *should* not work. Nevertheless, both women
and people with disabilities share the cultural status of nonworker.

This genealogy reveals that institutionalized work practices derive,
in part, from the ideologies, cultural meanings, and historically contingent conceptions of disability and gender that predominated during the
transition to modernity; they cannot be understood as simply the natural
product of material transformations in productive activities and technology. To say that work draws its meaning from the categories of gender
and disability is not the same, however, as the claim that work is built
around a "male" or "able-bodied" norm. The latter argument assumes
that there are stable, essential qualities of women or people with disabilities that exist independent of their relationship to work and that are
not accommodated by work. Instead, a genealogical analysis reveals that
work, gender, and disability have no essential or natural characteristics,
but constitute one another as the result of the historical process through

which modern work structures developed. Yet social conditions and the legal environment of workplaces are changing, raising the question of how work as an institution will respond to yet another major social transition.

Institutional Inequality and the Eroding Social Foundations of Work

Fundamental changes to institutions tend to occur when the social arrangements that supported institutional regimes erode and institutions suddenly appear problematic (DiMaggio & Powell 1991). Changing social arrangements reveal the social assumptions underlying institutions, destabilizing them and leaving them open to reinterpretation and challenge. Because institutions evoke automatic acceptance and normative approval, however, they can be a source of resistance to changes in the social arrangements that support them (Krieger 2000). In fact, institutions often persist long after the social conditions that gave rise to them have faded away, and such is the case with work.

The traditional family structure, in which a breadwinner supports a stay-at-home spouse who cares for the home and children, is a fundamental but rapidly changing social arrangement that historically has supported the institution of work. Although the family wage model was never universal, particularly among economically marginalized populations (Kessler-Harris 1982), this traditional conception of family was the most common and culturally approved social arrangement for the first half of the twentieth century (Hayghe 1990). Families structured around a (male) breadwinner and a (female) homemaker are compatible with and complement the traditional structure of paid employment on a full-time, year-round schedule, and increasing conflict between work and family reflects substantial changes in both families and work that make these institutions less compatible and symbiotic. Yet much recent theorizing about the problem of work/family conflict has noted how these two institutions remain mutually reinforcing, even in the face of substantial social change undermining both sides of the dyad (Albiston 2007).

Two recent dramatic changes have undermined the symbiotic relationship between male breadwinner model and traditional work structures: the increased participation of women in the labor force, including married women with children, and the growing number of single-parent families. The steep rise in women's workforce participation is stunning. The participation rate of women with children under six years of age was only 18.6 percent in 1960, compared with 30.3 percent in 1970, 45.5 percent in 1980, 62.7 percent in 1996, and 63.5 percent in 2006 (Commerce 1997; Statistics 2007). In addition, more women with very small children are working. In 1976, only 31 percent of mothers with a child under one year old were in the labor force, but by 2006, this figure increased to 54 percent (Reskin & Padavic 1994; Statistics 2007). Similar patterns emerged for women's participation rate in general (Hayghe 1997). Women and men now participate in the labor market at similar rates (Fullerton 1999), although a substantial percentage of employed women work part time (Cohen & Bianchi 1999; Kelly 2005).

Given this trend, it is not surprising that the proportion of families that fit the traditional breadwinner model has declined substantially. In 1940, 67 percent of families consisted of employed husbands with stay-at-home wives (Reskin & Padavic 1994). In 2006, that figure was only about 20 percent. Single-parent families also became more common as the result of increasing divorce rates and more never-married parents (Fields & Casper 2001; Hayghe 1990); in 2006, about 30 percent of families with children were supported by a single householder, mostly single women (Table 2.1). Dual-income families have become much more common, increasing the time pressure on many families (Jacobs & Gerson 2004). Married-couple families in which both spouses worked were 52 percent of all families in 2006, about twice the number of married-couple families in which only one spouse worked (Table 2.1). Married-couple families with children under 18 were even more likely to be dual worker families; both parents worked in 62 percent of these families (Table 2.1). These figures represent a radical undermining of the social arrangements that gave rise to the institutionalized work practices common today.

Table 2.1. *Family composition and worker configuration, 2006*

	Percent of All Families	Percent of Families with Children
Family Composition		
Married couples	74.8	70.3
Families maintained by women	18.4	23.6
Families maintained by men	6.9	6.1
Worker Configuration in Families[a]		
Married couples, percent who are:		
Dual workers	51.8	62.0
Father works, mother does not	19.8	30.5
Mother works, father does not	6.5	4.8
Families maintained by women, percent in which householder is working	63.8	72.0
Families maintained by men, percent in which householder is working	71.8	83.5

[a] Nonworking and other configurations omitted.
Source: Report, U.S. Department of Labor, Bureau of Labor Statistics, Employment Characteristics of Families in 2006 (May 9, 2007) (based on Current Population Survey 2006).

The institutional divide between work and disability also began to erode during this period. Although changes are more difficult to document quantitatively for a variety of reasons, broad trends can still be identified. During the twentieth century, the number of people with disabilities increased, as did the number of workers with disabilities. Some of this increase can be attributed to demographic trends. For example, the likelihood of having a disability increases with age (McNeil August 1997), and, as the baby boomer generation aged, the number of older Americans increased. Accordingly, the number of workers with potentially disabling chronic conditions such as cardiovascular disease, arthritis, and cancer also increased (Shapiro 1993).

In addition, significant medical advances improved the survival chances of individuals with serious illnesses or injuries. These include the development of antibiotic drugs, treatment for spinal cord injuries, insulin to treat diabetes, improved care for premature babies, and the development of trauma centers (Shapiro 1993). Developments in treatment also enabled some HIV-positive workers to remain in the workforce or to return to work. Improvements in medical technology, such as lighter and more portable wheelchairs, have made it possible for people with physical impairments to participate more fully in public life, including work (Shapiro 1993). In short, many Americans live and work with disabilities: In 2000, about 19 percent of the population 5 years and older reported having a disability, and about 60 percent of working-age men with disabilities and 51 percent of working-age women with disabilities were employed (Waldrop & Stern 2003).

Legal changes in civil rights doctrine suggest how these social changes destabilized work as an institution and undermined the social perceptions that set work in opposition to gender and disability. For example, in the 1960s Congress enacted the Equal Pay Act, which requires equal pay for men and women performing the same work, and Title VII of the Civil Rights Act, which prohibits discrimination in employment on the basis of sex. The more recent Family and Medical Leave Act requires employers to provide certain employees with up to 12 weeks of job-protected, unpaid leave to care for new children or ill or injured family members, helping ease the conflict between work and family responsibilities. This civil rights legislation, along with pressure from a resurgence of the women's movement in the 1970s, sought to change perceptions about women's roles in the workplace and the family (Ferree & Hess 1994). Legal changes in civil rights doctrine regarding disability also reconceptualized the relationship between disability and work. Educational reforms such as the IDEA required public education of children with disabilities and created graduates ready for the workforce. In addition, the Americans with Disabilities Act prohibits disability discrimination in employment and requires employers to provide reasonable accommodations to workers' disabilities (Shapiro 1993). These reforms helped reveal how disability is a socially constructed status, contingent upon the environment and social attitudes toward physical and mental impairments.

Despite these significant social changes and legal reforms, however, women, and especially women with family responsibilities, have found themselves marginalized with regard to work even as they enter the workforce in greater numbers. Women consistently earn only a fraction of what men earn (Bureau 2000). In addition, sample research makes clear that there is a significant wage penalty for motherhood (Kelly 2005). Mothers earn less than men, whether or not those men have children; mothers also earn less than women who do not have children. These wage penalties remain even after controlling for factors that might differentiate mothers and nonmothers, such as human capital investments, part-time employment, the mother-friendly characteristics of jobs held by mothers, and other important differences in the characteristics, skills, and behaviors of mothers and nonmothers (Anderson et al. 2003; Budig & England 2001; Waldfogel 1997).

People with disabilities also continue to be disadvantaged in the labor market despite the ADA. Although empirical research indicates that at least some workplaces did make small changes to remove barriers at work (Engel & Munger 1996; Harlan & Robert 1998), the larger employment picture for people with disabilities is more complex. Even though two-thirds of nonworking disabled Americans report that they want to work (Louis Harris and Associates 1986), the labor force participation rates of people with disabilities remained static nearly a decade after Congress enacted the ADA (Hale et al. 1998). In addition, workers with disabilities earn less and are more likely to work part time than workers without disabilities (Hale et al. 1998). Part-time work contributes to the difference in earnings, but even full-time workers with disabilities earn less than nondisabled full-time workers (Hale et al. 1998). Compared with people with no disabilities, people with moderate disabilities are twice as likely, and people with severe disabilities nearly three times as likely, to report that they are looking for work or that they were laid off (Hale et al. 1998).

One potential explanation for these lingering disadvantages lies in the persistence of the institutional relationship between work and conceptions of gender and disability, despite legal reforms. Institutionalized time standards built around the male breadwinner and able-bodied worker play an important role in this regard. Changes in time standards have been the most difficult to implement under the ADA. Empirical research shows that accommodations in the physical environment (ramps, etc.) are the least likely to be denied, whereas accommodations in the social work environment, such as schedule changes, are the most likely to be denied (Harlan & Robert 1998). In addition, disabled workers closest to the institutionalized standard of the able-bodied worker do best; that is, those whose disabilities permit them to work full time and year round are the closest in wages and employment to their nondisabled counterparts (Hale et al. 1998).

Workplace time standards also help to police traditional gender expectations. For example, experimental research shows that mothers who violate gender roles by working are not only perceived as less competent and less likely to be recommended for promotions or hiring than other workers, but are also held to a higher performance standard in terms of attendance and punctuality at work (Correll et al. 2007; Cuddy et al. 2004; Fuegen et al. 2004). More generally, workers who violate time norms by making use of family leave are evaluated more negatively than other workers in terms of perceived commitment and allocation of organizational benefits, regardless of performance (Allen & Russell 1999; Glass 2004; Judiesch & Lyness 1999; Wayne & Cordeiro 2003). Along these lines, detailed ethnographic research documents that many informal penalties and disincentives at work discourage workers from making use of leave policies (Fried 1998; Hochschild 1997). Time standards and gendered expectations are connected here as well: Although all leave takers are disadvantaged, men who use family leave are evaluated more negatively than men who do not use leave, and more negatively than women whether or not they make use of leave (Allen & Russell 1999; Wayne & Cordeiro 2003). Thus, workplace penalties are not directed solely at women who seek to break out of their nonworker status; men are penalized as well when they seek to depart from the breadwinner role. Workplace penalties associated with time norms are a subtle system for enforcing particular, historically contingent conceptions of gender roles based on the family wage model in which men work and women care for the home and children.

To understand why marginalizing work practices persist, it is necessary to understand that not only changing conceptions of gender and disability, but also resistance from the institution of work itself, affect the dynamics of social change. Even as the social foundations of work erode, institutionalized work practices and expectations persist. Because the features of work have become naturalized, however, social conflict seems to originate in external social changes, such as changing family structures or increasing numbers of people with disabilities, rather than within the relationship between the institution of work and outmoded conceptions of disability and gender. For example, the statement "conflict between work and family" obscures the gendered assumptions that construct both work and family. Work does not conflict with all family forms. It is compatible with, and therefore helps reinforce, a two-parent family supported by a working father and a mother who cares for the children and the home. Thus, work does not conflict with family per se, only with families that depart from traditional gender roles that reflect changing conceptions of gender. Similarly, the idea of "disability" itself, defined as the inability to work, is contingent upon whether the forms of work available accommodate more than a narrow range of abilities. Recognizing that the structure of work plays a central role in this conflict suggests a different solution to these social problems: changing the institution of work.

3 Institutional Inequality and Legal Reform

DESPITE THEIR HISTORY OF EXCLUSION FROM WORK, TODAY it is generally accepted that women and people with disabilities can be legitimate workers, and that parents with the responsibility of caring for children can and – at least in the context of welfare policy – should work (Orloff 2002). At the same time, it seems natural and normal to many people that part-time workers be laid off before full-time workers regardless of seniority, that employers be able to fire workers who miss some work because of serious illnesses or disabilities, that employers not be required to accommodate absences resulting from morning sickness or the normal physical challenges of pregnancy, and that employers control work schedules, including requiring overtime or changing workers' schedules with no notice.

These expectations have begun to change, however. Some states now provide paid family leave and require employers to accommodate pregnancy-related restrictions (Albiston 2005, 2007). The Pregnancy Discrimination Act (PDA) requires employers to provide pregnant workers with at least the same leave protections as they provide to other workers who are similar in their inability to work. The Americans with Disabilities Act (ADA) specifically states that modified schedules can be a reasonable accommodation within the meaning of the Act. The Family and Medical Leave Act (FMLA) requires employers to grant leave to qualified employees when those workers are seriously ill, are needed to care for seriously ill family members, or need time off for pregnancy, childbirth, or to care for a new child in the family.

A close look at how courts interpret these legal developments, however, reveals that historical patterns among work, disability, and gender persist. For example, despite the ADA's explicit language indicating that schedule adjustments and leave may be reasonable accommodations when an employee's disability requires periodic absences, many courts have held that time off can never be a reasonable accommodation because attendance is by definition an essential function of any job. Similarly, some courts have held that even when rigid attendance policies have a disparate impact upon pregnant women, these employment practices cannot be challenged under a disparate impact theory. Other courts have suggested that workers who are able to work a standard 40-hour work week are not entitled to FMLA leave, even if leave is needed to relieve them of mandatory overtime they are physically unable to do. In these cases, courts do not inquire whether the employer could easily have accommodated the illness, disability, or pregnancy. Instead, they simply enforce the time standard of the full-time, punctual, and always-ready worker despite legal reforms that attempt to change these practices when they exclude women, people with disabilities, and caretakers from the workplace.

Why have courts interpreted these civil rights statutes to be consistent with the workplace time standards these laws were designed to change? What do these cases reveal about the mutually constitutive relationships among work, gender, and disability? What do they tell us about the ability of law to remake historically constructed social institutions such as work? And, perhaps most importantly, what do they suggest about whether remaking the institution of work might also change the meaning of gender and disability?

This chapter draws upon sociological theory about the maintenance and recreation of cultural institutions to examine why workplace time standards seem to be impervious to restructuring by antidiscrimination law. I argue that work practices like time standards reflect what I call *institutional inequality*, that is, the way that institutions incorporate historical social practices that presumed that women and people with disabilities would be tangential workers or would do no market work at all. The analysis in this chapter shows that courts construe antidiscrimination rights to be consistent with patterns of institutional inequality at work, even though these work practices depend upon historically constructed and outmoded conceptions of disability and gender. As a result, when courts enforce time standards, they reinforce the societal patterns of inequality that existed when work institutions formed. These judicial interpretations not only fail to change the structure of work, they also permit employers to continue practices that reinforce inequality, thus undermining the transformative potential of civil rights legislation.[1]

Civil Rights Responses to the Institution of Work

The institutionalization of work created a web of interrelated social meanings, expectations, and naturalized concepts that tend to exclude women and people with disabilities from the workplace. Central among them is the notion that the most valuable work is full-time, year-round, and uninterrupted labor. These time standards construct – and are constructed by – particular conceptions of gender and disability. For example, family wage ideology assumes an implicitly gendered (male) worker who is autonomous, self-sufficient, and free from any caretaking responsibilities, and thus always available for work (Fraser & Gordon 1994; Okin 1989; Pateman 1988; Williams 2000). As part of a political decision to enforce wage labor as the primary means of support for citizens, disability has become defined as the inability to work (Stone 1984).

---

[1] This chapter takes as its starting point the existence of these statutes, and therefore does not engage in a comparative institutional analysis of courts and legislatures regarding the interpretation of rights. Indeed, where statutory rights are concerned, these two institutions play somewhat different roles in creating and interpreting the meaning of rights. Courts interpret rights through case-by-case adjudication, whereas legislatures enact the initial statute and engage in legislative override or revision as time goes on. Incremental decision making in the courts is especially receptive to the institutional processes examined here, but legislative processes may be subject to these institutional pressures as well.

Accordingly, workplace time standards are not ahistorical, apolitical realities produced by the demands of modern production; they are part of an interrelated system of meaning and practices that institutionalizes inequality.

As more women and people with disabilities enter the workforce, the social underpinnings of workplace time standards have begun to erode and the implicit contradictions between work on the one hand, and gender and disability on the other, have become more visible. Women and people with disabilities often lose their jobs when they need time off to care for others, for pregnancy, or to recovery from a temporary illness. In addition, work's culture of time constrains employment opportunities for workers who cannot work long hours or standard schedules, including women with caretaking responsibilities and people whose disabilities require shorter or interrupted work schedules. Although the structure of work makes these constraints appear to come from an individual's life choices or inherent limitations, reformers have questioned this assumption by pointing to the limitations that workplace practices place on the choices available to women and people with disabilities. These challenges eventually prompted reform legislation designed to increase access to work for women and people with disabilities.

Recent history has produced at least three broad legislative attempts to protect women and people with disabilities as workers, rather than as dependents: Title VII of the Civil Rights Act of 1964, the ADA, and the FMLA. Despite the apparent promise of these new laws, when individuals mobilize these rights in court their claims often founder on ingrained expectations about work. Courts interpret these new employment rights consistent with existing work practices and expectations. As a result, these legislative reforms do not live up to their transformative promise, and in some instances they actually reinforce institutionalized features of work that disadvantage women and people with disabilities.

Each of these statutes takes a slightly different approach. Title VII and the ADA incorporate two different doctrinal models: an equality model and an accommodation model, respectively. Title VII prohibits employers from treating workers differently on the basis of sex. The ADA not only prohibits discrimination, but also requires employers to accommodate workers' disabilities. Both statutes, however, create rights that are based on workers' identities. In contrast, the FMLA focuses directly on the characteristics of work. Rather than requiring equal treatment, it creates a substantive right to up to 12 weeks of job-protected unpaid leave per year. In this way, it is more like legislation that creates job-protected leaves for jury duty or military service than anti-discrimination legislation. The FMLA's structural approach offers more doctrinal avenues for interrogating workplace time norms built around historical conceptions of gender and disability.

Title VII and Its Discontents

Title VII of the Civil Rights Act of 1964, which prohibits discrimination based on sex, became one of the first legislative tools for opening work opportunities to women.[2] Although Title VII seemed to prohibit employment practices that rested on stereotypical assumptions that work and family responsibilities were mutually exclusive for women, the statute created only a broad and somewhat ambiguous prohibition against discrimination. For example, the statute did not explicitly specify whether discrimination on the basis of pregnancy was a form of sex discrimination or a permissible practice, leaving this issue for the courts to decide. Some of the most difficult questions under Title VII emerged in the context of pregnancy, not only when the physical demands of pregnancy required

---

[2] Section 703(a), 42 U.S.C. § 2000e-2(a) provides:It shall be an unlawful employment practice for an employer – (1) to fail or refuse to hire or to discharge any individual, or otherwise to discriminate against any individual with respect to his compensation, terms, conditions, or privileges of employment, because of such individual's race, color, religion, sex, or national origin; or to limit, segregate, or classify his employees or applicants for employment in any way which would deprive or tend to deprive any individual of employment opportunities or otherwise adversely affect his status as an employee, because of such individual's race, color, religion, sex, or national origin.

women to be absent from work but also when employers believed that pregnant women should not work. Pregnancy cases created particularly thorny issues because work and motherhood had historically been seen as mutually exclusive, and because pregnancy seemed to present real gender differences that some courts held could be legally considered in workplace decisions. The countours of conduct that constituted discrimination on the basis of sex were ambiguous and subject to judicial interpretation, and as a result, the appropriate interpretation of Title VII in pregnancy discrimination cases was highly contested.

The Supreme Court took up this question in *Gilbert v. General Electric Co.*, in which it held that Title VII's prohibition on discrimination on the basis of sex did not include discrimination on the basis of pregnancy.[3] This decision immediately came under heavy fire from critics who argued that *Gilbert* presumed that women were only supplemental or temporary workers who would soon return home to raise children full time (Frank & Lipner 1988). Congress rejected this approach by enacting the Pregnancy Discrimination Act (PDA), which defines discrimination on the basis of sex to include discrimination "on the basis of pregnancy, childbirth, or related medical conditions."[4] The PDA also provides that "women affected by pregnancy, childbirth, or related medical conditions shall be treated the same for all employment-related purposes ... as other persons not so affected who are similar in their ability or inability to work."[5]

Even after the PDA, however, pregnancy remains a difficult issue because it almost always requires working women to violate entrenched workplace time norms. For example, pregnant workers generally need time off for childbirth, and some workers may also require time off during the pregnancy. Although the PDA requires employers who grant time off for nonpregnancy-related disabilities to provide the same

---

[3] General Electric Co. v. Gilbert, 429 U.S. 125, 133–39 (1976).
[4] 42 U.S.C. §2000e(k).
[5] *Id.*

benefits for pregnancy-related disabilities, its language is less clear about whether employers that do not generally provide disability leave must grant leave to pregnant women. On the one hand, the first section of the PDA seems to prohibit discriminating against employees who are temporarily absent from work for medical reasons related to pregnancy and childbirth. On the other hand, other language in the PDA suggests that pregnant women merely must be treated no worse than other workers who are similar in their ability or inability to work.

Little legislative history exists for the prohibition against sex discrimination in Title VII because this prohibition was added at the last minute as an attempt to defeat the other antidiscrimination provisions of the bill.[6] In addition, although the PDA was a legislative override of the *Gilbert* decision, advocates framed its provisions narrowly to avoid political opposition to the amendment.[7] Thus, at the time the PDA was

---

[6] *See* 110 CONG. REC. 2577–84 (1964) (Floor Debate); CHARLES WHALEN & BARBARA WHALEN, THE LONGEST DEBATE: A LEGISLATIVE HISTORY OF THE 1964 CIVIL RIGHTS ACT 115–18 (1985). (Reading floor record to mean that the addition of "sex" was a racist joke to defeat the bill that backfired.) For a rejection of the popular interpretation that the last-minute addition of "sex" was a ploy to defeat the bill, see Jo Freeman, *How "Sex" Got into Title VII: Persistent Opportunism as a Maker of Public Policy*, 9 LAW & INEQ. 163, 176–78, 182 (1991) (noting, inter alia, that the "sex" amendment's sponsor, segregationist Rep. Howard W. Smith, had been an ERA sponsor since 1943 and twice during his floor comments said that he was "serious about" his addition of the term "sex"). Freeman concludes that "the overall voting pattern implies that there was a large group of Congressmen (in addition to the Congresswomen) that was serious about adding sex' to Title VII, but only Title VII. That is not consistent with the interpretation that the addition of 'sex' was part of a plot to scuttle the bill." *Id.* at 178. *Cf.* Robert C. Bird, *More Than a Congressional Joke: A Fresh Look at the Legislative History of Sex Discrimination of the 1964 Civil Rights Act*, 3 WM. & MARY J. WOMEN & L. 137 (1997) (documenting that feminists strongly supported inclusion of sex and secured passage). Bird concludes that Rep. Smith was "an opponent of civil rights legislation and introduced the sex discrimination provision to scuttle the bill. If the bill was to pass, however, Smith genuinely preferred a bill with a ban on sex discrimination.... The overwhelming evidence defies the conclusion that 'sex' was added as a mere joke." *Id.* at 157–58, 161.

[7] Both Senate and House reports, as well as the floor debates, emphasized the PDA's modest scope and analogousness to Title VII's preexisting provisions. S. REP. No. 95–331, at 4 (1977), *reprinted in* LEGISLATIVE HISTORY OF THE PREGNANCY

enacted, the meaning of these antidiscrimination provisions and the degree to which they would reach facially neutral structural barriers at work was largely an open question. *Griggs v. Duke Power Co.* had been decided, opening the door to challenges to facially neutral workplace practices that had a disparate impact on a protected class of workers, but there was as yet little judicial guidance about what disparate impact theories would mean in the gender discrimination context, particularly with regard to pregnancy.

How the PDA's prohibition against discrimination on the basis of pregnancy should be interpreted became a significant theoretical debate among feminist legal scholars because it tapped unresolved questions about what workplace equality required. Some argued that equality only required employers to give women equal access to existing workplace structures and practices, and that employers should treat pregnancy-related disabilities no better or worse than other disabilities. In their view, providing affirmative benefits to accommodate work to pregnancy would open the door to protectionist policies that reinforced and prioritized women's roles as mothers and wives rather than as workers.[8] Others argued that the law should value and reward the traditional family labor done by women, rather than requiring women to abandon the roles of mother and caregiver to claim the role of worker. Those who took this view did not believe that special treatment – such as pregnancy leave – paternalistically categorized women as "only mothers." They

DISCRIMINATION ACT OF 1978, at 41 (1980) ("the bill rejects the view that employers may treat pregnancy and its incidents as sui generis, without regard to its functional comparability to other conditions"); H. R. REP. No. 95-948, at 4 (1978), *reprinted in* LEGISLATIVE HISTORY OF THE PREGNANCY DISCRIMINATION ACT OF 1978, at 150 (1980); 123 CONG. REC. 29385 (1977) (Senator Williams providing illustrative description of the Senate bill as merely requiring equal treatment with other employees on the basis of their ability or inability to work); 123 CONG. REC. 29664 (1977). (Senator Brooke assuaging his colleagues' concerns by emphasizing that the PDA in no way provides special disability benefits for working women.)

[8] *See, e.g.*, Brief of National Organization for Women et al., amici curiae, California Fed. Sav. & Loan Ass'n v. Guerra, 758 F.2d 390 (9th Cir. 1985) (Nos. 84-5842 & 84-5844).

argued instead that antidiscrimination laws should change workplace practices to provide leave as a way to value women's traditional roles.[9] Thus, the early debate became: Should women be given the special treatment of pregnancy leave, reifying their roles as mothers, or should they be treated the same as other workers (i.e., men) and therefore have access to leave only if it is available to all workers for conditions other than pregnancy?

A third set of scholars challenged the unspoken assumptions in this debate by pointing out that defining equal treatment as equal access to the workplace as it is currently organized incorporates existing work arrangements into the legal standard, without questioning the socially determined and gendered history of work (MacKinnon 1987; Taub & Williams 1985). In this view, merely requiring the same treatment as men presumes that work practices and conventions are not discriminatory. In fact, they contend, even though each sex is equally dissimilar from the other, workplace practices privilege male physiology and ways of living without justifying why it is that *women's* differences should be devalued (MacKinnon 1987). One key example is how standard 40-hour work schedules and traditional career patterns of uninterrupted work leave little room for pregnancy, childbirth, or the ongoing care of children. This critique generated a rich scholarship that examines how work practices that are taken-for-granted are often implicitly gendered and recreate gendered systems of power and inequality (Abrams 1989; Acker 1990; Finley 1986; MacKinnon 1987; Williams 2000). This debate has been revisited recently by scholars who argue that antidiscrimination requirements inherently encompass accommodationist policies such as maternity leave, because even formal equality mandates will, in some instances, require substantive change (Jolls 2001; Williams & Segal 2003).

---

[9] *See, e.g.*, Linda J. Krieger & Patricia N. Cooney, *The Miller-Wohl Controversy: Equal Treatment, Positive Action and the Meaning of Women's Equality*, 13 Golden Gate U.L. Review 513 (1983); Brief of Equal Rights Advocates et al. as Amici Curiae supporting Respondents, Miller Wohl Co. v. Comm'r of Labor & Indus., 515 F. Supp. 1264 (D. Mont. 1981), *rev'd on procedural grounds*, 685 F.2d 1088 (9th Cir. 1982).

These theoretical debates deconstructed workplace practices to show that, rather than being natural, neutral, and inevitable, they are often gendered. In this way, feminist legal theorists have named an implicit and uninterrogated norm in workplace antidiscrimination doctrine – the male life experience around which wage work historically has been organized. New institutionalist and social constructivist theories show that this insight only gets us so far, however. Feminist legal theorists may have recognized that the structure of work rests on gender, but the discussion ever since has, by and large, been framed as how far work must (or should) change to accommodate the realities of gender – implying that work and gender exist as preexisting categories with independent and stable meanings, when in fact they are socially constructed and historically contingent. To state that the structure of work is "male" merely pushes the reification back one step, so that male ways of working become another socially constructed and unexamined category in the analysis of workplace practices. This formulation recreates new versions of the same gender divisions, rather than challenging the underlying structures of work – such as restrictive schedules and employers' control over time. It also fails to question how work's historically contingent characteristics organize employment-related *and nonemployment-related* social life in ways that construct the meaning of gender for both men and women.

Given the history of Title VII and the PDA, the story behind the evolution of interpretations of these statutes raises interesting questions about why particular interpretive paths were taken and others were not. There were several open interpretive paths when the PDA was enacted, including theories of discrimination focused on intent and unequal treatment, and others focused on structural barriers and disparate outcomes. The analysis that follows builds on the genealogy set forth in Chapter 2 to draw out the influence of institutions, including cultural and normative belief systems associated with work and gender, on the judicial interpretations of these rights. This analysis argues for an institution-focused social constructivist theory of interpretive development, rather than a theory that relies on political factors, academic commentary, or judicial decision making as explanatory factors for doctrinal development.

My approach departs from the antidiscrimination rubric in that it does not treat work as an ahistorical, objective structure, but instead recognizes how institutionalized work practices not only exclude women but also construct the meaning of gender. Rather than treat work and gender as objective, preexisting categories, institution-focused, social constructivist theory allows one to view them as contingent systems in which work gives meaning to gender and gender gives meaning to work. I argue that when courts interpret the meaning of the antidiscrimination provisions of Title VII, they make use of this mutually constitutive framework to determine what is appropriate and legitimate, as well as what is discriminatory and illegal.

Title VII and the PDA did not change work overnight; discriminatory practices persisted. For example, some employers continued to impose mandatory leaves during pregnancy,[10] restrict the type of work pregnant women could perform,[11] and limit the number of hours they could work.[12] In addition, when working women required pregnancy disability leave or other pregnancy-related accommodations, some employers refused to adapt workplace policies and simply fired these women.[13]

---

[10] Burwell v. Eastern Air Lines, Inc., 633 F.2d 361 (4th Cir. 1980) (mandatory leaves for pregnant flight attendants); deLaurier v. San Diego Unified School Dist., 588 F.2d 674 (9th Cir. 1978) (mandatory pregnancy leave policy for school teachers).

[11] International Union, UAW v. Johnson Controls, 499 U.S. 187 (1991) (rejecting employer's policy prohibiting fertile women from holding positions that involved the manufacture of batteries).

[12] Ensley-Gaines v. Runyun, 100 F.3d 1220 (6th Cir. 1996) (employer's refusal to allow pregnant woman to use a stool while sorting mail effectively limited her hours to four hours per day); EEOC v. Red Baron Steak Houses, 47 F.E.P. 49 (N.D. Cal. 1988) (employer reduced the number of hours it allowed a waitress to work after discovering she was pregnant).

[13] Spivey v. Beverly Enterprises, Inc., 196 F.3d 1309 (11th Cir. 1999) (employer denied a nurse's assistant's request for help lifting a particularly heavy patient during her pregnancy and instead terminated her employment); Lang v. Star Herald, 107 F.3d 1308, 1313 (8th Cir. 1997) (employer terminated an employee rather than allowing coworkers to cover her work while she was on pregnancy disability leave).

Most feminist legal scholars argued these practices to be obviously discriminatory, yet legal challenges to them often failed.

A close analysis of Title VII decisions reveals that courts have left little doctrinal room for challenging facially neutral work practices that nevertheless construct the meaning of gender. Legal challenges to discriminatory practices have been more likely to be successful when employers attempted to enforce traditional gender roles explicitly, and less likely to be successful (and more likely to be controversial) when plaintiffs challenge the taken-for-granted, historically determined relationship between work practices and gender norms. As a result, although the meaning of gender may have changed in the sense that women who are able and willing to meet institutionalized work norms are legally protected, the gendered provenance of those norms remains unexamined. In the sections that follow, I examine in detail the doctrinal opportunities and constraints Title VII creates for unpacking the relationship between work and gender, and show how this relationship informs courts' interpretations of Title VII.

Pregnancy discrimination cases illustrate how courts interpret the PDA's prohibition against gender discrimination in light of culturally resonant, common sense meanings of work and gender. Pregnancy cases are particularly useful examples because they often expose the unspoken expectations and assumptions about work, gender, and family that operate in the workplace. Because pregnancy almost always requires at least a short absence from work, these cases also tend to highlight the way time norms affect working women. These cases indicate that as long as women seek equal access to work on its own terms, courts generally find in their favor. Challenges based on legal theories that implicitly or explicitly called into question time norms, however, tend to produce doctrinal inconsistency and defeats for plaintiffs. Despite evidence that institutionalized time standards disproportionately disadvantage women, courts typically interpret the PDA and Title VII to reinforce work's culture of time. Accordingly, the law as it stands now tends to reinforce rather than change workplace time norms that exclude women.

As a preliminary matter, it is useful to review two of the primary legal theories for proving discrimination under Title VII and the PDA: disparate treatment theory and disparate impact theory.[14] Disparate treatment theory requires proof of intent to discriminate.[15] Disparate treatment claims address explicitly discriminatory policies (i.e., "no women may work here"), or employ other evidence, circumstantial or otherwise, to show intent to discriminate.[16] In contrast, disparate impact theory challenges employment practices "that are facially neutral in their treatment of different groups but that in fact fall more harshly on one group and cannot be justified on business necessity."[17] Disparate impact claims do not require proof of discriminatory intent, and thus can be understood as challenges to discriminatory structural barriers rather than to discriminatory animus.[18] Despite these differences, courts draw on the mutually constitutive relationship between gender and work when they evaluate claims brought under either theory.

Legal Challenges by Pregnant Woman Who Can Work

The most successful pregnancy-related challenges under the PDA have been brought by pregnant women seeking to maintain their access to employment without modifying the features of work. Generally, if they can do a job as specified even while pregnant, courts have been unsympathetic to employers who attempt to exclude pregnant women from the workplace. Even when employers claim that pregnancy prevents women from meeting work requirements because of safety concerns, courts usually require employers to prove rather than assert that facially discriminatory policies that exclude women – for example, "no women may

---

[14] International Bhd. of Teamsters v. United States, 431 U.S. 324, 335–36 n.15 (1977).
[15] *Id.*
[16] *See* Armstrong v. Flowers Hosp. Inc., 33 F.3d 1308, 1313 (11th Cir. 1994) (explaining the two kinds of disparate treatment theories).
[17] *International Brotherhood*, 431 U.S. at 335–36 n.15.
[18] Griggs v. Duke Power Co., 401 U.S. 424, 430–32 (1971).

hold positions manufacturing batteries" – are essential to their business. Thus, consistent with new institutionalist theories, when antidiscrimination principles do not require restructuring established work practices, legal challenges generally succeed.

Most successful pregnancy-related challenges under Title VII have involved facially discriminatory actions or employment policies that attempt to bar women from certain jobs, to place them on mandatory leaves, or to fire them solely because they are pregnant.[19] For example, in *Carney v. Martin Luther Home, Inc.*, the court held that the employer violated the PDA by forcing a pregnant woman who was able to perform her job to take involuntary unpaid medical leave.[20] The court noted how such policies resonate with the protective legislation of the past:

> By enacting the Pregnancy Discrimination Act, Congress rejected the outdated notions upon which many "protective" laws and policies were based, policies which often resulted from attitudes about pregnancy and the role of women in our economic system, and which perpetuated women's second class status in the workplace.[21]

Other courts reached the same conclusion when employers fired women because of their pregnancy even though they were able to work,[22] or sought to bar women from certain (often lucrative) jobs thought to be too dangerous for women who might become

---

[19] *See, e.g.*, International Union, UAW v. Johnson Controls, 499 U.S. 187 (1991) (holding that excluding fertile women from jobs manufacturing batteries violated Title VII); Carney v. Martin Luther Home, Inc., 824 F.2d 643 (8th Cir. 1987) (holding that the employer violated Title VII by placing a pregnant worker on mandatory unpaid leave when she remained able to perform her job); EEOC v. Red Baron Steak Houses, 47 F.E.P. 49 (N.D. Cal. 1988) (holding that terminating a pregnant cocktail waitress violated Title VII where the manager stated that pregnant cocktail waitresses were "tacky"); EEOC v. Corinth, Inc., 824 F. Supp. 1302 (N.D. Ind. 1993) (holding that firing a pregnant waitress who was able to work violated Title VII).

[20] *Carney*, 824 F.2d at 649.

[21] *Carney*, 824 F.2d at 647.

[22] *See, e.g.*, EEOC v. Red Baron Steak Houses, 47 F.E.P. 49 (N.D. Cal. 1988); EEOC v. Corinth, Inc., 824 F. Supp. 1302 (N.D. Ind. 1993).

pregnant.[23] In *International Union, UAW v. Johnson Controls*,[24] the Supreme Court rejected a battery manufacturer's claim that excluding fertile women from jobs manufacturing batteries was necessary to the operation of its business because lead exposure endangered the potential fetuses of these women. The Court held that an employer could explicitly exclude women only in "instances in which sex or pregnancy actually interferes with the employee's ability to perform the job,"[25] a situation the Court found was not presented in this case.

Rather than accepting the culturally resonant argument that pregnancy and motherhood justified excluding women from the workplace, the Court in *Johnson Controls* forced the employer to prove, rather than simply assert, that its gender requirements were related to job performance. The Court essentially enforced the right of women to choose for themselves whether to work in conditions that might be hazardous. The Court did not, however, create any doctrinal opening for considering whether antidiscrimination law requires those positions to be modified so that they are less hazardous for women (and less hazardous for men as well). Instead, even after *Johnson Controls*, pregnant workers' choices remained constrained by existing workplace practices.

Challenges to workplace practices encounter more difficulty when pregnancy causes working women to violate institutionalized time norms. In these cases, courts struggle with the difference between equal and "preferential" treatment, and with the question of whether an employer's assumption that a pregnant employee will need time off constitutes discrimination or good business judgment. How that struggle plays out depends on the doctrinal framework courts employ in deciding a case. As the following analysis shows, Title VII doctrine has evolved to leave little room for challenging institutionalized work practices, even when those practices disproportionately disadvantage working women.

[23] *See, e.g.*, International Union, UAW v. Johnson Controls, 499 U.S. 187 (1991).
[24] 499 U.S. 187 (1991).
[25] *Johnson Controls*, 499 U.S. at 192.

Doctrinal Barriers to Restructuring Institutionalized Work Practices

The majority of pregnancy employment discrimination claims involve disparate treatment theories of discrimination (Donohue & Siegelman 1991). Courts generally evaluate disparate treatment claims through a three-part inquiry.[26] First, the plaintiff must establish a *prima facie* case of discrimination.[27] Courts formulate this burden in various ways, but typically the plaintiff must show that (1) she was a member of a protected class, (2) she was qualified for her position, (3) she suffered an adverse employment action, and (4) others who were similarly situated but not in the protected class were more favorably treated.[28] After the plaintiff makes this showing, the burden shifts to the defendant to produce a legitimate, nondiscriminatory reason for its actions.[29] If the defendant articulates such a reason, then the plaintiff bears the burden of proving that the reason given is a pretext for discrimination.[30]

This doctrinal structure does little to challenge existing time standards and may even reinforce them. For example, in the disparate treatment context several courts have held that the PDA does not protect pregnant employees from being discharged for being absent from work, even if their absence is because of their pregnancy or complications of pregnancy, unless the employer overlooks comparable absences of nonpregnant employees.[31] As a result, a pregnant worker fired for taking

---

[26] This discussion leaves aside questions of mixed motive, in which the employee provides some direct evidence of discriminatory intent on the part of the employer. Price Waterhouse v. Hopkins, 490 U.S. 228 (1989). It is difficult to prove direct evidence of discrimination, so these cases are relatively rare.

[27] McDonnell Douglas Corp. v. Green, 411 U.S. 792, 802 (1973).

[28] For example, the Fifth Circuit in *Urbano* formulated the plaintiff's *prima facie* case as follows: "(1) she was a member of a protected class, (2) she was qualified for the position she lost, (3) she suffered an adverse employment action, and (4) that others similarly situated were more favorably treated." Urbano v. Continental Airlines, Inc., 138 F.3d 204, 206 (5th Cir. 1998).

[29] *Id.*

[30] *Id.*

[31] Stout v. Baxter Healthcare Corp., 282 F.3d 856 (5th Cir. 2002); Dormeyer v. Comerica Bank-Ill., 223 F.3d 579 (7th Cir. 2000); Wallace v. Methodist Hospital System, 271 F.3d 212 (5th Cir. 2001).

pregnancy leave must point to evidence that the employer gives non-pregnant workers leave when they are unable to work. If the employer's normal operating procedures track work's institutionalized time norms, however, the similarly situated inquiry incorporates those norms without questioning them. Typically in these cases, other workers are treated just as badly as pregnant women,[32] or there are no similarly situated workers to whom pregnant workers can be compared.[33] In either instance, the disparate treatment standard does not require courts to consider whether the workplace's policies are built around an outmoded conception of gender.

The second step in the disparate treatment analysis, in which the court considers the legitimate business reason proffered by the defendant for its adverse employment action, can also reinforce work's institutionalized time norms. Employers often offer an established work practice, such as attendance requirements or policies against leave, as a legitimate business reason for firing pregnant women. To overcome this justification, a plaintiff must show that the employer's explanation is not believable or that discriminatory animus was the real motivation.[34] Showing that the employer could have accommodated the pregnant worker's needs is not sufficient to demonstrate pretext, although it is not entirely clear why an employer's refusal to accommodate a pregnant woman, if it could be done easily, should not be evidence of animus toward pregnant working women. It may be that many of these practices seem so natural, normal, and intrinsic to how we understand work, that courts cannot imagine penalizing employers for refusing to change them, even though these practices have roots in the gendered history of work's development. In any event, under current interpretations courts treat an employer's ability to accommodate the worker as irrelevant.[35]

---

[32] Troupe v. May Dept. Stores Co., 20 F.3d 734, 738 (7th Cir. 1994).

[33] Illhardt v. Sara Lee Corp., 118 F.3d 1151, 1155 (7th Cir. 1997).

[34] Civil Rights Act of 1991, Pub. L. No. 102–166 §§ 703(m), 706(g)(2)(A), 105 Stat. 1071, 1075–76; Desert Palace, Inc. v. Costa, 539 U.S. 90, 99–100 (2003); see also St. Mary's Honor Ctr. v. Hicks, 509 U.S. 502 (1993).

[35] See, e.g., Lang v. Star Herald, 107 F.3d 1308, 1313 (8th Cir. 1997) (noting employee's argument that coworkers could have covered for her while on pregnancy leave was

Courts also generally defer to employers' assertions about the requirements of work,[36] unless there is evidence that those requirements were
applied unequally.[37] As a result, workers who advance a disparate treatment theory have no doctrinal opening to demonstrate that alleged work
requirements may not be related to the job, or that alternatives exist that
do not penalize pregnant workers.[38]

Two recent Seventh Circuit cases illustrate these dynamics. *Troupe v.
May Dept. Stores Co.*[39] involved a pregnant worker who changed to a
part-time schedule, took several days of sick time for morning sickness,
and then was fired the day before her maternity leave was to begin. She
was told that she was fired because her employer did not expect her to
return to work after her maternity leave ended. The court noted that
the plaintiff presented no evidence that other, similarly situated workers
with absences caused by nonpregnancy-related illness were treated more
favorably, and the lack of a comparator was enough to defeat her claim.
This outcome seems contrary to Title VII's prohibition against the use
of gendered stereotypes. The employer's statement references the stereotype that women with children will (or should) leave work to care for
their children, yet the *Troupe* court held, as a matter of law, that this motivation for terminating a pregnant woman did not violate the PDA.[40]

---

irrelevant; "The relevant question ... is whether the Star Herald treated Lang differently than nonpregnant employees on an indefinite leave of absence, not whether the
Star Herald could have made more concessions for Lang."). Decisions such as Lang do
not explain why the fact that an employer could easily change its practices to accommodate pregnant women but refuses to do so should not be evidence of animus. It may
be that many of these practices, although they rest on the gendered history of work,
seem so natural that courts cannot imagine asking employers to change them.

[36] *See, e.g., Illhardt*, 118 F.3d at 1155. ("We refused to act as a 'super-personnel department' and second-guess Sara Lee as to how best to staff its law department.")

[37] *See, e.g.,* EEOC v. Ackerman, 956 F.2d 944 (10th Cir. 1992) (holding that denying a
pregnant employee's request for a schedule adjustment when all other requests from
nonpregnant employees were granted violated Title VII).

[38] *See, e.g., Lang*, 107 F.3d at 1313 (noting employee's argument that coworkers could
have covered for her while on pregnancy leave was irrelevant).

[39] 20 F.3d 734 (7th Cir. 1994).

[40] *Troupe*, 20 F.3d at 738.

In another case, *Ilhardt v. Sara Lee*,[41] the employer fired a part-time attorney after her maternity leave. The court noted that because there were no nonpregnant part-time attorneys in the law department to whom she could be compared, she could not establish a *prima facie* case.

> [W]e must compare Ilhardt's treatment with that of a group of simi-
> larly situated nonpregnant employees to see if she was treated worse
> because she was pregnant, but because Ilhardt was the only part-
> time member of the law department, there are no other similarly
> situated employees with whom to compare her. It is also clear, how-
> ever, that we cannot compare Ilhardt with the nonpregnant full-time
> attorneys, as she suggests, because full-time employees are simply
> not similarly situated to part-time employees. There are too many
> differences between them: as illustrated in Ilhardt's case, part-time
> employees work fewer hours and receive less pay and fewer bene-
> fits. … Ilhardt must show that 'she was treated less favorably than
> a non-pregnant employee under identical circumstances.' [citations
> omitted] Because she was the only part-time attorney, she cannot
> do this.[42]

To attempt to show discriminatory intent through other evidence, the plaintiff cited her supervisor's comments that he was sure that she would not return to full-time work after her third child because his daughters were busy with just two children, and that he thought it was better for mothers of young children to stay at home.[43] The court held that "statements expressing doubt that a woman will return to work full-time after having a baby do not constitute direct evidence of pregnancy discrimination."[44]

Workplace time norms that reference and reinforce traditional gender roles pervade this opinion. The court finds that part-time workers are not similarly situated to full-time workers without explaining why time

---

[41] 118 F.3d 1151 (7th Cir. 1997).
[42] *Ilhardt*, 118 F.3d at 1155.
[43] *Id.* at 1156.
[44] *Id.*

worked should be a meaningful distinction in this case. Even though part-time status, pregnancy, and motherhood are all part of a system of meaning that portrays working mothers as less committed to their jobs than other workers, the court never considered how the employer's part-time justification incorporated family wage stereotypes and failed to interrogate why it seems natural and normal to fire part-time workers first.[45] Instead, the court accepted without challenge that the plaintiff's nonstandard hours justified her termination despite her superior performance and offer to return full time. Entrenched expectations about motherhood and work also made a supervisor's statements about a woman's presumed role as caretaker of her children seem natural and logical – to both workers and courts alike – rather than stereotypical assumptions about gender roles.

The courts' interpretations in *Troupe* and *Ilhardt* depart from Supreme Court precedent regarding stereotype theories in the gender discrimination context. In *Price Waterhouse v. Hopkins*, the Court found that Price Waterhouse violated Title VII when it denied a woman manager partnership because she failed to conform to gendered norms about walking, talking, and dressing in a feminine manner, wearing makeup and jewelry, and taking "a course at charm school."[46] The Court held that the failure to conform to gender stereotypes was not a legitimate factor to consider for employment decisions, noting that "we are beyond the day when an employer could evaluate employees by assuming or insisting that they match the stereotype associated with their group."[47]

---

[45] The plaintiff in *Illhardt* also raised a disparate impact challenge to the employer's practice of laying off part-time workers before full-time workers. The court rejected this claim, holding that the employer's one-time reduction in force could not be called an "employment practice" within the definition of Title VII. As a result, Illhardt has no practice against which to raise a disparate impact challenge. The court also refused to take judicial notice of evidence of studies from the 1970s and 1980s, that showed that the majority of part-time workers are women with childcare responsibilities, stating that "the decades-old conclusions of the studies ... are certainly subject to dispute." *Illhardt*, 118 F.3d at 1156.

[46] Price Waterhouse v. Hopkins, 490 U.S. 228, 235–36, 256 (1989).

[47] *Id.* at 251.

More recently, in *Nevada Department of Human Resources v. Hibbs*, the Court reiterated its view that stereotypical assumptions based on gender contribute to discrimination, noting that "stereotypical views about women's commitment to work and their value as employees ... lead to subtle discrimination."[48] Consistent with these Supreme Court precedents, other circuit courts have taken a different interpretive path and have held that stereotypical remarks expressing the view that mothers with young children are not as competent, committed, or valuable as other employees constitute evidence of gender discrimination.[49] In fact, at least one circuit court has held that evidence of stereotyping of women as caregivers could support a *prima facie* case of disparate treatment even without any evidence about the comparative treatment of similarly situated men.[50]

Although most circuit courts view the anticipatory firing of a pregnant employee due to a perceived, hypothetical, future need for leave as a violation of Title VII, an uncritical acceptance of time norms has led a few courts to disagree.[51] In *Marshall v. St. Louis Circuit Court*, the employer terminated a pregnant employee several months before her due date because she intended to take an eight-week unpaid maternity

---

[48] Nev. Dep't of Human Res. v. Hibbs, 538 U.S. 721, 736 (2003).

[49] Back v. Hastings on Hudson Union Free School Dist., 365 F.3d 107, 120 (2d Cir. 2004) ("[I]t takes no special training to discern stereotyping in the view that a woman cannot 'be a good mother' and have a job that requires long hours, or in the statement that a mother who received tenure 'would not show the same level of commitment [she] had shown because [she] had little ones at home.'"); Santiago-Ramos v. Centennial P.R. Wireless Corp., 217 F.3d 46, 57 (1st Cir. 2000) (holding that questioning whether the plaintiff would be able to manage her work and family responsibilities supported a finding of discriminatory animus); Sheehan v. Donlen Corp., 173 F.3d 1039, 1044–45 (7th Cir. 1999) (holding that statements to a pregnant employee that she was being fired so she could spend more time at home with her children and that she would be happier at home with her children reflected gender stereotypes and provided direct evidence of discriminatory animus).

[50] Back, 365 F.3d at 121–22.

[51] Marshall v. American Hosp. Ass'n, 157 F.3d 520 (7th Cir. 1998) (finding no Title VII violation); Marafino v. St. Louis County Circuit Court, 707 F.2d 1005 (8th Cir. 1983) (same); Maldonado v. U.S. Bank, 186 F.3d 759 (7th Cir. 1999) (finding such anticipatory firing to violate Title VII).

leave.[52] The plaintiff was fired long before she missed any work at all, yet the court held the employer did not violate Title VII by firing her. Other courts, however, have held that the PDA bars employers from taking anticipatory action against a pregnant employee unless it has "a good faith basis ... that the normal inconveniences of the pregnancy will require special treatment."[53] These courts reason that assumptions that pregnant women will require substantial absences from work reflect gender stereotypes, and therefore cannot be the basis for penalizing or refusing to hire pregnant women.[54]

When women actually do need to miss some work to accommodate pregnancy and childbirth, however, courts generally allow employers to terminate them, so long as they do not explicitly rely on the reason for that absence – pregnancy – in their decision.[55] Thus, courts have permitted employers to penalize pregnant women who miss work or will miss work because of childbirth,[56] whose absenteeism increases as a result of

[52] *Id.*

[53] Maldonado v. U.S. Bank, 186 F.3d 759 (7th Cir. 1999); see also Troy v. Bay State Computer Group, Inc., 141 F.3d 378 (1st Cir. 1998) (affirming a jury verdict where employer might have acted on unlawful, stereotypical speculation that a pregnant employee would have poor attendance).

[54] Maldonado v. U.S. Bank, 186 F.3d 759, 762 (7th Cir. 1999); Troy v. Bay State Computer Group, Inc., 141 F.3d 378, 380–82 (1st Cir. 1998) (holding it was reasonable for the jury to conclude that the plaintiff had been dismissed based on the "stereotypical judgment that pregnant women are poor attendees"); Wagner v. Dillard Dept. Stores, Inc., 17 Fed. Appx. 141, 151 (4th Cir. 2001) (holding the employer's refusal to hire pregnant plaintiff and the statement that she should reapply after her baby was born and after she had proper childcare reflect the stereotypical assumption that pregnant women will eventually require substantial absences from work) (unpublished decision); *see also* Deneen v. Northwest Airlines, Inc., 132 F.3d 431, 434 (8th Cir. 1998) (affirming the jury verdict that the employer discriminated against the plaintiff by placing her on medical leave while she was pregnant despite her doctor's approval for her to return to work).

[55] *See* Crnokrak v. Evangelical Health Sys. Corp., 819 F. Supp. 737, 743 (N.D. Ill. 1993).

[56] Marshall v. American Hosp. Ass'n, 157 F.3d 520 (7th Cir. 1998) (holding that a pregnant woman's need for pregnancy disability leave is sufficient justification for terminating her employment under Title VII); Marafino v. St. Louis County Circuit Court, 707 F.2d 1005 (8th Cir. 1983) (holding that Title VII does not prohibit refusing to hire

morning sickness,[57] or whose pregnancies prevent them from performing their employer's definition of the job's requirements.[58] Because of the structure of Title VII's disparate treatment standard, there is no requirement to show that these work-time requirements are significantly related to the job, unlike the substantial justification that courts demand for facially discriminatory policies. Nevertheless, in all these cases, pregnant women lost their jobs when they violated norms about the behavior of ideal workers and ideal mothers.

I make no argument here about whether the existing structure of disparate treatment analysis is jurisprudentially correct or incorrect in not requiring employers to demonstrate that the workplace practices they offer as legitimate reasons for terminating women are, in fact, related to the job. Instead, my point is that the doctrinal structure of disparate treatment effectively sidesteps any direct inquiry into the relationship between work practices and traditional conceptions of gender, except perhaps in those circumstances where an employer also articulates

a pregnant woman because she will require leave of absence in the first year of work). *But see* Abraham v. Graphic Arts Int'l Union, 660 F.2d 811 (D.C. Cir. 1981) (holding that terminating a pregnant employee for exceeding a 10-day absolute ceiling on disability leave violated Title VII).

[57] Dormeyer v. Comerica Bank-Illinois, 223 F.3d 579 (7th Cir. 2000) (terminating employees for absences resulting from morning sickness did not violate Title VII); Troupe v. May Dept. Stores Co., 20 F.3d 734 (7th Cir. 1994) (terminating an employee because of absences and tardiness resulting from morning sickness does not violate Title VII). *But see* Maldonado v. U.S. Bank, 186 F.3d 759, 766 (7th Cir. 1999) (holding that an employer cannot assume a pregnant worker will be absent in future based solely on her pregnancy); Roberts v. United States Postmaster Gen., 947 F. Supp. 282, 289 (E.D. Tex. 1996) (noting that an employer can violate Title VII under a disparate impact theory by failing to provide an adequate attendance policy for the needs of pregnant women).

[58] Urbano v. Continental Airlines, Inc., 138 F.3d 204 (5th Cir. 1998) (finding no violation of Title VII where a pregnant employee was denied light duty and forced to take unpaid leave, even though some other employees similar in their inability to work were offered light duty); Spivy v. Beverly Enter., 196 F.3d 1309 (11th Cir. 1999) (terminating a pregnant employee rather than providing light duty does not violate Title VII where some but not all other temporarily disabled employees are offered light duty). *But see* Ensley-Gaines v. Runyon, 100 F.3d 1220 (6th Cir. 1996) (a pregnant employee could not be denied light duty if any other employees were

discriminatory stereotypes about mothers. In circumstances that do not involve stereotypical remarks, however, disparate treatment analysis incorporates the contradiction between gender and work that is embodied in many institutionalized workplace practices, such as time norms. When courts adopt this approach, they obscure the ways in which standard work schedules and the beliefs that support them constrain women's choices and reinforce gendered expectations and behavior at work and at home.

When courts allow institutionalized work practices to justify penalizing pregnant workers, they recreate institutional inequality. They validate institutionalized time norms, such as firing part-time workers first and denying time off for pregnancy-related medical conditions, which implicitly rest on outmoded conceptions of gender. They reinforce perceptions that the barriers working women face arise from natural characteristics associated with their gender or pregnancy, rather than from work practices such as no-leave policies. Because courts treat work as a natural, normal, and unchanging given, the consequences for working women seem to flow from women's choices rather than the structure of work. As a result, disparate treatment analysis actually *legitimizes* institutionalized work practices that enforce traditional roles for women, thus limiting Title VII's potential for social change.

The Qualified Promise of Disparate Impact Theories

Unlike disparate treatment theory, disparate impact theory engages directly with work's structure. It allows plaintiffs to challenge employment practices "that are facially neutral in their treatment of different groups but that in fact fall more harshly on one group and cannot be justified by business necessity."[59] Although disparate impact theory requires no proof of discriminatory intent,[60] a plaintiff must identify a

---

offered light duty, even if all other employees with nonwork-related injuries were denied light duty).

[59] International Bhd. of Teamsters v. United States, 431 U.S. 324, 335–36 n. 15 (1977).

[60] Griggs v. Duke Power Co., 401 U.S. 424, 430–32 (1971).

specific employment practice and show that it causes a disparity in treatment.[61] Once a plaintiff makes this showing, the defendant may raise the defense that the "challenged practice is job-related for the position in question and consistent with business necessity."[62] If an employer successfully asserts business necessity, the plaintiff may still prevail by showing that less discriminatory alternatives exist to the challenged policy.[63]

Early disparate impact cases regarding time norms and pregnancy required employers to change workplace time standards that disproportionately disadvantage women (Jolls 2001; Krieger & Cooney 1983; Siegel 1985). For example, in *EEOC v. Warshawsky & Co.*, the court held that the employer's policy of not providing sick leave to first-year employees had a disparate impact on women because of their ability to become pregnant, and therefore violated the PDA. The court found that the policy could not be justified by business necessity given that "no one in management knew the reason for the policy; the policy just existed,"[64] a classic description of an institutionalized practice. In *Abrams v. Graphic Arts International Union*, a case in which a pregnant employee was fired because she took more than the allotted ten days of leave under the employers' policy, the court held that "[a]n employer can incur a Title VII violation as much by a lack of an adequate leave policy as by unequal application of a policy it does have."[65] Some courts have allowed disparate impact challenges to time-norm-based work practices such as selecting employees for termination based on their part-time status,[66]

---

[61] 42 U.S.C. § 2000e-2(k)(1)(A); Watson v. Fort Worth Bank & Trust, 487 U.S. 977, 994–95 (1988).

[62] 42 U.S.C. § 2000e-2(k)(1)(A)(i).

[63] 42 U.S.C. § 2000e-2(k)(1)(A)(ii), (k)(1)(C); Albemarle Paper Co. v. Moody, 422 U.S. 405, 425 (1975).

[64] 768 F. Supp. 647, 655 (N.D. Ill. 1991).

[65] 660 F.2d 811, 819 (D.C. Cir. 1981).

[66] Ilhardt v. Sara Lee Corp., 118 F.3d 1151, 1156–57 (7th Cir. 1997) (considering but then rejecting for lack of evidence plaintiff's disparate impact challenge to her termination on the basis of her part-time status).

terminating women for absenteeism caused by morning sickness,[67] and even denying the use of sick leave to tend to ill family members.[68] All these policies assume an ideal worker who will not be pregnant, will not have family responsibilities, and will work a full-time schedule – all assumptions based on a traditional division of labor between a breadwinner and a noncareer-oriented partner.

Despite the initial promise of these cases, disparate impact theory has not been a reliable avenue for restructuring work's time norms. Although courts recognize that disparate impact challenges are theoretically permissible, in practice few plaintiffs prevail. Plaintiffs must overcome significant evidentiary hurdles to make the required *prima facie* showing that a specific employment policy exists and has a disparate impact on a protected group.[69] As we just saw, institutionalized employment practices can be so deeply entrenched that they no longer appear to be business practices, but simply seem to define what work means. For example, inflexible work schedules, full-time or longer work hours, stingy absenteeism and leave policies, and penalties for part-time work

---

[67] Miller-Wohl Co. v. Commissioner of Lab. & Industry, 692 P.2d 1243, 1251–52 (Mont. 1984) (noting in state law claim that facially neutral policies may violate Title VII if they have a substantially disparate impact on members of one sex), vacated and remanded, 479 U.S. 1050 (1987), judgment and opinion reinstated, 744 P.2d 871 (Mont. 1987).

[68] Roberts v. United States Postmaster Gen., 947 F. Supp. 282, 289 (E.D. Tex. 1996) (holding that the plaintiff's allegation that the employer's policy of denying sick leave to attend to medical needs of family members stated a cause of action under Title VII's disparate impact theory).

[69] First, although courts differ on whether employees must present statistical evidence to show disparate impact, several look for statistical evidence to make a *prima facie* case. Lang v. Star Herald, 107 F.3d 1308, 1314 (8th Cir. 1997) (requiring statistical evidence of disparate impact); Armstrong v. Flowers Hosp. Inc., 33 F.3d 1308 (11th Cir. 1994) (requiring statistical evidence of disparate impact); Maganuco v. Leyden Community High Sch. Dist., 939 F.2d 440, 443–44 (7th Cir. 1991) (noting plaintiffs "generally rely on statistical evidence" to show disparate impact). *But see Garcia*, 97 F.3d at 813 (holding that statistical evidence would be unnecessary if the plaintiff demonstrated all or substantially all pregnant women would have lifting restrictions). Statistical disparities are difficult to demonstrate for small employers because statistical significance depends in part on the size of the sample. *See* Lang, 107 F.3d at 1314

seem to be natural, normal, and inevitable, rather than explicit employer policies subject to challenge under a disparate impact theory.[70]

If the plaintiff makes a *prima facie* showing of disparate impact, her claim can fail if an employer can successfully raise the defense of business necessity, a murky and contested standard.[71] Even if the requirements for disparate impact challenges were clear, however, the theoretical justification for this theory remains ambiguous. There is tension between a broad rationale for disparate impact theory as a means to reach practices that were adopted without discriminatory intent but that have a discriminatory impact, and a narrower vision of disparate impact as simply a doctrinal tool for smoking out subtle forms of intentional discrimination (Jolls 2001; Siegel 2000). Despite early successful disparate impact challenges to workplace time standards, it has become unclear exactly how Title VII applies to employers who adopt common business practices that are facially neutral but rest on, and reference, outmoded conceptions of gender. Employers may not have chosen those practices with the intent to exclude women, but instead merely adopted workplace

(noting that the employee admits she cannot show statistical disparity for her small employer). Second, it can be difficult to demonstrate that an adverse employment action flows from a "particular practice" rather than simply a one-time decision by the employer. *See, e.g., Illhardt*, 118 F.3d at 1156–57 (holding a reduction in force that eliminated a female employee because she was part time was an "isolated incident" rather than an employment practice).

[70] *Illhardt*, discussed above, illustrates how a disparate impact challenge to time norms can founder in this way on the evidentiary hurdles required for a *prima facie* case. Illhardt argued that terminating part-time employees had a disparate impact on professional women with young children. The court rejected this claim, holding that the employer's one-time reduction in force could not be called an "employment practice" within the definition of Title VII, thus evicerating Illhardt's disparate impact challenge.

[71] 42 U.S.C. § 2000e-2(k)(1)(A)(i). Employers asserting the business necessity defense must demonstrate that job characteristics are objectively necessary. Early decisions interpreting disparate impact theories required defendants that were asserting business necessity to show that the challenged employment practice was "related to job performance" and "consistent with business necessity." *Griggs*, 401 U.S. 424. In Ward's Cove Packing Co. v. Atonio, the Court held that an employer must demonstrate only that the practice had a "legitimate business purpose." 490 U.S. 642 (1989).

practices that were institutionalized among their peers, even though historically, those practices systematically excluded women.

Some commentators argue that because disparate impact theory requires no proof of intent, they allow women to challenge work's structural characteristics. In this view, disparate impact theory requires not only the absence of discrimination, but also changes to work's characteristics to adapt to women's needs, by providing pregnancy leave, for example (Jolls 2001; Williams 2000). Other commentators argue that disparate impact theory only creates another means of smoking out "covert" discriminatory intent that would be difficult to prove otherwise (Rutherglen 1987; Strauss 1989).[72] Indeed, consistent with the latter view, many early disparate impact cases involved facially neutral education or testing requirements imposed to screen out women and minorities after the Civil Rights Act of 1964 took effect.[73] This constrained view of disparate impact theory would limit it to these kinds of covertly discriminatory hurdles, and would not reach work practices that are so institutionalized that they have become standard and therefore seem free from discriminatory intent.

But what if institutionalized work practices do not reflect discriminatory biases but instead reflect what I call *institutional inequality* –

Ward's Cove threatened to eviscerate disparate impact as a separate theory, but the Civil Rights Act of 1991 rejected the decision, allowing the standard to revert to the relatively stable, but not uncontested, state of law prior to Ward's Cove. Disparate impact claims, although controversial, are relatively rare. John J. Donohue & Peter Siegelman, *The Changing Nature of Employment Discrimination*, 43 STAN. L. REVIEW 983, 998 (1991).

[72] *See also* Lanning v. Southeastern Pensylvania Transportation Authority, 181 F.3d 478, 490 (3rd Cir. 1999). ("The disparate impact theory of discrimination combats not intentional, obvious discriminatory policies, but a type of covert discrimination in which facially neutral practices are employed to exclude, unnecessarily and disparately, protected groups from employment opportunities. Inherent in the adoption of this theory of discrimination is the recognition that an employer's job requirements may incorporate societal standards based not upon necessity but rather upon historical, discriminatory biases. A business necessity standard that wholly defers to an employer's judgment as to what is desirable in an employee therefore is completely inadequate in combating covert discrimination based upon societal prejudices.")

[73] *See, e.g.*, Griggs v. Duke Power Co., 401 U.S. 424 (1971).

historical social patterns based on women's subordinate roles? Early disparate impact decisions such as *Warshawsky* and *Abrams* allowed challenges to institutionalized work practices that did not reflect discriminatory animus, but that stemmed from historical social practices that presumed women would be tangential workers. Moreover, the disparate impact theory codified in the Civil Rights Act of 1991 is not limited only to circumstances that involve subtle or covert discriminatory intent. Nevertheless, courts have suggested that the very fact that a work practice based on time norms has become institutionalized may insulate it from disparate impact challenges.

In *Dormeyer v. Comerica Bank-Illinois*, the plaintiff lost her job because of absences related to morning sickness. The Seventh Circuit recognized that disparate impact theory might apply if the absenteeism policy "weighed more heavily on pregnant employees than on nonpregnant ones and ... was not justified by compelling considerations of business need."[74] The court then suggested, however, that disparate impact theory should apply only to eligibility requirements that are not really necessary for the job, referencing the education and testing requirements challenged in past cases. In the court's view, any disparate impact challenge to an absenteeism policy would be an argument that employers "excuse pregnant employees from having to satisfy the legitimate requirements of the job...."[75] Although dicta, the court's conclusion was that "the concept of disparate impact [did] not stretch that far."[76]

The reasoning in *Dormeyer* fails to require the employer to demonstrate that restrictive attendance policies are consistent with business necessity; it merely assumes that they are legitimate requirements of the job. By implicitly deciding without inquiry what the legitimate requirements of work are, the court's dicta make a normative judgment about necessary work practices. This analysis sidestepped any meaningful inquiry into whether this particular absenteeism policy was necessary.

[74] 223 F.3d 579, 583 (7th Cir. 2000).
[75] *Id*. at 584.
[76] *Id*.

It also enforced and obscured the relationship between time norms and traditional gender roles by labeling restrictive absenteeism policies as natural and obvious, thus validating them and insulating them from challenge.

Other developments in the Fifth Circuit illustrate that institutionalized time standards may be particularly impervious to disparate impact reasoning even when other workplace policies are successfully challenged through disparate impact claims. *Stout v. Baxter Healthcare Corp.*[77] involved a challenge to a strict absenteeism policy that required the termination of any employee who missed more than three days during her 90-day probationary period. The Fifth Circuit had previously held in *Garcia v. Women's Hospital of Texas* that statistical evidence of disparate impact was unnecessary when all or substantially all pregnant women would be affected by a mandatory job requirement, in this case the requirement that employees be able to lift 150 pounds. The plaintiff in *Stout* argued that, like the lifting requirement in *Garcia*, the three-day absence rule would disproportionately affect all, or substantially all, pregnant women.[78] Although the Fifth Circuit agreed that the plaintiff had demonstrated that all or substantially all pregnant women who give birth during the probationary period would be terminated under the policy, the court refused to apply *Garcia* to claims in which the "only challenge is that the amount of sick leave granted to employees is insufficient to accommodate the time off required in a typical pregnancy."[79] To reach this conclusion, the court reasoned that:

> When the *Garcia* rule is applied to cases (such as this one) in which a plaintiff challenges only an employer's limit on absenteeism the rule produces an effect which is contrary to the plain language of the statute. It is the nature of pregnancy and childbirth that at some point, for a limited period of time, a woman who gives birth will be unable

[77] 282 F.3d 856 (5th Cir. 2002).
[78] The plaintiff provided expert testimony that no pregnant woman who gives birth would be able to work for at least two weeks afterward. *Id.* at 861.
[79] *Id.*

> to work.... If *Garcia* is taken to its logical extreme, then every preg-
> nant employee can make out a *prima facia* case against her employer
> for pregnancy discrimination, unless the employer grants special
> leave to all pregnant employees. This is not the law....[80]

The court locates the conflict between work's time standards and pregnancy not in the challenged work practice, but in the nature of pregnancy
and childbirth. This rhetorical move avoids any meaningful inquiry into
whether a three-day absenteeism policy is job related and consistent
with business necessity, or whether less discriminatory alternatives are
available. Other attendance policies are clearly possible without singling
out pregnant employees for different treatment. Not all employers have
three-day absenteeism policies, and many with more generous policies
provide no special leave to pregnant employees, so a disparate impact
challenge to this particularly restrictive policy should have been possible
in theory. But because this disparate impact challenge might require the
employer to change the taken-for-granted time standards of work (and
do so for a pregnant employee), the court categorically holds that disparate impact theory does not apply, even though after *Garcia* it logically
should have.

Why did the Fifth Circuit accept the disparate impact challenge
in *Garcia* but reject it in *Stout*? One answer is that 150-pound lifting
requirements are not as taken-for-granted as employer-imposed time
standards. Time standards implicate the relationship between work and
gender in a way that lifting requirements do not, and they also reach to
the heart of hard-won employer prerogatives to control the process of
production. To say that work must accommodate pregnancy leave is to
remake the divide between public and private life, and to accept that
barriers to women's employment are not inherent in their gender, but
are constructed by workplace policies such as unnecessarily restrictive
attendance requirements. That is, pregnancy renders women unable to
work only in a world in which institutionalized work practices require

[80] *Id.*

uninterrupted attendance and minimal leave, just as using a wheelchair renders one disabled only in a world without ramps. For this reason, courts may resist changing the time standards of work because to do so disrupts a far deeper social structure built around traditional conceptions of work and gender, the gendered meaning of public and private life, and employer controls over work time that rest on gendered conceptions of labor.

Even if an employer demonstrates business necessity in a disparate impact case, a plaintiff may still prevail by demonstrating that less discriminatory alternative practices exist.[81] This analysis provides another way to challenge institutionalized work practices because it involves articulating alternative ways of organizing work that do not rely on outdated conceptions of gender. It remains to be seen, however, whether courts will accept alternative practices that may increase costs and reduce efficiency. Some commentators and courts have expressed skepticism about less discriminatory alternatives that appear to be costly.[82] Institutionalization plays a role here as well: To the extent that practices such as restrictive absenteeism policies have become common, deviating from the norm is unlikely to be costless, just as installing a women's restroom in the lawyer's lounge at the Supreme Court to accommodate the growing number of women arguing cases before the Court was not costless (Quindlen 1992). The question is how costs like these should be understood. One can view the expense of deviating from institutionalized norms as costs imposed on employers by employment laws, or one can view these expenses as the product of historical factors that structured work in an inefficient way that excludes women from work. The former view assumes avoiding the cost of change is efficient, but the status quo is not necessarily the most efficient or optimal solution, even from a purely

---

[81] 42 U.S.C. § 2000e-2(k)(1)(A)(ii), (k)(1)(C); Albemarle Paper Co. v. Moody, 422 U.S. 405, 425 (1975).
[82] Watson v. Fort Worth Bank & Trust, 487 U.S. 977, 998 (1988); Note, business necessity under Title VII of the Civil Rights Act of 1964: A no-alternative approach, 84 Yale L.J. 98, 114–15 (1974).

economic perspective. Inefficient institutions can persist even as fundamental social conditions, such as the structure of families, change (North 1990; Pierson 2000). Institutional perspectives suggest that considering the cost of changing institutionalized practices without also interrogating the continuing necessity and utility of the practices themselves itself makes little sense. Considering only costs undermines attempts to challenge entrenched work practices that perpetuate inequality.

The latter view suggests a justification for imposing costs that the employer, or even society, should bear to eradicate institutionalized inequality, given that women primarily bear the costs of current institutional arrangements (i.e., inflexible workplaces). Allowing the workplace to remain the same is not costless; the costs of such a policy are borne by women workers who are excluded or penalized by existing arrangements. Treating the burden of change as an impermissible cost accepts the structure of work as the natural, rather than socially constructed, baseline.

The Failure to Contemplate Family Life

Pregnancy discrimination cases illustrate why Title VII and the PDA have limited potential for restructuring the institution of work. The limitations of these laws become even more apparent when accommodating family life beyond pregnancy is considered. Even after Title VII, employers remain free to structure their workplaces around a two-parent family in which work must be mutually exclusive from caring for children. For example, courts have held that Title VII does not require parental leave to care for new children after the mother is no longer physically disabled by childbirth.[83] Clearly, however, someone still must be available to care for children after they are born. Courts have also held that Title VII does

---

[83] *See, e.g.*, Maganuco v. Leyden Community High School, 939 F.2d 440, 444 (7th Cir. 1991) (holding leave policies that disproportionately impact women who "forego returning to work in favor of spending time at home with [their] newborn child" do not violate Title VII); Piantanida v. Wyman Ctr., Inc., 927 F. Supp. 1226, 1238 (E.D. Mo.

not require employers to provide part-time or flexible work schedules,[84] nor does it protect women who hold part-time positions from being the first to be laid off, even if those women have more seniority than full-time workers who are retained.[85] All these cases involved disparate treatment theories, however. It is an open question whether such policies could be challenged under disparate impact theory.[86]

1996) (denying relief to a mother seeking leave to take care of a newly adopted child because "new mother" is not a protected class under Title VII); Barnes v. Hewlett-Packard Co., 846 F. Supp. 442, 443–45 (D. Md. 1994) (holding employer's failure to provide parental leave to a female employee to care for her child does not violate Title VII); Wallace v. Pyro Mining Co., 789 F. Supp. 867, 870 (W.D. Ky. 1990) (holding that denying an employee leave to breast feed her child did not violate Title VII), aff'd, No. 90–6259, 1991 U.S. App. LEXIS 32310 (6th Cir. Dec. 19, 1991); Record v. Mill Neck Manor Lutheran Sch., 611 F. Supp. 905 (E.D.N.Y. 1985) (denying relief to female employee on the grounds that Title VII does not protect people who wish to take child-rearing leaves); EEOC v. Southwestern Elec. Power Co., 591 F. Supp. 1128 (W.D. Ark. 1984) (holding that firing a woman who requested six rather than four weeks of leave after giving birth did not violate Title VII where worker's doctor said she physically could go back to work after four weeks but he recommended the extra time in part to bond with her child). In some cases it seems clear that the key distinction for courts is "legitimate" physical incapacity compared to the "choice" of individuals physically able to work to care for new children in the family. See Barrash v. Bowen, 846 F.2d 927, 931–32 (4th Cir. 1988). ("One can draw no valid comparison between people, male and female, suffering extended incapacity from illness or injury and young mothers wishing to nurse little babies.")
[84] See Spina v. Management Recruiters of O'Hare, 764 F. Supp. 519, 536 (N.D. Ill. 1991) (holding that an employer was not obligated to provide part-time work to "rescue [an employee] from a predicament for which it was not responsible," i.e., health complications following pregnancy, even where male employees with health problems were given leave); Haas v. Phoenix Data Processing, Inc., No. 89-C-0305, 1990 U.S. Dist. Lexis 3797 (N.D. Ill. April 5, 1990) (holding Title VII did not prohibit terminating a pregnant employee who refused to work overtime due to pregnancy and child care issues because the employer had a legitimate expectation that the employee would work overtime).
[85] Illhardt v. Sara Lee Corp., 118 F.3d 1151 (7th Cir. 1997) (holding that Title VII did not prohibit terminating a part-time employee before full-time employees, even if the part-time employee was pregnant and had more seniority that employees who were retained).
[86] Roberts v. United States Postmaster Gen., 947 F. Supp. 282, 288 (E.D. Tex. 1996) (noting that whether the employer's policies denying parental leave could be

In *Armstrong v. Flowers Hospital, Inc.*,[87] the Eleventh Circuit summed up the constraints on choice that judicial interpretations of antidiscrimination law now create for working women. The court concluded that a woman faced with a workplace that fails to accommodate her pregnancy or her family responsibilities "may choose to continue working, to seek a work situation with less stringent requirements, or to leave the workforce. In some cases, these alternatives may, indeed present a difficult choice. But it is a choice that each woman must make."[88] She may not, however, rely on Title VII and the PDA to challenge the institutionalized features of her job that exclude her from work, no matter how arbitrary or nonessential they may be.

Of course, full-time work schedules, restrictive attendance policies, and lack of disability leave are not inherent in the nature of work, or is the fact that they are common practice unrelated to past gender discrimination. Current judicial interpretations of Title VII, however, obscure how these work practices rest on outdated conceptions of gender and work and how they constrain women's choices in the present. The result is that these barriers to employment are treated as natural consequences of gender and pregnancy, rather than as socially constructed features of work with roots in the family wage gender norms of the past.

Nevertheless, there is a growing recognition that workplace decision making based on gendered stereotypes about family caregiving is prohibited by Title VII. For example, Williams and Segal (2003) outline how existing theories under Title VII and other laws can be used to challenge discrimination against caregivers that is driven by stereotypes about women and mothers not being adequate workers. In addition, the

challenged under a disparate impact theory was an open question); *see also Record*, 611 F. Supp. at 907; 29 C.F.R. § 1604.10(c) (if the leave policy of a federal contractor has a disparate impact on pregnant employees, it must be justified by business necessity).

[87] 33 F.3d 1308 (11th Cir. 1994).

[88] *Id.* at 1315.

EEOC has issued enforcement guidance about unlawful disparate treatment of workers with caregiving responsibilities.[89] The guidance makes clear that Title VII prohibits gender role stereotyping of working mothers: Employers may not, for example, treat female workers less favorably because they assume women will perform caretaking or that care responsibilities will interfere with their work. The guidance also states that in stereotyping cases, comparator evidence from similarly situated men may not be necessary to establish a *prima facie* case of disparate treatment, an important interpretive guideline for avoiding some of the pitfalls presented previously.

Stereotype theories are enormously useful because they allow plaintiffs to proceed without difficult-to-obtain comparator evidence from similarly situated male employees, and without expensive and complicated statistical evidence. In addition, they allow plaintiffs to take into account the role of culture, history, and social meaning, in this way unearthing many of the gender dynamics discussed in the genealogy of work presented earlier in this chapter. But stereotype theories also run the risk of reifying time norms and work structures. These theories emphasize that employers may not presume that pregnant women will take time off from work, but they also suggest that if a pregnant woman needs time off or an accommodation, that would be a different situation with a different outcome. Although these developments make good use of existing laws to challenge disparate treatment of workers based on gendered stereotypes about care and work, even the EEOC guidance makes clear that employment decisions based on workers' actual performance do not generally violate Title VII. Accordingly, to the extent that a worker needs time off or other changes to existing work practices to manage work and family responsibilities, Title VII still offers little protection.

[89] EEOC Enforcement Guidance: Unlawful Disparate Treatment of Workers with Caregiving Responsibilities (May 23, 2007). EEOC Enforcement Guidance has no legally binding effect, but some courts consider it in interpreting the law.

Moving Beyond Antidiscrimination Models

Title VII has proven to be an inadequate tool for challenging institution-alized work practices such as time norms. It has been relatively successful in curtailing discrimination against women, including pregnant women, who continue to be able to do their jobs as those jobs are currently defined. However, for working women who cannot meet time require-ments because of pregnancy, childbirth, or related medical conditions, only disparate impact theory offers an avenue for directly challenging time norms that disproportionately affect women. Moreover, challenges to deeply entrenched workplace practices such as full-time schedules or rigid attendance policies are almost never successful. Although gendered restrictions that do not affect work's structure are no longer accepted, challenges to that structure are, for the most part, rejected. Women able to meet institutionalized work norms are legally protected, but the way those norms rest on and recreate outmoded notions of gender remains unchallenged.

This doctrinal landscape creates a set of limited choices for work-ing women that are constrained by the existing structure of work. For example, is pregnancy incompatible with employment because child-birth requires absence from work or because workplace policies pro-hibit more than a few days of sick leave? More generally, note that work and family do not *always* conflict; instead, it is those families that fail to adhere to traditional gender roles that experience problems balancing the two. Because Title VII tends to focus only on gender discrimination without interrogating work practices, it invites courts to locate barriers to working in the personal circumstances and choices of women, not in the structure of work itself. This approach reinforces work practices that push workers to adopt traditional gender roles at home.

New institutionalist approaches help to explain why courts are reluc-tant to interpret Title VII and the PDA as requiring time off for pregnant workers. First, as we have seen, the time norms of work have come to seem so natural, normal, and inevitable that to courts they seem not be policies at all but realities within which actors must function. They have become somewhat impervious to legal reforms because courts find it hard to imagine that work practices can be organized in alternative ways and still be recognizable as work as we know it in our culture. When time norms come to be seen as part of the landscape rather than policy choices, they become insulated from meaningful challenge under Title VII.

Second, because work and gender are mutually constitutive, attempts to change work by relying on the category of gender can inadvertently reify the current relationship between the two. The very process of defining what gender and work mean for purposes of legal analysis tends to naturalize our existing conceptions of these categories in ways that undermine change. For example, when courts analyze gendered patterns in part-time work or parental leave, they often fail to consider how workplace structures construct the social conditions that require such choices and that shape men and women's behaviors at work and outside the workplace. Understanding work and gender as mutually constitutive categories suggests a potential solution to the dilemma of accommodation versus equality. Rather than focusing on prohibiting discrimination on the basis of gender, one might also ask what work should look like. This strategy for reform is not unprecedented. As we've seen, some laws protect other types of temporary leave, such as jury duty[90] or military leave, which traditionally has been taken mostly by men.[91] In addition, our expectations of a 40-hour work week stem from Progressive Era legislation that sets the hours of work in a standard work week; historically, work weeks have been both much longer and shorter than this legal standard (Hunnicutt 1988, 1996).[92] Highly contested at one time, these restrictions on the schedule of work are taken-for-granted today. These laws balance the social importance of civic responsibility, military preparedness, and a reasonable life outside of work against our expectations regarding work.

[90] 28 U.S.C. § 1875.
[91] 38 U.S.C. § 4311.
[92] Fair Labor Standards Act, 29 U.S.C. §§ 201 *et seq.*

Merely prohibiting discrimination on the basis of gender leaves the historically determined relationship between work and gender unchallenged. Prohibitions on gender discrimination were necessary, but something more is needed for the next wave of antidiscrimination measures. Laws that focus on changing workplace practices directly are a more explicit reform to the other side of the equation, namely work. Moreover, because work organizes both workplace and nonworkplace social life, changes in the structure of work will change the meaning of gender as well.

When the focus shifts from who is protected by antidiscrimination statutes to what work should look like, the question changes. It is not whether women should get special treatment even though they cannot live up to deeply entrenched time norms in the workplace. Rather, the question becomes whether the institution of work itself should be restructured by law (and along with it both the workplace *and* the nonworkplace organization of social life around traditional gendered roles). This approach queries whether a work practice is necessary or desirable, and does not simply assume it is necessary because it is part of the way things have always been done. Moreover, by treating work and gender as an interrelated system of meaning and by considering directly how work should be structured, one also considers, implicitly, how certain workplace practices may operate to enforce particular gender roles. In this way, theorists can envision a broader range of meanings for work and gender, and avoid reifying any particular understanding of either category.

Cultural versus Legal Conceptions of Disability and the ADA

Title I of the ADA, another civil rights response to institutionalized work practices, seems to offer more promise in restructuring time standards and other workplace barriers to people with disabilities. The ADA prohibits discrimination against individuals with disabilities, much like Title VII prohibits sex discrimination.[93] The ADA also extends beyond equal

[93] 42 U.S.C. § 12112(a).

treatment within the existing structure of work to require employers to provide reasonable accommodations to qualified workers with disabilities.[94]
The statute does not completely restructure work, however. As a defense,
employers may argue that providing accommodations would impose an
undue hardship,[95] or that particular job requirements are essential and
therefore not subject to accommodation under the Act.[96] Nevertheless,
the ADA requires employers to show that particular job requirements
are essential and job related, rather than merely asserting that they are.[97]
Accordingly, the ADA does not take for granted that the features of the
job as it has always been done are natural, normal, and essential.

By requiring not only equal treatment but also accommodation, the
ADA undermines the idea that the structure of work is inevitable and
unchangeable. Indeed, advocates justified the need for disability legislation by pointing out that work's customary structure was frequently
viewed as unchangeable even when it was not essential:

> It is often incorrectly assumed that there is only one way of doing
> something – the customary way that 'normal' people do it....
> Although it is sometimes difficult to see alternatives when 'things
> have always been done that way,' the tasks that comprise most jobs
> are often easily changed. (United States Commission on Civil Rights
> September 1983: 90)

Advocates successfully argued that employers legally should be required
to accommodate the range of abilities present in the workforce, rather
than being allowed to structure work around an idealized able-bodied
worker. This approach had the potential to be transformative by break-
ing down implicit understandings that disability and work are mutually
exclusive.

[94] *Id* § 12112(b)(5)(A).

[95] *Id.*

[96] Ward v. Mass. Health Research Inst., Inc., 209 F.3d 29, 34–35 (1st Cir. 2000); 29
C.F.R. § 1630.2(n).

[97] Ward, 209 F.3d at 35 (holding that the employer bears the burden of proving that a
given job function is an essential function).

The language of the statute makes some startling moves that reveal institutionalized inequalities in work's structure and that attempt to provide the legal means to challenge those inequalities.[98] First, the Act explicitly recognizes that an individual can be both disabled and a worker. The ADA prohibits employers from discriminating against "a qualified individual with a disability."[99] The Act defines a "qualified individual with a disability" to be

an individual with a disability who satisfies the requisite skill, experience, education and other job-related requirements of the employment position such individual holds or desires, and who, with or without reasonable accommodation, can perform the essential functions of such position.[100]

The statute defines "disability" to mean

(A) a physical or mental impairment that substantially limits one or more of the major life activities of such individual;
(B) a record of such impairment; or
(C) being regarded as having such an impairment.[101]

Major life activities include "caring for oneself, performing manual tasks, walking, seeing, hearing, speaking, breathing, learning, and working."[102] An impairment is "substantially limiting" if it renders an individual

---

[98] The ADA incorporates many regulatory definitions of disability developed in connection with the Rehabilitation Act of 1973, which prohibits discrimination against people with disabilities in federal employment and contracting. *See* Jonathan C. Drimmer, *Cripples, Overcomers, and Civil Rights: Tracing the Evolution of Federal Legislation and Social Policy for People with Disabilities.* 40 UCLA L. REVIEW 1341–410 (1993). In addition, both the Rehabilitation Act and the ADA prohibit discrimination against people with disabilities in other contexts not relevant here, such as public accommodations, federal programs, and transportation. For ease of presentation, in the following discussion, I treat the ADA and the Rehabilitation Act as synonymous.
[99] 42 U.S.C. § 12112(a).
[100] 29 C.F.R. § 1630.2(m).
[101] 42 U.S.C. § 12102(2).
[102] *Id.* § 1630.2(i).

unable to perform a major life activity that the average person in the general population can perform, or if it significantly restricts the condition, manner, or duration under which an individual can perform that activity as compared to an average person in the general population.[103] Thus, for purposes of the ADA an individual may be both a qualified worker and disabled, notwithstanding cultural presumptions that these categories are mutually exclusive.

Second, the Act requires employers to modify existing work structures to accommodate a worker's disability. For example, the concept of "qualified individual with a disability" incorporates consideration of possible accommodations. To be "qualified," one must show (1) minimum qualifications and skills for the position, and (2) the ability to perform the essential functions of the position with or without a reasonable accommodation.[104] The second requirement creates a doctrinal avenue for restructuring work through reasonable accommodations, which are:

> Modifications or adjustments to the work environment, or to the manner or circumstances under which the position held or desired is customarily performed, that enable a qualified individual with a disability to perform the essential functions of that position.[105]

Reasonable accommodations may include, among other things: "job restructuring, part-time or modified work schedules, ... and other similar accommodations...."[106] Thus, time standards are included among the job features than are subject to accommodation.

In the courts, however, the cultural conceptions of work and disability that the ADA attempts to challenge have also been its downfall. When considering whether a plaintiff is disabled within the meaning of the Act, courts often rely on popular understandings of disability as the complete inability to work, rather than applying the legal definition of

---

[103] 29 C.F.R. § 1630.2(j)(1)(i)–(ii).
[104] 29 C.F.R. §§ 1630.2(m), (q).
[105] 29 C.F.R. §§ 1630.2(o)(ii).
[106] 42 U.S.C. §12111(9)(B).

disability set forth in the statute. Many courts require individuals to be nearly completely unable to work to qualify as disabled, which then tends to render them not "otherwise qualified" and therefore not protected by the statute. Alternatively, courts tend to assume that individuals who are otherwise qualified, and therefore able to work in some capacity, cannot, by definition, be disabled despite the contrary language of the statute. In many cases, this definitional catch-22 prevents courts from ever reaching the question of reasonable accommodation, thus cutting off the primary doctrinal avenue for reshaping existing work structures that create barriers to workers with disabilities.[107] Even when courts reach the question of reasonable accommodations, they are generally skeptical of proposed accommodations that change time standards. Courts tend to assume time standards and work schedules are essential and therefore not subject to accommodation, effectively closing any legal avenues for challenging those practices. As a result, the ADA does little to change institutionalized time standards at work despite its expansive language.

Several areas of ADA doctrine illustrate how cultural presumptions about work and disability have shaped judicial interpretations of the ADA. First, for a time, courts applied judicial estoppel (a doctrine that prevents parties from asserting contradictory legal arguments) to reject ADA claims from plaintiffs who also sought disability benefits

[107] For example, in Sutton v. United Air Lines, 526 U.S. 471 (1999), the employer refused pilot positions to two workers who had impaired vision that was easily corrected by glasses, arguing that it required pilots to have near-perfect uncorrected vision. Rather than considering whether a reasonable accommodation could include relaxing that rule, which would have allowed the plaintiffs to perform the job, the Supreme Court ruled that the plaintiffs were not, in fact, disabled because they were not impaired in the major life activity of seeing once their corrective lenses were taken into account. The Court also held that the plaintiffs were not impaired in the major life activity of working because other airlines that had no comparable rule would hire them as pilots. Somewhat paradoxically, these myopic plaintiffs were deemed sufficiently impaired to be rejected for employment but not sufficiently impaired to be protected by the ADA because other jobs, albeit less desirable ones, remained open to them. The Court never considered, however, whether the rule against corrected vision was truly an "essential function" of the position, even though the fact that other airlines did not have this rule suggested it was not.

from the state. The theory in these cases was that plaintiffs could not be "otherwise qualified" to perform their jobs if they claimed that they were unable to work for purposes of disability benefits. Second, courts have made it especially difficult to prove that one is both "qualified" and "disabled" when plaintiffs attempt to show disability through substantial limitations in the major life activity of working. In these cases, courts often apply "common sense" reasoning to find it paradoxical for plaintiffs to claim that they are qualified if their disabilities impair their ability to work. Third, courts avoid considering accommodations that would change the time standards of work, even though the statutory language explicitly contemplates such accommodations. Taken together, these developments generally prevent courts from even considering the Act's most transformational features in most ADA claims.

Legal and Social Meanings of Disability

The application of judicial estoppel doctrine is one of the clearest examples of how social and legal definitions of disability have come into conflict in judicial interpretations of the ADA. The doctrine of judicial estoppel prevents a litigant from asserting inconsistent legal positions in two different judicial proceedings in order "to protect the integrity of the judicial process, avoid inconsistent results, and prevent litigants from playing fast and loose in order to secure an advantage."[108] For a time, courts applied this doctrine to preclude plaintiffs who applied for state disability benefits from also claiming they were able to perform the essential functions of their positions with or without accommodation. As one court put it, "[i]t is impossible for [the plaintiff] to have been both disabled under social security law and able to perform the essential functions of his work under the ADA."[109] In these instances, courts

---

[108] Grant v. Lone Star Co., 21 F.3d 649, 651 n.2 (5th Cir. 1994). In the majority view, judicial estoppel precludes a plaintiff from asserting a position inconsistent with a previous position only if the plaintiff prevailed in the earlier proceeding. Britton v. Co-Op Banking Group, 4 F.3d 742, 744 (9th Cir. 1993).

[109] Nguyen v. IBP, Inc., 905 F. Supp. 1471, 1485 (D. Kan. 1995).

assumed that the ability to work and claims of disability are, by definition, mutually exclusive, rather than analyzing whether the statutory
definitions of disability in the ADA and the Social Security Act could
be compatible.[110] Some courts went so far as to hold that a claim that one
was both a qualified worker for purposes of the ADA and also disabled
for purposes of Social Security was not only legally incorrect, but also
morally suspect and fraudulent.[111]

The problem with these interpretations is that disability is not an
inherent, objective characteristic of individuals. It is a social and legal
construct that can have different meanings within different statutory
schemes. For example, the ADA's definition of qualified person with a
disability includes an assessment of whether an individual could work
with reasonable accommodations. The Social Security Administration,
however, determines disability without reference to whether a reasonable accommodation would enable a claimant to work.[112] Accordingly,
an individual could be able to work if given accommodations, thus meeting the definition of disability in the ADA, while also being unable to
find work due to a lack of available accommodations in the labor market,
thus meeting the definition of disability for purposes of state disability benefits. Culturally, however, claiming one is both a worker and disabled violates implicit norms that only those who are completely unable
to work should be supported by the state, and that those with residual
working capacity should rely on the labor market for survival.

The difficulties ADA plaintiffs face as they attempt to navigate this
statutory scheme reveals how work as an institution and disability as
an identity are constitutive of each other. Disability has been culturally defined not in terms of specific impairments, but in reference to
the labor market – as the complete inability to work. As Stone (1984)

---

[110] Reiff v. Interim Personnel, Inc., 906 F. Supp. 1280, 1291 (D. Minn. 1995).
[111] McNeill v. Atchison, Topeka & Santa Fe R.R., 878 F. Supp. 986, 991 (S.D. Tex. 1995);
Harden v. Delta Airlines, 900 F. Supp. 493, 496 (S.D. Ga. 1995); Reigel v. Kaiser
Found. Health Plan, 859 F. Supp. 963, 970 (E.D.N.C. 1994). ("Plaintiff ... cannot
speak out of both sides of her mouth with ... credibility before this court.")
[112] *See* Cleveland v. Policy Management Systems Corp., 526 U.S. 795, 802–04 (1999).

notes, this social definition reflects political pressures to force as many individuals as possible into an emerging wage-labor market during the historical transition to a modern capitalist economy. Judicial interpretations that treat working and disability as mutually exclusive implicitly accept the state's narrow definition of disability, without taking into account whether the structure of employment has disadvantaged people with impairments. Even though the ADA adopts a much different, more modern, approach that defines disability in terms of the environment, including accommodations (or lack thereof) at work, some courts had difficulty seeing how an individual could legitimately claim both protection from the ADA and benefits from Social Security Disability Insurance (SSDI). By applying judicial estoppel, courts enforced a choice between claiming disability benefits and claiming civil rights protections for workers who wanted to work but could not gain access to employment without accommodations. In these instances, plaintiffs' ADA challenges failed on the definitional question of whether they were both qualified and disabled, never reaching the structural question of whether a change to the workplace in the form of a reasonable accommodation might have enabled them to work.

Some courts recognized the catch-22 presented to workers who are fired in violation of the ADA and find themselves with no means of support because of their impairments. In *Fredenburg v. Contra Costa Department of Health Services*,[113] the Ninth Circuit articulated the bind created in these circumstances:

> [The plaintiff's] case illustrates the problem faced by a worker in her position. Her employer concluded that she could not perform her job, and placed her on unpaid leave. She disagreed with her employer's determination and unsuccessfully challenged it. Then, without pay because of her asserted disability, she applied for temporary disability benefits and received them. What else was she to do?[114]

---

[113] Fredenburg v. Constra Costa Dept. of Health Services, 172 F.3d 1176 (9th Cir. 1999).
[114] *Id.*, 172 F.3d at 1179.

The majority in *Fredenburg* concluded that judicial estoppel should not apply. The dissent, however, disagreed based on an implicit shirker logic. The dissenting judge argued that the majority looked away "with a wink and nudge because [the plaintiff] was 'forced' to lie in order to finagle benefits from the welfare state."[115] Implicit in this statement is the idea that the plaintiff's disability claim must be fraudulent if she was, as she argued, able to work. In this dissenting judge's view, worker status and disability are inherently incompatible; to claim financial support from the state legitimately, one must forgo all claims to the status of worker.

Other courts resolved this conundrum by directly recognizing that disability could have different meanings for purposes of the ADA and the Social Security Act. In *Overton v. Reilly*,[116] the Seventh Circuit held that the Social Security Administration's definition of disability was neither the same as nor determinative of the status of qualified individual with a disability under the ADA and the Rehabilitation Act.[117] The court reasoned that the facially objective medical definition of disability employed by the Social Security Administration contained an implicit administrative judgment:

> [A finding of disability by the SSA] is consistent with a claim that the disabled person is "qualified" to do his job under the Rehabilitation Act. First, the SSA may award disability benefits on a finding that the claimant meets the criteria for a listed disability, without inquiring into his ability to find work within the economy. As it turns out, the SSA granted benefits to Overton on this basis. Second, even if the SSA had looked into Overton's ability to work in the national economy, its inquiry would necessarily be generalized. The SSA may determine that a claimant is unlikely to find a job, but that does not mean that there is no work the claimant can do. In sum, the determination of disability may be relevant evidence of the severity of Overton's

---

[115] *Id.*, 172 F.3d at 1185 (Kozinski, J., dissenting).
[116] 977 F.2d 1190 (7th Cir. 1992).
[117] *Id.*, 977 F.2d at 1196.

handicap, but it can hardly be construed as a judgment that Overton could not do his job at the EPA.[118]

After *Overton*, federal courts continued to struggle with how the definitions of disability in these two statutes interact. A split in the circuits developed regarding whether claiming disability benefits precluded plaintiffs from demonstrating they were otherwise qualified within the meaning of the ADA.[119]

The Supreme Court finally resolved this question in *Cleveland v. Policy Management Systems Corp.*,[120] when it recognized that disability had no inherent meaning but instead was defined differently by different statutes with different remedial purposes. In *Cleveland*, the Court held that applications for SSDI benefits do not automatically legally estop individuals from pursuing ADA claims, nor do they create a strong presumption against a benefit recipient's success on an ADA theory.[121] The Court reasoned that SSDI and the ADA employed different definitions of disability: The ADA's definition includes an assessment of whether an individual could work with reasonable accommodations, whereas the SSDI system does not consider reasonable accommodations when assessing whether an individual is disabled.[122] The Court also recognized that discrepancies between ADA claims and SSDI benefit applications

---

[118] *Id.*

[119] *See, e.g.*, Rascon v. U.S. West Communications, Inc., 143 F.3d 1324, 1332 (10th Cir. 1998) (application for and receipt of disability benefits does not legally estop plaintiff from bringing an ADA claim); Griffith v. Wal-Mart Stores, Inc., 135 F.3d 376, 382 (6th Cir. 1998) (same); Swanks v. Washington Metro. Area Transit Auth., 116 F.3d 582, 586 (D.C. Cir. 1997) (same); McNemar v. Disney Store, Inc., 91 F.3d 610, 618–620 (3rd Cir. 1996) (applying judicial estoppel); *see also* Kennedy v. Applause, Inc., 90 F.3d 1477, 1481–1482 (9th Cir. 1996) (declining to apply estoppel but holding that the plaintiff who claimed total disability in benefits application failed to raise a genuine issue of material fact as to whether she was a qualified individual with a disability).

[120] 526 U.S. 795 (1999).

[121] *Id.* at 797–98.

[122] *Id.* at 802–04. The Court also noted that in some instances, even working individuals could receive SSDI benefits. *Id.* at 805.

could be explained by other factors, including changes in an individual's disability status over time.[123] Accordingly, the Court concluded that there are "many situations in which an SSDI claim and an ADA claim can comfortably exist side by side."[124] More specifically, "an ADA suit claiming that the plaintiff can perform her job with reasonable accommodation may well prove consistent with an SSDI claim that the plaintiff" is unable to work.[125] Accordingly, the Court concluded, "despite the appearance of conflict that arises from the language of the two statutes, the two claims do not inherently conflict to the point where courts should apply a special negative presumption."[126]

Although the Court rejected a presumption against allowing ADA claims from SSDI applicants to go forward, it also held that "a plaintiff's sworn assertion in an application for disability benefits that she is, for example, 'unable to work' will appear to negate an essential element of her ADA case – at least if she does not offer a sufficient explanation."[127] The court held that "an ADA plaintiff cannot simply ignore the apparent contradiction that arises out of the earlier SSDI total disability claim."[128] Instead, plaintiffs must provide "an explanation of any apparent inconsistency with the necessary elements of an ADA claim. To defeat summary judgment, that explanation must be sufficient to warrant a reasonable juror's concluding that, assuming the truth of, or the plaintiff's good-faith belief in, the earlier statement, the plaintiff could nonetheless 'perform the essential functions' of her job, with or without 'reasonable accommodation.'"[129] This interpretation leaves workers who

---

[123] *Id.*
[124] *Id.* at 803.
[125] *Id.*
[126] *Id.* at 803.
[127] *Id.* at 805.
[128] *Id.*
[129] *Id.* Although the Court couches this as an application of the plaintiff's burden of proof on summary judgment, as a practical matter *Cleveland* creates a new affirmative obligation on plaintiffs to demonstrate that their claims to SSDI and their rights under the ADA are not mutually exclusive.

claim disability benefits after being fired in a precarious legal position; they must claim disability benefits in a way that preserves their rights under the ADA, while still showing enough impairment to qualify for benefits. This requirement is particularly troublesome because most plaintiffs are neither aware of this issue nor represented by counsel when they apply for SSDI benefits.

Disabled Worker as a Cultural Oxymoron

Courts also draw on cultural assumptions that disability and work are incompatible when they evaluate whether a plaintiff is a qualified individual with a disability protected by the ADA. In particular, courts find it difficult to understand how a plaintiff could ever be sufficiently impaired in their ability to work to be protected by the ADA, yet retain enough capacity to work to remain "otherwise qualified" for her position, even though the Supreme Court explicitly recognized that this was possible. *School Board v. Arline*,[130] in which the Court considered this issue, made clear that, legally, an individual could be "handicapped" in her ability to work and still be "otherwise qualified" within the meaning of the Rehabilitation Act, a precursor to the ADA. In *Arline*, the defendant school district fired an elementary schoolteacher after she suffered a third relapse of tuberculosis within two years. The plaintiff claimed disability based on substantial limitations on working as a result of her illness. The defendant argued that although the regulations listed working as a major life activity, "disability" did not include a condition that impaired only the activity of working and no other. To contend otherwise, the defendant claimed, was to make "a totally circular argument which lifts itself by its bootstraps."[131]

The Court rejected this argument, reasoning that "Congress plainly intended the Act to cover persons with a physical or mental impairment

---

[130] 480 U.S. 273 (1987).
[131] *Id.*, 480 U.S. at 283 n.10.

(whether actual, past, or perceived) that substantially limited one's ability to work."[132] The Court reasoned that an actual impairment "might not diminish a person's physical or mental capabilities, but could nevertheless substantially limit that person's ability to work as a result of the negative reactions of others to the impairment."[133] The Court also reasoned that "[t]he fact that *some* individuals who have contagious diseases may pose a serious health threat to others ... does not justify excluding from the coverage of the Act *all* persons with actual or perceived contagious diseases." Further, the Court concluded that evaluating whether the plaintiff was "otherwise qualified" would require an individualized inquiry and deference to reasonable medical judgments regarding the threat her disease posed to others.[134]

Arline seemed to reject out of hand arguments that an individual could not be "otherwised qualified" if her claim to disability rested on a substantial limitation in her ability to work. Nevertheless, courts subsequently have struggled to determine the point at which an individual becomes sufficiently or substantially limited in the major life activity of working to be covered by the ADA, but still remains qualified to perform the position. Plaintiffs face an uphill battle if they claim disability based on limitations on their ability to work. On the one hand, most authorities agree that impairments that interfere with an individual's ability to perform only a single job are not "substantially limiting" within the meaning of the statute.[135] On the other hand, the ADA's regulations clearly state that "an individual does not have to be totally unable to work to be considered substantially limited in working...."[136] Instead, a plaintiff must show that he or she is significantly restricted in the ability

---

[132] *Id.* at 283.

[133] *Id.*

[134] 480 U.S. at 287–88.

[135] *See* Taylor v. United States Postal Serv., 946 F.2d 1214 (6th Cir. 1991); *see also* Forrisi v. Bowen, 794 F.2d 931, 935 (4th Cir. 1986) (rejecting a per se rule that every unsuccessful applicant who was rejected because of a job requirement would qualify as handicapped under the Rehabilitation Act).

[136] 29 C.F.R. § 1630.2(j)(3)(i), pt. 1630, app. A § 1630.2(j).

to perform a class of jobs or a broad range of jobs in various classes,[137] yet still able to perform some work. The Supreme Court elaborated on this requirement in *Sutton v. United Air Lines, Inc.*,[138] holding that "[t]o be substantially limited in the major life activity of working ... one must be precluded from more than one job, a specialized job, or a particular job of choice."[139]

Demonstrating that one is both substantially impaired in the ability to work and otherwise qualified is exceedingly difficult given the way courts have construed this requirement. Courts tend to reject claims of disability if the plaintiff exhibits any residual working capacity, rather than evaluating whether the plaintiff's ability to work is substantially impaired relative to the abilities of nondisabled individuals. As a result, evidence that a plaintiff might be able to find *any* other employment, even less lucrative employment that does not make full use of his or her skills and training, tends to undermine the plaintiff's ability to show substantial limitation in the ability to work.[140] This approach is hard to square with the regulations, which require workers to be substantially limited "in [their] ability to perform either a class of jobs or a broad range of jobs in various classes *as compared to the average person having comparable training, skills and abilities.*"[141] Nevertheless, some courts refuse to infer

---

[137] *Id.*

[138] 527 U.S. 471 (1999).

[139] Id. at 492.

[140] *See* Forrisi, 794 F.2d at 935 (noting the plaintiff was able to find employment); *see also* Gutridge v. Clure, 153 F.3d 898, 901 (8th Cir.) (holding no evidence of a substantial limitation in working where plaintiff found other employment), *cert. denied* 119 S. Ct. 1758 (1998); Patterson v. Chicago Ass'n for Retarded Citizens, 150 F.3d 719, 726 (7th Cir. 1998) (finding no substantial limitation where plaintiff found other employment); Halperin v. Abacus Tech. Corp., 128 F.3d 191, 200 (4th Cir. 1997), abrogated on other grounds by Baird v. Rose, 192 F.3d 462 (4th Cir. 1999) (finding "absolutely no indication that Halperin's lifting restriction significantly limits his ability to perform a wide range of jobs" where plaintiff found employment with a different employer); Zirpel v. Toshiba Am. Info. Sys., Inc., 111 F.3d 80, 81 (8th Cir. 1997); Gupton v. Virginia, 14 F.3d 203, 205 (4th Cir. 1994).

[141] *Id.* § 1630.2(j)(3)(I)(emphasis added). The EEOC has made clear that this standard is not intended to require an onerous evidentiary showing. 29 C.F.R. pt 1630, app, 56 Fed Reg 35726, 35741 (July 26, 1991).

limited employment opportunities from evidence of the plaintiff's substantial limitations relative to nonimpaired workers with similar skills and experience.[142] So, for example, a person with a significant hearing impairment might not be able to perform telemarketing, customer service, or other hearing intensive jobs. Although this person would fit the statutory definition of disabled because of substantial impairment in his or her ability to work relative to nonimpaired workers, courts applying the residual working capacity logic would conclude that this person was not disabled because he or she could still work in nonhearing intensive positions, such as factory assembly line tasks.

When courts employ the cultural definition of disability, which focuses on residual working capacity, rather than comparing plaintiffs' limitations to similar nondisabled workers as the statute requires, any ability to work tends to exclude the plaintiff from the protection of the ADA. This result is more than a little ironic given that the statute was designed to protect disabled individuals who were able to work in at least some capacity. When plaintiffs claims disability based on limitations on working, the social meaning of the identity "disabled" eclipses the legal reforms that were designed to challenge prevailing notions that individuals with impairments are not qualified to work.

Demonstrating that one is both "substantially limited in the major life activity of working" and a "qualified" worker has become an exceedingly narrow bridge to cross because many courts interpreted disability consistently with its historical and cultural meaning – the inability to work at all – rather than examining how the statute defined disability. The Ninth Circuit recognized these contradictions in *Mustafa v. Clark County School District*, albeit in reference to the defendants' position.

---

[142] Bolton v. Scrivner, Inc., 36 F.3d 939 (10th Cir. 1994) (holding plaintiff, a former warehouse worker, was not substantially limited in his ability to perform a class of jobs despite evidence in the record that he could no longer perform jobs that required him to stand for prolong periods); cf. Ray v. Glidden Co., 85 F.3d 227, 229–30 (5th Cir. 1996) (holding plaintiff could not demonstrate he was regarded as having an impairment that substantially limited his ability to lift, reach, or work because there was no evidence that plaintiff had been denied another job based on this perception).

The plaintiff in *Mustafa* argued that his depression, posttraumatic stress disorder, and panic attacks substantially limited him in the major life activity of working as a teacher.[143] The plaintiff's doctor released him for nonclassroom work only, such as tutoring or administrative work, and the defendant refused to accommodate this limitation. The defendant argued both that the plaintiff was not disabled and that he was no longer qualified for any teacher's job.

In reversing the district court's grant of summary judgment, the court noted the contradictions inherent in the defendant's position:

> It is not lost on the court that [defendant] adopts arguably contradictory positions in attempting to show that Mustafa cannot prove that he is disabled under the Rehabilitation Act, when it contends, on the one hand, that classroom teaching is an essential function of any teacher's job, but, on the other hand, that the inability to teach in a classroom does not disqualify a teacher from a broad range of jobs.[144]

In other words, the defendant made the contradictory argument that teachers were required to teach, but that the inability to teach did not disqualify the plaintiff from jobs as a teacher. To show substantial impairment in the ability to work within the meaning of the ADA, however, every plaintiff must prove the mirror image of this cultural contradiction. That is, the plaintiff must simultaneously show that he is unable to work in a class of jobs and that he is able to perform the essential functions of the job – that he is able to do the job as the employer has historically defined it. So long as "disability" is defined to mean no residual working capacity, and "qualified" is defined as the ability to meet institutionalized work expectations, the relationship between disability and work will prevent any meaningful restructuring of work through the ADA.

---

[143] Mustafa v. Clark County Sch. Dist., 157 F.3d 1169, 1174 (9th Cir. 1998).
[144] *Id.* at 1175 n.5.

Judicial Resistance to Accommodations That Change Time Standards

Even when a plaintiff manages to show sufficient impairment in working to be deemed disabled, she often faces difficulty proving she is nevertheless qualified within the meaning of the Act. At this point in the analysis, courts tend to refocus the inquiry away from whether a plaintiff has any residual working capacity and toward her ability to perform the essential functions of the job with or without accommodation. Here the plaintiff faces a catch-22: Courts frequently find that the impairment that demonstrates that she cannot perform a class of jobs is evidence that she is not qualified for the position. In particular, courts often reject as "unreasonable" any accommodation that might modify institutionalized time standards, without inquiring whether modification could be easily accomplished.[145]

How is this slight of hand accomplished, given that the statute requires reasonable accommodations, including part-time and modified schedules? Although the ADA requires employers to provide reasonable accommodations to workers with disabilities, the EEOC interpretive guidance states that employers are not required to provide accommodations that change the essential functions of a job.[146] The statute also states that "consideration shall be given to the employer's judgment as to what functions of a job are essential," although additional objective measures are to be considered as well.[147] The regulations provide only a vague definition of essential

---

[145] *See, e.g.*, DePaoli v. Abbott Lab., 144 F.3d 668 (7th Cir. 1998) (finding that plaintiff was disabled because she was substantially limited in the major life activity of working, but that her disability rendered her no longer "qualified" to work for the defendant); Maziarka v. Mills Fleet Farm, Inc., 245 F.3d 675, 681 (8th Cir. 2001) (holding that plaintiff whose disability caused erratic absences was substantially limited in the major life activity of working, but was also not qualified to perform his job because of those absences).

[146] The EEOC's interpretive guidance on the ADA states that "an employer or other covered entity is not required to reallocate essential functions" of a job. Interpretive Guidance on Title I of the Americans with Disabilities Act, 29 C.F.R.App. § 1630.2.

[147] 42 U.S.C. § 12111(8).

functions,[148] and the EEOC's regulatory definition of essential functions emphasizes how the employer defines the position and how it historically has been performed.[149] Thus employer's historical decisions about how to structure work receive considerable weight in the reasonable accommodation analysis.

Nevertheless, the ADA expressly authorizes some modifications to existing work arrangements, including changing the time standards of work.[150] For example, the statute explicitly states that reasonable accommodation may include "job restructuring [and] part-time or modified work schedule[s]...."[151] Despite this explicit statutory language, courts have had great difficulty dealing with unpredictable absences,[152] leaves of absence,[153] and requests for part-time schedules,[154] all of which

---

[148] *Id.* § 1630.2(o), pt. 1630, app. A § 1630.2(o). ("The essential functions are by definition those that the individual who holds the job would have to perform, with or without a reasonable accommodation, in order to be considered qualified for the position.")

[149] *Id.* § 1630.2(n)(3); *see also* 42 U.S.C. § 12112(8) ("consideration shall be given to the employer's judgment as to what functions of a job are essential").

[150] The concept of "reasonable accommodation" is relevant to several stages of the analysis of an ADA claim. First, it is relevant to demonstrating membership in the protected class. *See* 42 U.S.C. § 12112(b)(5) (prohibiting discrimination against qualified individuals with disabilities); *id.* § 12111(8) (defining qualified individual with a disability as an individual with a disability who is able to perform the essential functions of her position with or without reasonable accommodation). Second, reasonable accommodation is relevant to proving a plaintiff's claim of disability discrimination. *See id.*, § 12112(b)(5) (defining discrimination as "not making a reasonable accommodation"). Third, reasonable accommodation is relevant to the defense of "undue hardship." *See id.* § 12112(b)(5) (specifying defense if a reasonable accommodation would create an undue hardship).

[151] *Id.* § 12112(9)(B); *see also* 29 C.F.R. § 1630.2(o)(2)(ii).

[152] *See, e.g.,* Buckles v. First Data Resources, 176 F.3d 1098 (8th Cir. 1999) (citing the need for predictable attendance).

[153] *See, e.g.,* Hudson v. MCI Telecomm. Corp., 87 F.3d 1167, 1168 (10th Cir. 1996) (holding unpaid leave of indefinite duration is not a reasonable accommodation); Rogers v. International Marine Terminals, Inc., 87 F.3d 755, 759 (5th Cir. 1996) (same). *But see* Haschmann v. Time Warner Entertainment Co., 151 F.3d 591 (7th Cir. 1998) (two to four week leaves of absence reasonable); Criado v. IBM Corp., 145 F.3d 437 (1st Cir. 1998) (one month leave may be reasonable).

[154] *See, e.g.,* Terrell v. U.S. Air, 132 F.3d 621 (11th Cir. 1998) (rejecting plaintiff's argument that part-time work was a reasonable accommodation).

undermine core institutionalized expectations about time and work. In these instances, institutionalized time standards influence how courts interpret the meaning of essential functions. Courts have been reluctant to find workers qualified if their disabilities require them to interrupt a regular schedule of work, and many courts have ruled that timely and regular attendance is an implicit essential function for most jobs.[155] Consequently, courts have generally held that granting long leaves of absence or unpaid leaves of indefinite duration are not reasonable accommodations.[156] Similarly, courts have ruled that permitting excessive or erratic absences are not reasonable accommodations, even when those absences are caused by a worker's disability.[157] Some courts have also construed reasonable accommodation to include only accommodations that would enable workers to perform the essential functions of their jobs immediately or in the near future, rejecting accommodations that temporarily suspend those essential functions or adapt them to the workers' limitations.[158]

[155] Carr v. Reno, 23 F.3d 525, 529 (D.C. Cir. 1994) (holding that "coming to work regularly" is an "essential function"); Law v. United States Postal Serv., 852 F.2d 1278, 1279–80 (Fed. Cir. 1988) (holding that attendance is a minimum function of any job); Walders v. Garrett, 765 F. Supp. 303, 309 (E.D. Va. 1991) (holding that "reasonably regular and predictable attendance is necessary for many [jobs]"), aff'd, 956 F.2d 1163 (4th Cir. 1992); Santiago v. Temple Univ., 739 F. Supp. 974, 979 (E.D. Pa. 1990) ("attendance is necessarily the fundamental prerequisite to job qualification"), aff'd, 928 F.2d 396 (3d Cir. 1991).

[156] Hudson, 87 F.3d at 168 (holding unpaid leaves of indefinite duration are not reasonable accommodations); Rogers v. International Marine Terminals, Inc., 87 F.3d 755, 759 (5th Cir. 1996) (holding employee who is not able to attend work is not qualified, and that an employer is not required to provide leave for an indefinite period as a reasonable accommodation); Myers, 50 F.3d at 283. A few courts have held that leaves of short and definite duration may be reasonable accommodations. See Haschmann v. Time Warner Entertainment Co., 151 F.3d 591 (7th Cir. 1998) (two to four week leaves of absence reasonable); Criado v. IBM Corp., 145 F.3d 437 (1st Cir. 1998) (one month leave may be reasonable).

[157] See, e.g., Carr, 23 F.3d at 530; Walders, 765 F. Supp. at 311. ("[R]easonable regular and predictable attendance was implicit job requirement for plaintiff, as it is for many.")

[158] See Myers v. Hose, 50 F.3d 278, 283 (4th Cir. 1995) ("[R]easonable accommodation is by its terms most logically construed as that which presently, or in the immediate

These interpretations of the ADA ignore statutory and regulatory definitions of essential functions, instead applying a "common-sense idea ... that if one is not able to be at work, one cannot be a qualified individual."[159] The problem with this approach is that it requires the plaintiff to demonstrate that he or she is qualified through more than skill, experience, education, or adequate performance, the factors set out in the regulations, which also explicitly indicate that schedule adjustments can be a reasonable accommodation.[160] Current judicial interpretations require, in addition to the statutory factors, that workers meet implicit time norms regarding work to be deemed qualified. The court in *Tyndall v. National Education Center*[161] summarized this judicially imposed requirement this way:

> [A]n evaluation of the quality of Tyndall's performance does not end our inquiry. In addition to possessing the skills necessary to perform the job in question, an employee must be willing and able to demonstrate these skills by coming to work on a regular basis. Except in the unusual case where an employee can effectively perform all work-related duties at home, an employee "who does not come to work cannot perform any of his job functions, essential or otherwise." [Citation omitted.]

This "common sense" standard is contrary to the statute, the regulations, and the EEOC's interpretive guidance for the ADA, all of which state that changes in the schedule of work, including reduced time at work, are reasonable accommodations.[162] Nevertheless, courts ignore this authority because regular, uninterrupted attendance at work has become so

---

future, enables the employee to perform the essential functions of the job in question."); *Hudson*, 87 F.3d at 169 (citing *Meyer*); *Tyndall*, 31 F.3d at 213.

[159] Waggoner v. Olin Corp., 169 F.3d 481, 482 (7th Cir. 1999). This court also stated "We think it also fair to conclude that in most instances the ADA does not protect persons who have erratic, unexplained absences, even when those absences are a result of a disability. The fact is that in most cases, attendance at the job site is a basic requirement of most jobs." *Id.* at 484.

[160] *Cf.* 29 C.F.R. §1630.2(m).

[161] 31 F.3d 209 (4th Cir. 1994).

[162] 42 U.S.C. § 12112(9)(B); 29 C.F.R. § 1630.2(o)(2)(ii), App. part 1630, § 1630.2(o).

taken-for-granted that courts cannot imagine work organized any other way. These institutionalized time standards are so deeply entrenched that they override explicit statutory language that allows schedule changes and part-time work as accommodations.

The way courts analyze poor attendance or interrupted work reveal how social ideas about time discipline inform their opinions. In *Buckles v. First Data Resources*,[163] the court concluded, after the plaintiff won at trial, that the plaintiff's attendance record rendered him not "qualified" within the meaning of the ADA.[164] The plaintiff experienced acute reactions to environmental irritants on the job that occasionally required him to leave work for the day. He requested the accommodation of an irritant free workplace and additional unpaid sick time. In vacating the jury's verdict, the court demanded no evidence from the employer that regular attendance was in fact an essential element of the plaintiff's job, instead deferring to the company's unilaterally imposed attendance policy:

> First Data contends that Buckles is not qualified because of his excessive absences. In the context of the ADA, we have recognized that "regular and reliable attendance is a necessary element of most jobs." *Nesser*, 160 F.3d at 445. First Data is no exception and considers attendance to be an "essential function," as illustrated by the detailed attendance policies and procedures. Buckles, an hourly employee, disputes that attendance is essential to First Data since there are numerous employees and the company accounts for possible absences. We are not persuaded by such a conclusory argument, [footnote omitted] which runs contrary to the express policies and procedures of First Data.[165]

The echo of E. P. Thompson's time discipline can be heard in the court's dismissive statement that "[u]nfettered ability to leave work at any time

---

[163] Buckles v. First Data Resources, 176 F.3d 1098 (8th Cir. 1999).
[164] To vacate a jury verdict for the plaintiff, the court must find that no reasonable juror could have returned a verdict for the plaintiff based on the evidence presented at trial. Buckles v. First Data Resources, 176 F.3d 1098, 1100 (8th Cir. 1999).
[165] *Id.* at 1101.

is certainly not a reasonable accommodation here."[166] The court found it unthinkable to consider relaxing attendance requirements, even though this type of accommodation was explicitly contemplated by the statute and even though a jury found in the plaintiff's favor. To change these time standards would threaten taken-for-granted expectations about work that reflect the historical ways in which control over time was a means of asserting employer power and a mechanism for excluding certain groups from employment (Boydston 1990; Thompson 1967).

The Eleventh Circuit took a similar approach in *Jackson v. Veterans Administration*,[167] a Rehabilitation Act case in which a Veterans Administration hospital fired a veteran with a service-connected disability caused by rheumatoid arthritis. The veteran lost his job after missing six days of work during the first three months of his employment as a housekeeping aide because of adverse reactions to his bi-weekly arthritis treatment and a flare-up of his condition. His absences did not exceed his accrued sick leave. The majority opinion held that regular attendance was an essential function of the plaintiff's job, and that his unpredictable absences demonstrated that he could not perform this essential function. The plaintiff argued he could perform his work – cleaning the hospital – with a reasonable accommodation:

> Jackson sought the following accommodations: when he receives his bi-weekly treatment for arthritis, the VA could either schedule a regular off day or delay the start of Mr. Jackson's shift. In the event of a flare-up due to his condition, Jackson could swap off days with other employees, delay his shift start time, or defer more physically demanding and less time sensitive job duties until the next day.[168]

The majority rejected this argument, concluding that "requiring the VA to accommodate such absences would place upon the agency the burden of making last-minute provisions for Jackson's work to be done

---

[166] *Id.*
[167] Jackson v. Veterans Administration, 22 F.3d 277, 279 (11th Cir. 1994).
[168] *Id.*

by someone else."[169] Without explanation or analysis of the burden the requested accommodation would place on the hospital, the majority ruled that the hospital had no obligation to accommodate the plaintiff's absences.

The dissent in *Jackson* pointed out that employers routinely accommodate unpredictable absences and reallocate work through the provision of sick leave, and that the plaintiff's situation was no different. The dissent also noted that "the essential function of Jackson's job appears to be less the actual presence of Jackson himself than the completion of his work."[170] The dissent contended that by holding as a matter of law that employers are not required to accommodate unpredictable absences, the district court improperly avoided analyzing whether any of the accommodations proposed by Jackson were reasonable. It also argued that summary judgment was particularly inappropriate where essential elements of the job and the reasonableness of proposed accommodations were factual issues for the jury, "where the VA has shown no interest in accommodating Jackson, and where no attempt has been made to determine the reasonableness of the requested accommodations."[171] The dissent in *Jackson* revealed that the majority relied on assumptions rather than evidence about the job's actual requirements, thus cutting off any analysis of whether the plaintiff's requested accommodation was reasonable.

Defining regular attendance as an essential function effectively prevents courts from considering whether changing time standards to accommodate a worker's disability would impose an undue hardship on the employer.[172] Once attendance is assumed to be essential, employers

---

[169] *Id.*

[170] *Id.* at 284.

[171] *Id.*

[172] Of course, like the term "reasonable," the term "undue hardship" may also be an opening for institutionalized ideas about which features of work are and are not legitimately changeable can come in. Very few cases reach the question of undue hardship, however, as most claims fail on the definitional questions of who is disabled and otherwise qualified.

prevail simply by asserting, rather than demonstrating, that reasonable accommodations do not include changing a job's time components. Only the narrow question of whether an accommodation would improve the plaintiff's attendance is left on the table, and courts fail to consider whether changing the attendance standard itself should be the accommodation.[173] Thus, treating uninterrupted attendance as essential reifies institutionalized work schedules as unchangeable givens, even if changing a work schedule would create few problems for an employer, preventing any meaningful restructuring of institutionalized time norms.

This doctrinal slight of hand has not gone unnoticed. A few courts have recognized that treating attendance as an essential function effectively creates a presumption that changes in the time requirements of work can never be reasonable accommodations. In *Cehrs v. Northeast Ohio Alzheimer's Research Center*,[174] the Sixth Circuit declined to treat attendance as an essential function, noting that this approach would evade the undue hardship analysis required by the statute:

> The presumption that uninterrupted attendance is an essential job requirement improperly dispenses with the [employer's burden to show undue hardship]. Under such a presumption, the employer never bears the burden of proving that the accommodation proposed by an employee is unreasonable and imposes an undue burden upon it. [citation omitted] If an employer cannot show that an accommodation unduly burdens it, then there is no reason to deny the employee the accommodation. ... In addition, the presumption eviscerates the individualized attention that the Supreme Court has deemed "essential" in each disability claim. ... If we were to presume that uninterrupted attendance in all instances is a mandatory job requirement, then the policies and needs of both the individual employer and employee would never be considered.[175]

---

[173] *See, e.g.*, Carr v. Reno, 23 F.3d 525, 529 (D.C. Cir. 1994); Walders v. Garrett, 765 F. Supp. 303, 314 (E.D. Va. 1991).

[174] *See, e.g.*, Cehrs v. Northeast Ohio Alzheimer's Research Center, 155 F.3d 775, 782 (6th Cir. 1998); Norris v. Allied-Sysco Food Services, Inc., 948 F. Supp. 1418, 1439 (N.D. Cal. 1996).

[175] *Cehrs*, 155 F.3d at 782.

This court reversed the district court's grant of summary judgment to the employer, finding that the plaintiff raised a question of fact about whether a leave would constitute a reasonable accommodation under the ADA.

Similarly, in *Ward v. Massachusetts Health Research Institute, Inc.*,[176] the court rejected the employer's claim that regular and timely attendance was an essential function of the plaintiff's data entry position. The plaintiff requested a flexible work schedule, including permission to arrive at work after 9:00 A.M., to accommodate his severe arthritis, which substantially limited his mobility in the mornings. Although the defendant argued that a regular and predictable schedule was an essential function of the plaintiff's job, the court did not accept this argument without evidence. Instead, it held that "the defendant, who has better access to the relevant evidence, should bear the burden of proving that a given job function is an essential function,"[177] and noted the lack of evidence in the record that the plaintiff's position required him to be present during specific hours of the day. The court was similarly unsympathetic to the employer's quite revealing argument that the requested change to time standards would undermine work discipline:

> [The defendant] has offered only general statements regarding the snowball effect of such an accommodation – it would eliminate employers' control over the workplace and ability to maintain any standards. Such an argument runs counter to the general principle behind the ADA that imposes a duty on the employer to modify some work rules, facilities, terms, or conditions to enable a disabled person to work, and if [the employer's] position were given credence, it would defeat almost any reasonable accommodation.

The employer's argument makes clear how resistance to modifying time standards is rooted in the historical role that control over time has played in maintaining power over workers. Although the court rejected

---

[176] 209 F.3d 29 (1st Cir. 2000).
[177] *Id.*, 209 F.3d at 35.

the employer's justification for denying accommodations, this outcome is unusual.

Another way that courts avoid addressing whether changes in time standards could be reasonable accommodations is to treat a request for a modified work schedule as a request to create a new part-time position. Because several courts have held that employers are not required to "create a new position" as a reasonable accommodation,[178] characterizing modified work schedules as new positions evades any meaningful analysis of whether changing work's time requirements would create an undue hardship for the employer. The Eleventh Circuit employed this technique in *Terrell v.U.S. Air*,[179] in which the plaintiff, a reservations sales agent, suffered from carpal tunnel syndrome and could type only four hours per day. She argued that her employer should have accommodated her disability by allowing her to work part time, rather than placing her on unpaid medical leave. The evidence suggested that her position did not necessarily require full-time work, as in the past the employer had allowed the plaintiff to work part time for 60 days, according to its light duty policy, and then placed her on unpaid medical leave.[180] In addition, several intermediate reservation sales agents worked six hours per day, rather than eight.[181] The plaintiff argued that once she identified a part-time schedule as a potential accommodation, the burden shifted to the employer to prove undue hardship.

The Eleventh Circuit rejected this argument, stating that part-time work was not always a reasonable accommodation and that the employer had decided to eliminate part-time positions. Accordingly, the court concluded, the employer was not required to create a new part-time position for the plaintiff as a reasonable accommodation. Without a single citation to the ADA or its legislative history, the court stated that:

---

[178] *See, e.g.*, White v. York Int'l Corp., 43 F.3d 357, 361 (10th Cir. 1995); Gomez v. American Bldg. Maintenance, 940 F. Supp. 255, 260 (N.D. Cal. 1990).

[179] 132 F.3d 621 (11th Cir. 1998).

[180] *Id*. at 623.

[181] *Id*. at 625 n.5.

Whether a company will staff itself with part-time workers, full-time workers, or a mix of both is a core management policy with which the ADA was not intended to interfere.[182]

Thus, despite explicit statutory language that reasonable accommodation includes part-time and modified work schedules, the court rejected any restructuring of the plaintiff's schedule that might interfere with management control over work time without any inquiry into whether part-time work would be an undue hardship for her employer.

A part-time schedule could be framed alternatively as restructuring the schedule of the plaintiff's existing job, rather than as creating a new job. The interpretive move of labeling a schedule change "job creation," however, effectively takes schedule changes off the list of potential accommodations, even if the plaintiff only requests to perform her current job for fewer hours per week. Moreover, by deferring to management policy rather than requiring employers to demonstrate that part-time schedules would create a hardship, courts insulate work's time norms from any meaningful change.[183] In this way, courts avoid altogether the question of whether time standards are essential to the job.

---

[182] *Id*. at 626–27.

[183] The way courts resist changing work schedules is only one example of how institutionalized work practices permeate ADA doctrine; there are others. For instance, whether working at home constitutes a reasonable accommodation is another fertile area of conflict. The D.C. Circuit has ruled that working at home can be a reasonable accommodation in appropriate circumstances. Langdon v. Department of Health & Human Serv., 959 F.2d 1053, 1060–61 (D.C. Cir. 1992); see also Carr v. Reno, 23 F.3d 525, 530 (D.C. Cir. 1994). ("[I]n appropriate cases, [the Rehab Act] requires an agency to consider work at home, as well as reassignment in another position, as potential forms of accommodation.") Other courts, however, have held that an employer is not required to accommodate a disability by allowing the disabled worker to work at home, sometimes presuming without evidence that working at home will produce an inevitable disruption and reduction in workers' productivity. *See, e.g.*, Vande Zande v. Wisconsin Dep't of Admin., 44 F.3d 538, 546 (7th Cir. 1995) ("An employer is not required to allow disabled workers to work at home, where their productivity inevitably would be greatly reduced."); see also Law v. United States Postal Serv., 852 F.2d 1278 (Fed. Cir. 1988) (Rehab Act). ("[A]n agency is inherently entitled to require an employee to be present during scheduled work times and, unless an agency is

Restructuring Work through the FMLA

The fundamental difference between the FMLA and the ADA or Title VII is that the FMLA focuses on the structural features of work itself, rather on the identity of the class of persons protected by the law. That is, it focuses on the work side of the equation, rather than on the identities of gender or disability that implicitly construct the meaning of work. The FMLA restructures work's time norms by providing for up to 12 weeks of job-protected, unpaid leave each year for pregnancy disability, parental care of a new child, the care of a worker's own serious health condition, and the care of a child, parent, or spouse with a serious health condition.[184] Employers are required to reinstate workers to the same or equivalent position after a leave.[185] The FMLA also prohibits interfering with, restraining, or denying the exercise or attempt to exercise the rights to leave.[186]

The legal theory behind the FMLA is very different from the anti-discrimination provisions of the ADA and Title VII. The FMLA is "based on the same principle as the child labor laws, the minimum wage, Social Security, the safety and health laws, the pension and welfare benefit laws, and other labor laws that establish minimum standards for

notified in advance, an employee's absence is disruptive to the agency's efficient operation.")

Requests to work at home are particularly interesting because working at home actually challenges an institutionalized feature of work that was constructed in connection with gender, rather than disability. That is, "work" came to mean only labor outside the home through the gendered division of labor in the transition to modernity. Siegel R. B. *Home As Work: The First Woman's Rights Claims Concerning Wives' Household Labor, 1850–1880*. 103 YALE L. J. 1073–217 (1994); VALENZE D. 1995. THE FIRST INDUSTRIAL WOMAN. New York: Oxford University Press. Nevertheless, attempting to expand work to include accommodations such as working at home still violates institutionalized understandings of work. Accordingly, when working at home is proposed as a reasonable accommodation, institutionalized ideas about work and gender also create resistance to reasonable accommodation of disabilities.

[184] 29 U.S.C. § 2612(a).

[185] 29 U.S.C. § 2614.

[186] 29 U.S.C. § 2615(a).

employment."[187] The legislative history of the Act discusses how each of these laws responded to specific problems with broad societal implications, such as avoiding exploitative wages or child labor, and states that the FMLA likewise responds to the pressures placed on families by the changing demographics of both families and the workplace. The legislative history specifically mentions many of the societal trends detailed in Chapter 2, including the increased participation of women in the workforce, rising divorce rates and single parenthood, and the aging of the American population.[188] Congress also recognized how these social changes have eroded the structural relationship between work and family, noting that "the crucial unpaid caretaking services traditionally performed by wives … [have] become increasingly difficult for families to fulfill."[189] To bring the substantive point home about the importance of these caretaking activities, the Senate report makes an explicit analogy to employment protections that ensure that veterans are reinstated to their previous job with full retention of seniority, pay, and other benefits.[190] By treating family and medical leave like leave for jury duty or military service, the FMLA explicitly recognizes the value of caring for others, rather than focusing only on questions of identity and equal treatment.

This choice of legal theory was no accident; by establishing the FMLA as a minimum labor standard rather than an antidiscrimination statute, Congress sought to avoid many of the limitations of Title VII and the ADA as they are currently interpreted. It also sought to avoid special protection based on group identity to avoid the risk of discriminatory treatment of that group.[191] It mandates leave for pregnant workers, rather than leaving to the courts the question of whether equal treatment for pregnant workers requires employers to grant leave.

---

[187] S.Rep. No.3, 103d Cong., 1st Sess. at 4, *reprinted at* 1993 U.S.C.C.A.N. 3, 6–7.

[188] S.Rep. No.3, 103d Cong., 1st Sess. at 6–7, *reprinted at* 1993 U.S.C.C.A.N. 3, 8–9.

[189] S.Rep. No.3, 103d Cong., 1st Sess. at 7, *reprinted at* 1993 U.S.C.C.A.N. 3, 9.

[190] S.Rep. No.3, 103d Cong., 1st Sess. at 4–5, *reprinted at* 1993 U.S.C.C.A.N. 3, 7.

[191] S.Rep. No.3, 103d Cong., 1st Sess. at 16, *reprinted at* 1993 U.S.C.C.A.N. 3, 18.

The FMLA also requires employers to provide job-protected leave for childbirth even if they do not provide short-term disability leave in any other circumstances. Employers cannot fire or replace pregnant workers because they need time off from work unlike the comparative standard under Title VII, which allows employers to deny time off as long as they do so even-handedly.

For workers with short-term impairments that prevent them from working, the FMLA requires employers to provide time off, rather than allowing courts to interpret what is a reasonable accommodation. As we have seen, the ADA has done little to change time standards because courts interpreting the scope of reasonable accommodation tend to find regular attendance and full-time work to be essential functions of most jobs. The FMLA, however, requires employers to provide time off for certain illnesses and injuries, including intermittent time off and reduced work schedules.[192] By requiring intermittent time off when necessary, the FMLA challenges work's standard schedule of full-time, year-round, and continuous labor to the exclusion of other needs. This direct approach precludes courts from defining modified schedules or periodic absences as impermissible encroachments on employer discretion and control. As one court put it when considering the FMLA's application to mandatory overtime, "because the FMLA expressly contemplates that employees who are otherwise capable are entitled to work their jobs either 'intermittently or on a reduced leave schedule' ... working more than full-time cannot logically be an essential part of one's job under the FMLA."[193]

Perhaps most importantly, the FMLA requires employers to grant time off to care for new children and sick family members, two needs that for the most part are not covered by Title VII or the ADA. The statute also provides these forms of family leave in a gender-neutral manner. Women and men can take job-protected leave to care for new children or for their seriously ill children, spouses, or parents. These provisions

[192] 29 U.S.C. § 2612(b).
[193] Verhoff v. Time Warner Cable, Inc., 299 Fed. Appx. 488, 497 (6th Cir. 2008).

undermine the implicit expectation that caring for family members is a responsibility handled by a worker's stay-at-home partner, not by the worker him- or herself. They force work to acknowledge workers' family responsibilities, and chip away at the cultural divide between the public life of work and the private life of family.

Opposition to the FMLA centered on arguments that the market would provide a better range of leave options for employees, and that the costs of unpaid family and medical leave, in terms of administering the benefit and keeping jobs open for absent employees, would be prohibitive for businesses. Extensive empirical research had demonstrated, however, that market provision of leave benefits was sparse and uneven; leave was available to highly skilled professional employees but not to low-wage workers (Kamerman et al. 1983). In addition, some employers who already provided leave noted that a uniform legal requirement would take away any competitive advantage for firms that chose not to provide this benefit. Congress addressed the issue of cost by setting a high threshold – fifty employees – before an employer was covered by the Act. It also provided funds to study the administrative burden on new employers of implementing the new law; this study showed that most employers found little to no effect of the FMLA on profitability or productivity, and most employers found the FMLA easy to administer (Commission on Leave 1996).

The evolving debate over the FMLA suggests that employer opposition may be more about managerial prerogatives to use time standards to control workers than it is about costs. Arguments based on overall cost have faded in the face of evidence that the FMLA does not affect profitability. In fact, many employers simply shift the work of employees on leave to other workers rather than hiring temporary replacements, which saves salary costs during the employee's leave (Bond et al. 1991). Research also indicates that providing unpaid leave costs less than allowing employees to quit and then hiring and training replacements (Trzcinski & Alpert 1990). Since the law has passed, employer advocacy around regulatory change has focused increasingly on limiting intermittent leave, the form of leave that most directly challenges attendance policies and employer control over schedules. This shift highlights how political opposition to the FMLA is based on maintaining power in the form of control over time, rather than avoiding expense.

What difference does the minimum labor standards approach make? Situations that under Title VII or the ADA often resulted in no relief for workers have different outcomes under the FMLA. For example, in *Whitaker v. Bosch Braking Systems*, the plaintiff requested FMLA leave to avoid working overtime during her pregnancy.[194] Her doctor provided medical documentation stating that, owing to the plaintiff's normal pregnancy, she should not work more than eight hours per day or more than 40 hours per week. Her employer denied the plaintiff FMLA leave, she refused to work overtime anyway, and as a result the defendant required her to take short-term disability leave.[195] Her employer argued that she did not have a serious health condition because her pregnancy was normal and she could work a full-time schedule, ironically using her ability to meet time norms as a justification for refusing her request to limit her schedule. Here the employer drew upon cultural conceptions of disability to suggest that a worker is only entitled to claim medical leave if she is completely unable to work. The court rejected this argument, noting that "nothing in the FMLA provides that a pregnancy can constitute a serious health condition only if the pregnancy is abnormal or if the employee is physically unable to perform her job."[196] Instead, the court reasoned, a pregnant employee can establish a serious health condition if her doctor determines that her particular job duties present a risk to her health or pregnancy, in this case, working overtime.[197]

---

[194] 180 F.Supp.2d 922, 924–25 (W.D. Mich. 2001).
[195] The plaintiff sought to recover the difference between the wages and bonus she would have earned working 40 hours per week less the amount she received from short-term disability. *Id.*, 180 F.Supp.2d at 925.
[196] *Id.*, 180 F.Supp.2d at 931.
[197] *Id.*

Similarly, in *Treadaway v. Big Red Powersports, LLC*,[198] the pregnant plaintiff requested leave because of dangerous levels of carbon monoxide at the all-terrain vehicle factory and showroom where she worked. Rather than grant her leave and address the problem, her employer replaced her. The employer argued that the plaintiff was not eligible for FMLA leave because she was not incapacitated due to pregnancy.[199] To support its argument, the employer pointed to plaintiff's testimony that "[t]he restriction was in the environment, not my disability" and that "pregnancy wasn't the problem. It was the carbon monoxide fumes ... that [were] the problem."[200] The employer argued that this testimony demonstrated that the plaintiff's pregnancy did not prevent her from working. The court rejected this argument, noting that the plaintiff's physician concluded that the plaintiff should not return to work until the carbon monoxide problem was resolved, and that the employee was covered by the FMLA.[201]

By refocusing the analysis on the characteristics of the job rather on the question of whether these plaintiffs' pregnancies were normal, these courts recognized that many existing workplace conditions are incompatible with even a normal pregnancy. In this view, an employee's ability to work depends not only on her physical restrictions, but also on the particular duties and circumstances of her job. The *Whitaker* court rejected the argument that the ability to work a standard full-time schedule precluded a worker from using FMLA leave to avoid mandatory overtime, rather than reflexively accepting workplace time standards as definitive of the (in)ability to work. Similarly, the *Treadaway* court recognized that it was the interaction between the plaintiff's pregnancy and dangerous working conditions that rendered her unable to work, refusing the defendant's interpretation that only incapacity resulting solely from the effects of pregnancy warranted protection by the FMLA.

---

[198] 611 Fed. Supp.2d 768 (E.D. Tenn. 2009).
[199] *Id*. at 776.
[200] *Id*.
[201] *Id*.

In this way, these courts locate the conflict between work and pregnancy not in the nature of pregnancy, but in the specific characteristics of the workplace and how those characteristics limit pregnant women's ability to work. They recognized that the FMLA was created to overturn workplace time standards that exclude women when they become pregnant, even when the pregnancy-related symptoms that affect women's ability to work result from a normal pregnancy.[202]

Because the FMLA creates a minimum employment standard, several courts have emphasized that the FMLA's substantive entitlement to leave is not contingent on the employer's needs and that employers have no discretion to deny family leave to eligible employees.[203] Courts reason that in cases involving denial or interference with leave, the employer's subjective intent is irrelevant; instead, the question is whether the employee received the benefit to which he or she was entitled.[204] As one court points out, "[t]he employee need not show that the employer treated other employees less favorably, and an employer may not defend interference with the FMLA's substantive rights on the ground that it treats all employees equally poorly without discriminating."[205] This approach contrasts sharply with Title VII's equal treatment standard, which allows employers to deny workers time off as long as they do so even-handedly. Because leave is an entitlement rather than a discretionary benefit, an employer cannot defend against liability by simply asserting a legitimate business reason for denying leave. Congress made clear

---

[202] *Id.*
[203] Nevada Dep't of Human Resources v. Hibbs, 538 U.S. 721, 732 (2003) (noting the FMLA was enacted to respond to the serious problem with the discretionary nature of family leave); Hodgens v. General Dynamics Corp., 144 F.3d 151, 159 (1st Cir. 1998); Diaz v. Fort Wayne Foundry Corp., 131 F.3d 711, 712–13 (7th Cir. 1997); Lui v. Amway Corp., 347 F.3d 1125, 1135 (9th Cir. 2003) (noting that FMLA leave for baby bonding time is not contingent upon an employer's needs); Nero v. Industrial Molding Corporation, 167 F.3d 921, 927 (5th Cir. 1999) (noting the FMLA creates a series of entitlements or substantive rights, including the right to reinstatement after a leave).
[204] Hodgens v. General Dynamics Corp., 144 F.3d 151, 159 (1st Cir. 1998).
[205] Hodgens v. General Dynamics Corp., 144 F.3d 151, 159 (1st Cir. 1998).

that any such legitimate business concerns have already been taken into account and balanced against the needs of workers in the drafting of the statute.

The FMLA also addresses some of the shortcomings of the ADA as it has been interpreted by the courts. When it enacted the FMLA, Congress explicitly found that despite the protections of the ADA, "there is inadequate job security for employees who have serious health conditions that prevent them from working for temporary periods."[206] Accordingly, a serious health condition as defined by the FMLA can be temporary, unlike a disability, which must be long term or permanent, as defined by the ADA. The FMLA also provides for intermittent time off and leaves for extended periods, whereas the ADA generally does not.[207] In addition, because FMLA leave is an entitlement, questions of reasonableness and hardship are not relevant. In contrast, an ADA plaintiff must demonstrate that a requested accommodation is reasonable, and an employer can defend against an ADA claim by asserting that an accommodation would be an undue hardship.

Finally, the FMLA and its implementing regulations make clear that employers cannot continue to apply the usual attendance policies and evaluation criteria when a worker's absences or reduced schedule are covered by the FMLA. Requests for a reduced work schedule as the result of serious health condition qualify as medical leave under the FMLA.[208] In addition, the regulations specifically provide that "employers cannot use the taking of FMLA leave as a negative factor in employment actions, such as hiring, promotions or disciplinary actions; nor can FMLA leave be counted under 'no fault' attendance policies."[209]

---

[206] 29 U.S.C. § 2601(a)(4).
[207] 29 U.S.C. § 2612; cf. Byrne v. Avon Products, Inc., 328 F.3d 379, 381–382 (7th Cir. 2003) (holding that although "[in]ability to work for a multi-month period removes a person from the class protected by the ADA," a plaintiff could be entitled to two months leave under the FMLA to recover from major depression).
[208] Rowe v. Laidlaw Transit, Inc., 244 F.3d 1115, 1119 (9th Cir. 2001); 336 F.Supp.2d 1129, 1140 (D. Or. 2004).
[209] 29 C.F.R. § 825.220(c).

Lui v. Amway Corporation illustrates how this approach makes a difference in changing workplace time standards. In this case, the employer treated the plaintiff's FMLA leave as personal leave, gave her a negative evaluation after her leave based solely on subjective factors, and fired her based on that evaluation.[210] The supervisor in *Lui* exercised a classic pattern of managerial discretion by applying workplace time norms that suggest that a worker who takes leave is not a valuable employee. In a legal regime without the FMLA, violation of these time standards would have been sufficient justification for firing this worker. Instead, the court concluded that the employer violated the Act by taking the plaintiff's leave into account in her final performance evaluation, and by terminating her employment based on that evaluation. By taking away managerial prerogatives to penalize workers who need time off, the FMLA directly challenges these norms and the implicit model of a good worker that they embody.

Although the FMLA's approach overcomes several limitations of antidiscrimination statutes like Title VII and the ADA, the FMLA has some limitations. It does not protect employees who change their work schedules to accommodate family care responsibilities but do not reduce the hours they work.[211] It does not solve the problems that arise when a pregnant worker wants to continue working but requires some changes in her job duties to do so. For example, in *Harvender v. Norton Co.*,[212] the plaintiff, a lab technician, submitted a note from her doctor indicating that she should not work around chemicals. She neither requested nor wanted FMLA leave; she only wanted to change her duties to avoid these chemicals, as 60 percent of her job duties did not require working around them. Rather than granting this request, her employer placed her on forced leave when she was two months pregnant, and indicated that she would be terminated if she did not return to work after 12 weeks of

---

[210] *Lui,* 347 F.3d at 1134–37.

[211] *See* Giles v. Christian Care Centers, No. 3: 96-CV-2168-G, 1997 U.S. Dist. LEXIS 20351 (N.D. Tex. Dec. 11, 1997).

[212] 4 Wage & Hour Cas. 2d 560 (N.D.N.Y. 1997).

leave. The court held that employers were not required to change job duties so that work would be compatible with pregnancy, and could place pregnant women unable to perform the essential functions of their positions on involuntary leave. So, although the FMLA provides pregnancy disability leave, it does not require employers to structure work so that pregnant women can continue working during their pregnancies.[213] This lack of legal protection for women who could continue working with some minimal accommodations reinforces the implicit cultural conflict between the status of worker and (expectant) mother.

In addition, time norms still influence the way in which some courts interpret the FMLA. For example, some courts have expressed a dim view of the legitimacy of FMLA leave in light of employers' historical control over the timing and nature of work. They describe the statute as the "so-called Family and Medical Leave Act,"[214] and note that "FMLA makes incredible inroads on an at-will employment relationship."[215] A few courts express their skepticism by focusing on FMLA's preamble, which states that the FMLA provides for leave "in a manner that accommodates the legitimate interests of employers" and the "demands of the workplace."[216] A few have invalidated a FMLA regulation that could require more than twelve weeks leave when an employer fails to notify an employee of his or her leave rights, with one court pointedly noting that the "FMLA never provides that an employer must retain an employee who works fewer that 40 weeks a year."[217] This reasoning treats

---

[213] Some state laws do provide such accommodations, however. *See, e.g.*, California Civil Code § 12945.

[214] *See* Hott v. VDO Yazaki Corp., 922 F. Supp. 1114, 1127 (W.D. Va. 1996).

[215] Satterfield v. Wal-Mart Stores, Inc., 135 F.3d 973, 977 (5th Cir. 1998); *see also* Cox v. Autozone, Inc., 990 F. Supp. 1369, 1372 (M.D. Ala. 1998). ("[The FMLA is o]ne of the newer nation-wide restrictions on employers" that requires leave "for what Congress considers to be a good reason.")

[216] *See, e.g.*, Cox v. Autozone, Inc., 990 F. Supp. 1369, 1373 (M.D. Ala. 1998), *aff'd sub nom* McGregor v. Autozone, Inc., 180 F.3d 1305 (11th Cir. 1999) (citing the preamble of the FMLA, 29 U.S.C. § 2601).

[217] *Cox*, 990 F. Supp. at 1376; *see also* Ragsdale v. Wolverine Worldwide, Inc., 218 F.3d 933, 939 (8th Cir. 2000); Neal v. Children's Habilitation Ctr, 1999 WL 706117 (N.D.

a worker's failure to meet the institutionalized norm of year-round work as a self-evident justification for firing.

In addition, at least one court has suggested that work need not accommodate pregnancy except when serious complications arise. In *Gudenkauf v. Stauffer*,[218] the court held that the FMLA's definition of serious health condition excludes normal pregnancies. The employer fired the plaintiff one day after she missed a day of work because of the onset of preterm labor. She testified that she had been experiencing back pain, nausea, headaches, and swelling during her pregnancy, and consequently had requested leave to work a part-time schedule. The plaintiff brought a FMLA claim because the FMLA specifically requires employers to reduce a worker's schedule for "[a]ny period of incapacity due to pregnancy, or for prenatal care."[219] Nevertheless, the court held the plaintiff was not entitled to use FMLA leave to reduce her schedule because her normal pregnancy was not a serious health condition.

The court relied on the fact that the plaintiff's medical records indicated "her pregnancy was normal and that her complaints about the symptoms and conditions commonly associated with pregnancy were not unusual or severe."[220] The employer admitted that the plaintiff had fallen behind in her work and been unable to perform some tasks because of her pregnancy, indicating that she was impaired in her ability to work and therefore qualified for leave under the FMLA. Nevertheless, the court held that the employer need not accommodate normal pregnancy-

---

Ill. Sept. 10, 1999) (adopting the reasoning of *Autozone*). *But see* Chan v. Loyola Univ. Med. Ctr, No. 97-C-3170, 1999 U.S. Dist. LEXIS 18456 (N.D. Ill. Nov. 18, 1999) (rejecting the reasoning of *Autozone* and deferring to the Dept. of Labor's regulation).

[218] 922 F. Supp. 465 (D. Kan. 1996).

[219] 29 C.F.R. § 825.114(a)(2)(ii); *see also id.* § 825.112(c) (An expectant mother may take FMLA leave prior to the birth of her child, if it is required for prenatal care or because her condition makes her unable to work).

[220] Gudenkauf v. Stauffer Communs., 922 F. Supp. 465, 476 (D. Kan. 1996). Although the court also noted that plaintiff's doctors had not certified her need for time off from work, her employer fired her before she could see her doctor regarding her recent contractions and her need for leave.

related complaints. Nowhere in the opinion does the court acknowledge that the symptoms of normal pregnancy might limit the plaintiff's ability to work because work's existing structure does not accommodate those physical limitations. Instead, the plaintiff's only choices were to do her job as usual, despite her pregnancy-related limitations and early contractions, or be fired. In this court's view, the institutionalized attendance and time requirements of work need not yield to normal pregnancy, even though the intermittent inability to work due to pregnancy is explicitly covered by the statute.[221] This case is difficult to square with the holdings in *Treadaway* and *Whitaker* discussed previously.

Some courts have also relied on cultural understandings of disability and work as incompatible to suggest that plaintiffs were not sick enough to come within the FMLA's protections, even when their illnesses met the statutory definition of serious health condition. In *Reich v. Standard Register Co.*,[222] the plaintiff, a machine operator with metatarsalgia (a form of arthritis), requested FMLA leave to cover mandatory overtime so that his hours would not exceed 40 hours per week, the maximum number of hours he was able to work given his arthritis. The court acknowledged that the regulations explicitly include arthritis within the definition of serious health condition, but held that the worker's arthritis was not severe enough to qualify given that he had managed to work at least 40 hours per week. The court reasoned that if the worker could work a regular full-time schedule, then he was not "unable to perform the functions of his position" according to the definition of serious health condition.[223] Under the examples given in the FMLA's intermittent leave provisions, however, if the plaintiff could only work 32 hours per week, he would be considered to be within the definition of serious health condition and thus be able to use leave to reduce his schedule from 40 to 32 hours per week.[224] Institutionalized expectations

---

[221] 29 U.S.C. §§ 2611(11), 2612(a), 2612(b)(1).
[222] 1997 WL 375744 (W.D. Va. 1997).
[223] *Id.* at *3.
[224] *See* 29 C.F.R. § 825.205.

about standard work schedules make 40 hours the magic number, even though there is no logical reason why the need to reduce hours from 50 to 40 should be different than the need to reduce hours from 40 to 32. Here again, the court adopted the cultural meaning of disability as the complete inability to work, rather than applying the statutory definition of serious health condition, which is far less restrictive. The plaintiff's ability to meet a standard work schedule meant, in this cultural context, that he was not sufficiently disabled to claim to be unable to work. Like courts' interpretations of the ADA, this interpretation managed to ignore his work limitations by simply asserting without analysis that he was able to do his job.

Despite these few problematic cases, however, most judicial interpretations suggest that the FMLA solves many of the doctrinal difficulties presented by Title VII and the ADA. It does so by avoiding jurisprudential debates about what equality for women and people with disabilities requires, and by avoiding doctrinal avenues through which institutionalized work practices become legitimate defenses for unequal treatment. Instead, the statute takes on a structural limitation of work directly, and by doing so, changes both work and the identity categories of gender and disability that institutionalized work patterns construct.

Conclusion

The complex process through which the meaning and structure of work changed in the transition to modernity built on existing inequalities to form new standards for productive labor. Ownership of time was a central battle in this transition. Gender and disability (and their socially constructed meanings) were infused in this battle, and its resolution continues to give meaning to these identities. As a result, institutionalized time standards at work incorporate not only power relationships between employee and employer, but also power relationships among different classes of workers in ways that marginalize women and people with disabilities. Over time, the historically contingent and socially constructed nature of these time standards have been forgotten, so that these workplace features now appear to us as the natural, normal, objective, and inevitable nature of work. To accept them as such, as many courts have done, is to accept institutionalized inequalities deep within work's structure.

Over the last two decades, employment civil rights statutes have shifted toward substantive reform of work's institutional features. Disparate impact theories under Title VII, the reasonable accommodation requirements of the ADA, and the mandatory time off required by the FMLA, are all examples of this shift. These changes increasingly locate barriers to employment in work itself, rather than in the limitations imposed by worker's identities as women or people with disabilities. So, for example, both courts and reformers reference the idea that disability is a product of the interaction between impairments and the environment, rather than a naturalized characteristic of individuals. Similarly, courts have recognized how workplace practices such as denying leave, particularly parental leave for men, are based on outmoded conceptions of gender that treat caring for family members as women's work. In this way, law has begun to acknowledge how institutionalized workplace practices give rise to and reproduce relationships of inequality, rather than merely asking whether different groups are treated the same within a given set of institutional arrangements.

Title VII, the ADA, and the FMLA all have the potential to rework time standards, but often the underlying symbiosis among work, gender, and disability derails this potential for change. Claims challenging time standards under these laws must contend with implicit institutional frameworks that link time standards to gender and disability. Individuals who mobilize these laws run up against these frameworks when judges make "common sense" assumptions about the meaning of work and equality when they evaluate antidiscrimination claims. For example, when courts hold that regular attendance is an essential function of work, or that rigid schedules can never be challenged under disparate impact theories, they reinforce both beliefs and practices that define work as full-time labor and treat those who cannot meet this standard as legitimately excluded. Cultural beliefs about the meaning of work, disability, and gender obscure flaws in judicial reasoning when courts enforce the taken-for-granted features of work. Moreover, unlike the initial legislative push to establish a new right, individual rights mobilization is an ongoing process in which each individual claim is an opportunity for courts to interpret rights consistent with these implicit cognitive frameworks.

Analyzing Title VII and the ADA together reveals how judicial interpretations of both these statutes shore up existing workplace practices to reproduce institutional inequality. For example, when courts reject the idea that schedule modifications can be reasonable accommodations to disability or pregnancy, they also reinforce perceptions that individuals who need these accommodations are not legitimate workers. Similarly, when courts hold that an employer's statement that a pregnant woman cannot be both a good worker and adequately care for her children does not constitute gender discrimination, they legitimize beliefs that the roles of motherhood and worker are mutually incompatible.

The comparative analysis of Title VII, the ADA, and the FMLA set forth in this chapter teaches that changing work structures such as time standards requires more than an antidiscrimination strategy. A strategy that focuses solely on the identities incorporated into work's structure risks inadvertently reinforcing institutionalized inequalities on the basis of gender and disability. Focusing on how work must change to accommodate disability and gender marks women and people with disabilities as separate and different from all other workers, who become normalized in the process. In contrast, substantive strategies like the FMLA seem more promising than the strategies of Title VII or the ADA, because they target directly institutionalized work features that reinforce outmoded conceptions of gender and disability and set specific and detailed requirements for change. In this way, institution-focused legal reforms not only have a better chance of success, but also potentially benefit all workers rather than fostering divisions among workers.

4 Mobilizing the FMLA in the Workplace
Rights, Institutions, and Social Meaning

O THE EXTENT WORKERS INVOKE RIGHTS IN WORKPLACE interactions and negotiations about leave, workplaces are an important place to study how institutions shape the way FMLA rights operate in practice. How do workers who need leave but encounter resistance from their employer make sense of their situations? How do they view conflict over leave and evaluate their choices about how to respond? How do institutionalized expectations and norms about work give meaning to these workplace interactions? More broadly, how do these institutional processes inhibit or facilitate social change through law?

These questions can be addressed, in part, by interviewing workers who negotiated contested leaves in the workplace but did not take their disputes to court. This approach serves two broad theoretical objectives. The first is to examine how established power dynamics and social meanings in the workplace shape informal rights negotiations. Understanding this process is important because the vast majority of disputes never make it as far as a formal complaint (Miller & Sarat 1981), yet most studies of rights mobilization focus on litigation or collective action (see, e.g., Burstein 1991; Burstein & Monahan 1986; McCann 1994; Rosenberg 1991; Schultz 1990), rather than on more informal ways of using rights. Although a handful of qualitative studies examine how social frameworks affect individuals' interpretations of their experiences and decisions about claiming their rights (Marshall 2003; Morgan 1999; Quinn 2000; see also Felstiner et al. 1981), most of these studies pay little attention to the broader institutionalized structures and practices that affect rights mobilization. To address these questions, this chapter draws on qualitative interview data to analyze how institutions affect informal mobilization of rights in the workplace.

The second objective is to examine how workers' experiences with FMLA rights in the workplace connect to larger social institutions. This focus on institutions extends beyond the familiar claim that law is always shifting, contingent, and dependent upon social context and considers how the local systems of ordering that compete with law relate to larger social structures. This analysis reveals how institutions give rise to cultural frameworks that enable systems of power and inequality to reproduce themselves through everyday interactions, even when workers attempt to assert legal rights. These data also suggestion, however, that workers can mobilize law to challenge these cultural frameworks and change entrenched workplace practices and norms.

How Do Workers Decide Whether to Mobilize Rights?

Mobilization decisions are often viewed as rational calculations by individuals who assess the costs and benefits of claiming rights according to their preferences, particularly in studies that adopt classical rational actor assumptions. Other sociolegal theories, however, offer a richer and more complex understanding of mobilization that is based in social interaction and context, rather than individual preferences and cost/benefit analysis. These approaches connect microlevel processes to broader systems of power and inequality to explain how institutions constrain individual choice and give meaning to rights in the workplace.

Rational Actor Models

American civil rights statutes incorporate a model of rights mobilization implicitly based on individual choice and agency exercised according to rational actor assumptions. Employment rights are enforced primarily by individual workers mobilizing private rights of action. Individuals, not government officials, decide whether to sue when they believe their workplace rights have been violated, and individuals bear some of the costs associated with pursuing their rights.[1] An individual is assumed to make mobilization decisions by assessing the costs and benefits of pressing a legal claim, and presumably decides to go forward only if the claim serves his or her self-interest. This system of private rights of action is said to democratize and decentralize enforcement, rather than vesting enforcement authority solely with the government (Burke 2002).

Although individuals who believe their rights have been violated can seek a remedy from the courts, formal legal action is not necessarily required to obtain redress. When problems come up, the parties can informally negotiate a solution without going to court, a process sometimes called "private ordering." One classic model of private ordering posits that these informal negotiations take place in the "shadow of the law" (Mnookin & Kornhauser 1979). That is, rational actors bargain for settlements in their self-interest, but do so by drawing on "bargaining endowments" granted by law and with an eye toward the likely outcome if they decide to litigate their claims instead. In this way the law constrains informal negotiations, but within those constraints an actor is free to seek a solution that best satisfies his or her preferences, even one that markedly departs from the remedy provided by law.

One important implication of this rational actor model is the corollary that social behavior cannot be legislated directly. Private ordering allows actors to choose not to pursue legal claims or to waive legal entitlements in exchange for some other desired outcome. This feature of private enforcement seems desirable because the theory assumes that parties accept deviations from their legal rights only when they believe

---

[1] Most employment statutes also include fee shifting provisions that award attorney's fees to "prevailing" parties, so that successful plaintiffs can recover at least a portion of the costs of the lawsuit. Both doctrinal and practical constraints, however, mean that even successful plaintiffs rarely recover all of their attorney's fees (Albiston & Nielsen 2007).

those deviations are better than the likely outcome in litigation. These assumptions give rise to an elegant model of dispute resolution that relies on private negotiations to satisfy the parties' preferences, and that does not require extensive government intervention for optimal outcomes.

Sociolegal Alternatives to Rational Actor Models

Law and society scholars have long challenged this model of private ordering and the normative conclusions that flow from it (Bumiller 1987, 1988; Felstiner, Abel, & Sarat 1981; Merry & Silbey 1984). Rather than treating disputes as natural occurrences to be negotiated according to individual preferences, sociolegal scholars conceptualize disputes as social constructs. In this view, through a subjective and contingent process of "naming, blaming, and claiming," individuals recognize (or fail to recognize) injuries, assess fault for those injuries, and claim their rights by demanding redress (Felstiner, Abel, & Sarat 1981). Sociolegal scholars question rational actor assumptions that treat individuals' preferences as stable, internal personal attributes. Instead, they posit a contingent, reactive, and shifting process of social construction through which individuals' actions and preferences take shape in relation to the social context of potential disputes.

Like rational actor models, sociolegal models of mobilization conclude that behavior cannot be legislated directly, but sociolegal theorists are more pessimistic about outcomes that depart from the legal remedies available. Sociolegal approaches model mobilization as an interactive process shaped by a social context that encompasses more than just bargaining endowments, and they argue that power, inequality, and deeply entrenched expectations limit the effects of legal reforms (Bumiller 1987, 1988; Edelman et al. 1993; Galanter 1974). Rather than reforming problematic social relations, these theorists argue, rights can end up legitimizing inequality by appearing to provide a remedy even though contextual constraints mean that those rights are rarely mobilized (Bumiller 1987, 1988; Quinn 2000; Scheingold 1974). Nevertheless, at least some scholars contend that rights, even if largely symbolic, can empower individuals whose grievances otherwise would be ignored (Minow 1987; Williams 1991). Moreover, to the extent that both the powerful and the powerless buy into the legitimacy and authority of legal rights, individuals can sometimes obtain success even by informally referencing rights (McCann 1994).

Sociolegal researchers who draw on this theoretical framework have generally taken a qualitative, interpretive approach to studying informal mobilization (Bumiller 1988; Engel and Munger 1996, 2003; Morgan 1999; Quinn 2000). Like interpretive studies of litigation as a mobilization strategy (McCann 1994), these microlevel studies examine how rights work as cultural discourses or "schemas" in informal settings and everyday life (Bumiller 1988; Ewick and Silbey 1998; Hull 2003; Marshall 2003; Nielsen 2000; Quinn 2000). For example, Bumiller (1988) found that potential civil rights claimants chose not to pursue their rights because they did not want to take on a victim identity. Quinn (2000) found that workplace norms framed sexual harassment as harmless joking or chain pulling, making it difficult for women who were harassed to name and pursue harassment as a legal injury, even when it caused them significant emotional stress. Methodologically, these studies expand the inquiry beyond observable action to include individuals' subjective processes, including the ways in which actors "redefine their perceptions of experiences and the nature of their grievances in response to the communications, behaviors, and expectations of ... opponents, agents, authority figures, companions and intimates" (Felstiner et al. 1981: 638).

Institutional Perspectives on Rights Mobilization

Conceptualizing the decision to mobilize rights as a social process embedded within existing social relations turns the inquiry toward determination of which contextual factors affect actors' perceptions and preferences about rights. Institutions come into play by shaping behavior to be consistent with established practices and by molding consciousness to fit within existing ideas about work and leave. In workplace interactions over leave, law is only one of many available interpretive frames for understanding conflict and resistance to family and medical leave. Models of rights mobilization must also consider other available frames, which interact with legal discourse to shape actors' perceptions and preferences. These alternative frames often connect to broader systems of power and control.

Social change can be both facilitated and constrained by the interaction of these competing interpretive frames. Change is possible when actors draw on frameworks in new ways to reinterpret established meanings and to change social structure (Sewell 1992). Change is constrained, however, by established practices and expectations that generate resistance to restructuring deeply entrenched social patterns. Institutionalization of these linked sets of practice and meaning – in workplace rules and behavior, for example – helps naturalize, normalize, and make invisible those presumptions about how things should be done that otherwise might be open to question. Over time, institutions become self-sustaining and resistant to change because they come to define what constitutes legitimate action and to channel behavior to be consistent with established practices and norms.

If the meaning of rights is constructed not only by law, but also by the cultural and social institutions that shape everyday interactions, then studying mobilization requires going beyond simple questions of legal entitlements, individual preferences, and available resources (Ewick & Silbey 1998; Harrington & Merry 1988; Sarat 1990). For example, not only observable actions but also the complex subjective processes in which individuals engage to interpret workplace conflicts become important objects of inquiry. Similarly, one must take into account social interactions with potential "agents of transformation" – opponents, friends, coworkers, and family members – who draw on both legal and nonlegal cultural frameworks to interpret workplace experiences (Felstiner, Abel, & Sarat 1981; Morgan 1999).

In the context of the FMLA, these frameworks include the practices and implicit expectations that construct the meaning of work. Although the FMLA attempts to change the time standards of work, the long-standing patterns of behavior and belief that give meaning to work do not disappear overnight. Workers mobilize their rights to family and medical leave in workplaces where workplace rules, coworkers' expectations, and employers' demands continue to reflect the historical ways in which work has been organized and performed. Although FMLA rights state that leave taking is legitimate, implicit beliefs and expectations about work, gender, and disability may give rise to very different interpretations of the same behavior. How do these competing systems of meaning shape the practical meaning of FMLA rights?

Method and Data

The analysis that follows draws on semistructured telephone interviews with workers who experienced conflict over leave but did not take their disputes to court. Data such as these are difficult to obtain because informal disputes generally do not produce court files or other easily identified records of a dispute. Also, employers are rarely enthusiastic about allowing their employees to talk to researchers about conflict over legal rights. To overcome these problems, this study located respondents through a state-wide telephone information line in California, run by a nonprofit organization that gives informal legal assistance to workers. Attempts were made to contact those individuals who called the information line with questions about family and medical leave during a one-year period. Twenty-four of the thirty-five individuals in this group agreed to be interviewed, a response rate of almost 70 percent.[2] Despite the small size of this group of workers, these respondents were fairly diverse in terms of age, race, education, marital status, income, and occupation (see Appendix A). Accordingly, although this small sample does not permit detailed comparison across these factors or across workplace

---

[2] Four individuals could not be contacted after multiple attempts, four individuals refused to be interviewed, one number had been disconnected, and two numbers were incorrect.

characteristics, these interviews do provide information about common patterns across multiple organizations, rather than relying on data from only one workplace. They also come from a group of respondents that is not racially homogeneous or uniformly economically privileged.

The phone interviews, which typically lasted about 45 minutes, were recorded and transcribed. These data were analyzed using qualitative analysis software that allows researchers to identify and code themes as they emerge from the transcripts. The analysis identified factors that influenced workers' decisions about whether to mobilize or not mobilize their rights, and the problems they experienced taking leave. Multiple readings of the interview transcripts identified significant themes in respondents' interpretation and understanding of the mobilization process, such as "gender," "slackers," and the meaning of "time." The analysis then went back and systematically coded each instance of these themes, and analyzed patterns among them. The software greatly simplifies this process by allowing the researcher to mark interview segments associated with a theme, to sort and index these segments by theme, and to identify patterns among themes.

Although the small number of subjects in qualitative studies such as this requires caution in drawing generalizations, the in-depth approach made possible by qualitative interviewing reveals considerable nuance and detail about the mobilization process that would be lost in a larger, quantitative survey. Because this study focuses on the experiences of workers who anticipated or experienced some difficulty in obtaining leave, the subjects are not and were not intended to be a random sample of the population of potential leave users. For this reason, this study makes no claims about how frequently problems with the FMLA arise or about the differences between workers who experience problems and those who do not. Instead, the analysis focuses on how social institutions give meaning to leave conflicts and constructs workers' preferences about mobilizing their rights. This theory-building inquiry examines the significance of broader social institutions for the microlevel process of informal rights mobilization and the implications of these social institutions for inhibiting or facilitating social change.

By recruiting subjects from an information line utilized by workers seeking help with their rights, this study identifies potential legal disputes in several workplace settings. This data-collection approach is superior to snowball sampling, which often presents homogeneity problems, or interviews from only one workplace, which cannot show patterns across workplace boundaries. In addition, because many workers called the information line seeking help to informally negotiate their rights, these data provide valuable information about disputes that do not become formal legal proceedings — those that reside at the bottom part of the dispute pyramid (Felstiner, Abel, & Sarat 1981). This stage of disputing is rarely studied because methodologically it is difficult to identify potential legal claims before they reach a legal forum.

The qualitative data from this study complement other ethnographic and quantitative studies of family and medical leave (Commission on Leave 1996; Fried 1998; Gerstel & McGonagle 1999; Hochschild 1997). These data add to quantitative research about patterns of leave taking in general (see, e.g., Gerstel & McGonagle 1999) because they access the cognitive processes that contribute to choices about leave and rights. This study also differs from recent ethnographic studies of leave taking and corporate culture within a single organization (see, e.g., Fried 1998; Hochschild 1997), because it reveals social patterns that bridge multiple workers and workplaces. This approach helps identify patterns that operate across workplaces and across organizational boundaries, patterns that show how social institutions such as work can shape and transform legal rights on a broader scale.

The Process of Rights Mobilization in the Workplace

The sections that follow outline two broad themes regarding the process of mobilization: how workplace rights mobilization is embedded in relations of power, and how institutionalized conceptions of work affect the practical meaning of FMLA rights.

Power and Workplace Rights Mobilization

Unequal power in the workplace can affect rights mobilization in several ways. First, to the extent that power consists of superior strength or resources, employers who have more resources than their workers may be more likely to prevail in conflicts over rights. Second, power includes employers' ability to prevent grievances from becoming full-blown public conflicts. For example, employers can create internal procedures to divert grievances from public forums (Edelman, Uggen, & Erlanger 1999), and workers may not mobilize their rights if they fear they will be penalized or fired in response (Bumiller 1988; Tucker 1993). Third, power can be deployed to keep grievances from being recognized at all. For example, employers may withhold information or use persuasion to make their actions seem natural and normal, rather than problematic or unfair (Felstiner, Abel, & Sarat 1981; Gramsci 1971; Lukes 1974). Power also operates through more impersonal cultural forces that shape how actors interpret their experiences. Many workplace frames are not deployed solely by employers, but instead are shared by both employers and workers as part of the broader culture. These ideologies often reinforce current relations of power and control, and shape how actors understand workplace experiences in ways that legitimize and maintain existing social arrangements (Bourdieu 1977; Foucault 1979; Gramsci 1971; Sewell 1992).

Information Control, Agents of Transformation, and Worker Solidarity

One important theme that emerged from these interviews is that unequal power in the workplace affects how workers think about rights mobilization. Most respondents mentioned at least one power dynamic that influenced how they thought about responding to conflict over leave, sometimes with tragic consequences. For example, threats of termination could silence resistance to unfair treatment:

> [W]hen I was pregnant, my doctor put in writing that I could not, he didn't want me bending for long periods of time, or looking up for long periods of time because I have a tendency to get dizzy and get off balance when you're pregnant.... So, everything that [my supervisor] wanted me to do was four to six inches from the floor. And there were other courtesy clerks there that could have done the job, but she wanted me to do it. She didn't care if my stomach is showing and everything. There were guys there that were courtesy clerks that could have did the job. And when I told her, "I don't think I'm supposed to be doing this." She'd tell me, "You don't like your job?" You know. And I felt that was pretty cruel, you know for her to treat me that way ... So ... [I did the work and] I ended up losing my baby.... When I returned to work, she started right back up. She told me that she did everything while she was pregnant with no restrictions. That's what she told me.[3] [1017]

An explicit threat of termination may not be necessary if workers fear other penalties at work. For example, the following respondent did not pursue her right to return to the same or equivalent job after leave, even though her hours were cut in half when she returned to work.

> I just didn't want to make – cause he's a new manager and I hadn't worked with him – I didn't want to come back with an attitude and then him kind of be negative toward me. It hurt, but I thought well, I still have my job. It's going to be rough because, you know, twenty hours a week. [1018]

Some respondents worried that being fired would not only deprive them of a job, but also harm their ability to find future employment. They

---

[3] This particular respondent's situation was covered by state law in California, rather than the FMLA. California law requires employers to accommodate pregnancy-related restrictions on the tasks a worker can perform by transferring her to a less strenuous or hazardous position where that transfer can be reasonably accommodated. Cal. Gov. Code § 12945. This passage also suggests that the respondent's

justified voluntarily quitting rather than pursuing their rights and risking termination by pointing out that no one wants to hire a fired worker, particularly a "troublemaker" who sued a former employer.

Power in the employment relationship also operates in subtle ways to shape how workers come to understand their workplace rights. Along these lines, one theme that emerged from these interviews is that control over information about rights yields an advantage in workplace negotiations over leave. Information is critical to "naming," or saying to oneself that a particular experience has been injurious, and "blaming," or holding another responsible for the injury (Felstiner, Abel, & Sarat 1981). The FMLA recognizes this link between information and enforcement by placing affirmative obligations on employers to tell workers about their leave rights.[4]

Virtually all respondents mentioned how important it was to have accurate information about their rights when deciding how to deal with conflict over leave. Many respondents indicated that their employers attempted to control information in ways that discouraged them from claiming rights and even prevented them from realizing they might have a legal claim. For example, when workers request leave, employers can stonewall by asserting that the statute does not apply unless the worker can prove otherwise.

> I mean the initial reaction ... was just sheer, "We're not going to even use this law because we don't know what we can get away with. We don't know ... if you qualify so until we do, you don't." That was my feeling that's how they treated that law.... Their whole attitude is stalwart it or whatever the word is, block it the best you can. Make these folks fight for it.... That's the reaction I got. [1002]

Some employers simply remain silent and wait to see whether workers recognize that leave rights might apply.

---

supervisor is applying certain norms about ideal workers. That dynamic is discussed in more detail later in the text.

[4] 29 C.F.R. §§ 825.301, 825.302.

[T]he way [R's employer] is, ... if you don't do your homework they'll let you ride with what you know and if you don't know enough then you shorten yourself. So you had to go in there with as much knowledge as I had you know, to talk to them. [1010]

Informal practices such as these give employers more control over the use and length of leave, and thus can transform a legal entitlement into a discretionary benefit. These findings are consistent with research that indicates that information about legal rights is hard to find yet essential to negotiating successfully with employers (Harlan & Robert 1998). Respondents across diverse work situations described common patterns of limiting and withholding information about rights, suggesting that control over information is a common strategy for limiting the impact of legal rights.

Employers can also act as agents of transformation through internal processes that affect how workers understand conflict over leave (Edelman, Erlander, & Lande 1993; Felstiner, Abel, & Sarat 1981). These processes can "drain the dispute of moral content and diffuse responsibility for problems" (Felstiner, Abel, & Sarat 1981). For example, one respondent's concerns about being denied leave were diverted into the Employee Assistance Program (EAP), a counseling program paid for by the employer. The counselor interpreted the respondent's problem as a personal issue rather than a legal violation.

[T]he EAP person at work [was helpful].... He was very understanding and he felt that [my problem] was a rotten deal but, you know, "Hey, there's nothing anybody can do about it." [1006]

By framing this respondent's conflict between work and the need for medical leave as a product of her personal circumstances rather than of the structure of work, the counselor helped diffuse conflict about leave and deflect a potential legal claim.

Although employers shape respondents' perceptions by controlling information about FMLA rights, most respondents also talked with friends, family, and others to gather information about the law and to mull over possible responses to conflict over leave. These conversations helped frame the meaning of workplace events, sometimes in terms of legal rights, but not always. For example, this respondent indicated that friends encouraged her to see her situation as a legal violation and to pursue her rights.

> I felt like I was kind of in a situation that nobody had really been in, and so I didn't really know what to do. So people's opinions and their thoughts of what I should do made a big impact because I really had no idea of where to go from here. And I have some friends who were very supportive of this and said, "No, you have to go forward with this. You have to go through with it because they can't get away with this." [1015]

Although her friends encouraged her to mobilize her rights, her stepmother interpreted the situation differently based on her experience losing her job before the FMLA was enacted.

> I talked to my stepmother, who had three children, and, um, I guess had had maternity leave for each child, for each birth. And she told me, "That's just the way it is." You know, I shouldn't try to fight it, I shouldn't get myself all upset. That it's what happens. [1015]

These conflicting interpretations illustrate how different cultural frameworks – in this case, acceptance of gender inequality versus empowerment by legal norms – can be deployed by agents of transformation in the mobilization process. For this respondent, legal norms facilitated mobilization by undermining her stepmother's interpretation that losing one's job when one has a baby is "just the way it is." Her experience suggests how legal discourse can generate alternative interpretive frameworks that challenge established patterns of acquiescence to inequality.

For these respondents, mobilization was not a solitary decision based on preexisting, endogenous preferences; it was a social process in which others' opinions about what they should do shaped the respondents' choices. In part, they formed their preferences in response to norms and perceptions communicated by others. As I will explain in more detail, those norms and perceptions, in turn, were shaped by actors' experiences within existing systems of inequality in the workplace, and by institutionalized conceptions of work, gender, and disability.

Friends, family, and others can act as agents of transformation in several ways. They can encourage workers to mobilize their rights, sometimes by framing a particular experience as unacceptable or illegal.

> I talked to ... the guy I was co-managing the store with and I talked to another manager [about my situation].... Both of them felt like I had been misled [by the company]. And that [it] had been done purposely.
>
> Interviewer: And did that influence what you did in your situation in any way?
>
> It made me want to talk to somebody in the law. [1008]

Exchanges with others can also warn workers about the risks of claiming rights, however.

> [Y]ou know I've heard horror stories about people taking time off when their baby was born and were getting a lot of flack from their bosses because they took the time.... I heard, there was this one guy, he has a shift that is mid-shift, 12 – 8:30 and when he came back to work they changed it on him.... They changed his shift to a graveyard shift, Monday through Friday when he came back.... I worked graveyard for four years, I didn't want to go back to that. [1010]

This last example suggests how actions taken against only one worker can influence how many others think about mobilizing their rights. Stories of retaliation that are passed through social networks in the workplace can discourage workers from requesting leave even absent any explicit threat directed toward them.

Social interactions about rights can also, however, build solidarity among workers. By discussing problems with leave with others, workers may uncover a larger pattern of shared grievances. As the following example illustrates, conversations about rights can also help build informal networks for pooling knowledge about the law.

Several of us were tempted to get together and get a suit going, but getting together with a lawyer is very difficult. And no one is really willing
to commit to helping at all to start it. But all of us had had issues as
far as FMLA, knew each others' issues ... So ... we would advise new
employees a lot of the time if they had issues come up, they would come
to us. ... As new people came in we would let them know, we've gone
through quite a bit if you need any help with anything as far as your
benefits, your health or whatever, just let us know ... [W]e all kind of
pooled our knowledge. We all had a much more expansive knowledge
of what was going on. As far as influencing me, I didn't think that I
could get FMLA [leave] for my condition and one of my coworkers
said, "Yes you can." So it did directly affect the course I took. [1021]

In this way, negotiating individual rights can become a collective concern, and workers can gain greater leverage in negotiations over leave.

This last point contradicts the critique that individual rights undermine collective action by atomizing disputes and isolating grievances
from their social context (McCann 1986; Scheingold 1974). This critique
may place too much emphasis on how formal rights claims in court narrow disputes to legally relevant facts and individualized remedies, strip-
ping them of their social context. It also assumes that rights mobilization
is a solitary rather than a social process. This assumption overlooks the
ways in which the informal process of mobilizing rights – finding information about rights and caucusing with other workers about what is
appropriate and legal – builds connections and common interests among
grievants. The social process of mobilization may also show workers how
rights claims extend beyond their individual interests. In fact, several
respondents said they took steps to pursue their rights to prevent future
workers from having a similar experience.[5]

This insight is important because it suggests that individuals who
mobilize their rights in informal settings can set in motion a framing
process that may lead to eventual collective action (Snow 2004; Snow

---

[5] Similar findings on a more macrolevel have emerged from recent research about
rights mobilization by social movements (see McCann & Silverstein 1998).

et al. 1986). Just as rights litigation in courts can provide a public rallying point and publicity for a social movement (McCann 1994), informal rights mobilization through workplace interactions can build solidarity among workers who share common grievances. It can also encourage workers to see their problems as part of a broader system of power and control. Accordingly, the findings reported here do not support the argument that rights are inherently limited as a social change strategy because they frame broader grievances as individual problems. Individual rights do not necessarily create an ideological framework that always causes workers to conceptualize difficulties as individual problems rather than collective concerns. Instead, these findings suggest that the process of sharing information can give rise to collective oppositional consciousness by drawing on rights discourse, even if power disparities or coordination problems sometimes prevent formal collective action.

Law as a Symbolic Resource in Leave Negotiations

Even for those workers who negotiate their rights on their own, legal rights can be an important symbolic resource. As Ewick and Silbey (2003: 1331) point out, both power and resistance to power "draw from a common pool of sociocultural resources, including symbolic, linguistic, organizational, and material phenomenon." Legal rights insert new cultural discourses into that pool of resources, and workers draw on these new resources in workplace negotiations over leave. For example, most respondents reported that they felt empowered by the legal entitlement to leave as they negotiated with their employers. In addition, many respondents said they felt morally justified in pursuing claims to leave once they knew that their employer acted illegally, and without that information they felt unsure of the legitimacy of their requests for leave. As one worker put it,

> [Information about FMLA rights] gave me a leg to stand on. And some kind of moral or ethical support knowing that this is what my rights were.... [1003]

In addition, many respondents described law as a pragmatic resource for confronting employers, even when they did not make a formal legal claim. For example, this worker used legal knowledge to negotiate successfully with her employer:

> [When my employer denied my leave request] I didn't say, "It's not legal," I said, "According to this state statute …" I put the statute number and stuff, so that they know that I know what I'm talking about … [A] lot of people will go, "Are you sure this is legal?" … and then they'll try and like moonshine their way around it. And rather than have people do that to me, I just got to where when stuff comes up, I'll learn the legal statute numbers and it's more effective for me that way.… [Information about my rights] gave me knowledge which gave me the power to act on what was going on. [1021]

Learning about their rights helped these workers frame their experiences in both legal and moral terms, and gave them the confidence to press for time off. Some workers also drew on law to interpret leave as an entitlement rather than as a personal problem. Thus, even workers who lack financial resources for a court battle can still mobilize law informally to validate their claims to leave.

A prior study of mobilization by Bumiller (1988) suggested that civil rights construct meanings that are disempowering rather than empowering. She found that some individuals chose not to pursue civil rights claims to avoid taking on a victim identity. Respondents in my study did not express similar concerns. Of course, not all laws construct the same symbolic meaning. The FMLA frames leave as an entitlement rather than a protection based on status, which may avoid constructing claimants as victims. Also, the respondents in this study differ from the unmobilized subjects in Bumiller's study in that they took some steps toward mobilization. Nevertheless, even respondents who abandoned potential claims did not say they did so to avoid the victim label. Accordingly, it may be that whether actors see the law as empowering or disempowering varies with the substance of particular rights.

Social Institutions and the Social Construction of Rights to Leave

Perhaps the most subtle form of power is the way institutionalized practices and expectations shape social interactions to recreate inequality. Three themes emerged from these interviews that show how workers' leave negotiations are embedded with existing relations of power and inequality. First, family wage ideology, or the assumption that the normative worker is a male breadwinner with a stay-at-home wife, shapes how workers and others think about the meaning of leave rights. Second, the belief that workers who take sick leave are slackers undermines the FMLA in ways that subtly reinforce the constitutive relationship between disability and work. Finally, some employers reinterpret leave rights in terms of management objectives, weakening the normative power of the law relative to the institution of work.

Family Wage Ideology

Most respondents who took pregnancy or parental leave discovered that despite the law, family wage discourse framed the meaning of their leave. Indeed, many women found that taking leave changed perceptions of them at work because it seemed to signal that they were no longer committed to their jobs. For example, one respondent reported that even though her performance reviews had been very good, her supervisor's attitude changed after her leave to care for her ill daughter.

> He's like, "Well she's having a problem with her kid." … [Now] he makes me feel like I'm inadequate. Like I can't do the job, like I'm not bright enough. [1018]

Virtually all the female respondents initially had no difficulty taking leave. When they attempted to return, however, they encountered resistance and perceptions that they were less reliable and committed to their work after their leave.

The experience of a respondent who took pregnancy leave when she gave birth to twins illustrates this phenomenon. She worked as a manager for her employer, a large company, for 16 years before she needed leave. Nevertheless, her employer assumed she would not return and canceled her health insurance while she was in the hospital. Her boss also told coworkers that she did not need her job because her husband could support her.

> [T]hey were saying, "Well she doesn't need to get paid." My boss was saying, "She has money – her husband is a doctor." [1009]

Despite her years of service, her employer presumed her husband was the breadwinner and that she therefore did not need her job. Her supervisor attempted to justify letting her go by mobilizing a cultural discourse that women (particularly mothers) are and should be economically dependent upon their husbands.

Legal rights also framed this worker's understanding of her situation, however. A friend who was a lawyer told her that she would have a strong legal claim if she tried to return and was fired, and she expressed outrage that her employer ignored her legal entitlement to leave. Nevertheless, she feared that no future employer would hire her if she were fired. She knew that her employer had fired other long-term employees who needed leave, and she decided to quit.

> [T]hose two got fired first and then I just said, you know, I don't want to get fired. I mean I have a good record and I would hate to have to go and start somewhere at, in your mid-thirties and then your employer that you've worked for 16 years fired you? That doesn't look good. And my husband said, "Is it really worth it all?" [1009]

When she left, however, she told her supervisor she could not return to work because she lacked childcare to avoid a confrontation with her employer.

This respondent's experience illustrates how legal and nonlegal frames for interpreting leave can shape informal rights negotiations. To decide whether to mobilize her rights, this respondent had to reconcile legal discourse with family wage ideology in a context already structured by power, gender, and taken-for-granted expectations about work. Her problems with leave arose in part because gendered assumptions about work and family gave meaning to her use of leave. This same family wage discourse helped obscure how her employer's power to fire her influenced her decision. Although she subjectively interpreted her experience as a violation of her rights, she avoided conflict by drawing on a gendered discourse to give a culturally acceptable reason to quit: lack of childcare. As a result, her actions communicated a putatively voluntary choice to stay home and care for her children because her husband could support her, and the roles that law and power played in her decision remained invisible. In this way, gendered assumptions about women and work are reinforced, and legal entitlements to leave are simultaneously undermined and obscured.

The male respondents who took family leave had somewhat different experiences. In fact, both male and female respondents reported informal workplace norms against men taking all the parental leave legally available to them. For example, in one respondent's workplace, it was unthinkable that a new father would take more than a week or two of leave.

> [T]here was another guy who was having a baby and I think that they got more pressure to come back to work, okay, "It's okay for you to take a week off and maybe a week and a half off, but let's not go crazy here." And that wasn't, I don't think they would have been open for the FMLA for the men. At least the men I knew just took their vacation and didn't take, didn't use the FMLA when they could've. Because they were pressured to come back to work, like "Hey, *you* didn't have a baby."
>
> Interviewer: And there wasn't the same kind of pressure on women?
>
> No. [1020]

Although female respondents typically found that employers expected them to take leave to care for others, all the male respondents reported that their employers and coworkers were incredulous and even hostile when they decided to take family leave. Thus, the same family wage discourse constructed different social meanings for respondents' leaves depending upon their gender.[6]

These deeply entrenched expectations about work and gender also shape the legal consciousness of workers. For example, some male respondents who took unpaid family leave struggled to reconcile leave rights with norms that men should prioritize work over family needs. The experience of the following respondent who took leave to care for his terminally ill wife illustrates this point. He had worked as a laborer for seven years for a public agency in the San Francisco area. When he took leave to care for his wife, he encountered criticism from coworkers for missing work, and also received a disciplinary letter from his employer telling him to keep his leave use to a minimum. When his coworkers, his employer, and even his wife questioned his time away from work, he drew on legal norms to legitimize his leave:

> I always made them understand that I'm under Family Leave … and that allows me the right [to take leave].… [M]y wife a lot of times, says "Babe, you can't miss this much work," this and that, and I'd say "Honey, you know, I'm not missing work to miss work. You're sick or whatever and if you need me, I'm here and that's what Family Leave is, that's why I'm under it, and that's why we fill out the Certification papers with your medical provider to protect me in these times of need." [1012]

At the same time, however, he believed he should not seek advancement at work while he might need family leave.

> [T]here has been plenty of opportunities for me to move up and stuff, but I didn't pursue them because … I'm not ready to give 100% responsibility. My responsibility deals with my wife and family at

---

[6] Other studies have demonstrated consistent and widespread employer hostility toward male workers taking parenting leave. For example, one study found that 63 percent of large employers considered it unreasonable for a man to take any parental leave at all, and another 17 percent considered a reasonable leave to be no longer than two weeks (see Malin 1998: 39–40).

this time. And I've known how sick she is so I didn't pursue any of those advancements for that reason. It was that my priorities are with my family and not moving up at this time. ... [W]e are pretty middle class. I mean there is nothing we are deprived of. We probably have more things than what most people got, but that has never been a priority to me, like having more or whatever. You know, my priority is my family and that's how I'd like to keep it. [1012]

This respondent knew about his legal rights, and he was aware that the FMLA prohibits employers from taking leave into account in promotion decisions.[7] Nevertheless, he understood leave and advancement at work to be an either/or choice – he could not pursue a promotion and also care for sick family members. When he justified taking leave by saying he passed up opportunities for advancement, he accepted and reinforced the family wage norm that ideal workers should have no responsibility to care for others. At the same time, his statement that his family is "pretty middle class" despite his choice to put family first implicitly references cultural expectations about the male breadwinner role and justifies his choice against those norms.

In mobilizing his rights, this respondent ran up against implicit, gendered expectations about what work and being a good worker mean. By referencing his legal rights, he legitimized his choice to put his family first both to himself and to those who question his absence. The fact that his choice to care for his wife requires justification, however, reveals how leave rights interact with other systems of meaning that construct this choice as illegitimate. He reconciled legal rights with these ideologies by simultaneously asserting his rights and voluntarily compromising advancement at work. In this way, legal and nonlegal discourses interact to shape his understanding of his legal rights as well as their practical meaning.

The conflicting expectations about being a good worker and the family caretaker also affected female respondents, but female

---

[7] 29 C.F.R. § 825.220.

respondents struggled with the contradiction between being "good workers" and "good mothers." The following respondent's experience illustrates this conflict. She had worked in the human resources department of a hotel before taking leave for pregnancy disability and childbirth. When she tried to return to work after her leave, she discovered that her employer had filled her position. She was angry, and when friends suggested that she contact a lawyer about pursuing her rights, she did. At the same time, she worried that she was to blame for her situation, and that she had violated norms about being a good worker.

> I was speaking with a lawyer all that time, trying to get back my job and see if they would offer me anything else, but they just wanted to put me in housekeeping. They couldn't find anything for me. At least that's what they were saying. Other situations they were hiring for, other things like sales. And I was like, "Well I can learn sales, anything." A lot of my friends tell me that it's not my fault, that people are just like that. I felt like I was to blame. I even talked to my boss about it. I said, "Didn't I do a good job?"... [1013]

Although her boss assured her that she had performed well, he also demoted her from human resources assistant to hotel housekeeper. She continued to work as a housekeeper for several months while her lawyer negotiated for her job.

Although she continued to negotiate her rights, she worried about failing to meet her obligations as a mother. She said, "I just felt that no one else would take care of [my child] like a mother would." She was ambivalent about returning to work because she no longer had the job she loved, and she had to leave her child with another caretaker to work in a less desirable job for reduced pay.

> I felt bad in my own way and I was very sad. And I think a lot of it was because I knew my child was with this other person. I couldn't do anything about it. My job went to another woman and what was I going to do? All I could do is cry. [1013]

Although some of her friends thought she should continue to fight, others suggested a different solution:

> I have one friend, she was always telling me, "[Maria] if you feel this way why don't you just quit your job and just take care of your son?" Then my husband got a better job offer so that's when I said, I think I will do that. [1013]

Eventually, she gave up her negotiations with her employer and quit her job.

This respondent negotiated her rights within three overlapping and contradictory frames: legal entitlements to leave, institutionalized expectations about what it means to be a good worker, and deeply entrenched norms about what it means to be a good mother. The conflict among these frames made claiming her rights psychologically taxing. She hired a lawyer to fight for her job, but she also felt unsure of her claim of being a good worker after missing work for pregnancy leave. At the same time, she worried about not meeting an idealized norm of a mother's intense and personal care of her children (Hays 1996). Her comments reveal the contradictory legal and cultural schemas about the meaning of leave that framed her decision about mobilization.

She decided to quit, but it is simplistic to interpret her choice as the result of immutable gendered preferences without considering how institutionalized work norms and structural conditions shaped those preferences. Perhaps she would have made a different choice if her employer had allowed her to return to her former management position rather than demoting her to housekeeper. As some feminist scholars have suggested, for working-class women and women of color such as this respondent, meeting the demands of ideal motherhood can be a haven of respectability from race and class discrimination in the job market (Davis 2000). By demoting her from manager to housekeeper, the employer may have tipped the balance away from low-status work in favor of motherhood. Also, by suggesting that she should quit and care for her son, her friend framed her situation as a choice between work and motherhood, rather than as a legal violation. Norms about the mutually exclusive roles of mother and worker undermined her resolve to pursue her legal rights, and constructed a culturally acceptable solution for resolving her stress. Her choice, channeled in part by the cultural conflict between being a good worker and being a good mother, helped reinforce that cultural bind despite the protection of the law.

As these examples illustrate, respondents who took family leave negotiated their rights within a web of meaning made up not only of law, but also of deeply entrenched assumptions about work and gender. Although these respondents negotiated rights within the same social context, the interpretations that flow from that context varied with gender. As the responses of their employers, friends, and families suggest, culturally, women are expected to quit work to care for new children, whereas men are expected to make work their first priority (Epstein & Kalleberg 2001; Malin 1998). By deploying this cultural frame, agents of transformation help define the meaning of leave, and sometimes identify a path of least resistance for resolving conflict over leave. In this way, institutions can shape workers' preferences and choices about rights mobilization by providing a graceful explanation for the first respondent to quit, by defining a compromise through which the second respondent justifies his decision to take leave, and by suggesting to the third respondent that quitting to care for others is the solution to her dispute. Because they reinforce gendered conceptions of work and family, however, these paths of least resistance help recreate the inequalities that FMLA rights were meant to change.

Slackers and Workers

Respondents who needed leave for their own serious health condition navigated somewhat different informal workplace norms that labeled leave taking as shirking. Virtually all these respondents reported that in their workplaces, "committed" workers were expected to come to work even when sick despite legal entitlements to medical leave. Conversely, workers who were unwilling or unable to work while sick were perceived as less valuable.

There seemed to be kind of, I forgot the proper way to word this, the company's attitude towards people working when they're ill and working to the point of causing illness, that was sort of a badge of courage. And I had seen other people in the company pretty much be discounted as valuable employees because they wouldn't or couldn't work when they were sick. And I think that's where my fear came from. [1008]

Coworkers as well as employers sometimes interpreted taking leave as shirking, as this long-time employee of a public transit company explains.

Well some people consider that you're a slacker or whatever ... because you're off. They don't consider sick at any point. They know I'm very energetic and hyper and all this stuff, but I should just retire or quit or whatever. I'm in the way.... [S]ome people who are real company oriented or upward, yuppy types feel like you're not being a good employee if you're off. Even if you do the job efficiently. [1003]

Employers communicated this norm through concrete practices: by passing over leave takers for promotion, by transferring (or refusing to transfer) them, by cutting their hours, or by assigning them undesirable work or shifts. These responses mark those who take leave as poor workers, despite legal rights to leave.[8]

Everyday workplace practices can help reinforce perceptions that taking leave for an illness is a form of shirking. For example, not replacing workers who take leave can encourage hostility toward leave takers, as this employee of a large health-maintenance organization describes, because employers require the remaining workers to take on the increased workload.

Like for instance the, well, the FMLA they have to give you. But what they do is some departments and most of the departments actually, they won't replace you when you get sick, so it causes peer pressure

---

[8] Many of these practices are technically illegal. For example, the FMLA prohibits discrimination against workers who use leave rights, including using the taking of leave as a negative factor in employment actions such as hiring, promotions, or disciplinary actions. 29 C.F.R. § 825.220. These kinds of claims can be very difficult to prove, however.

and creates hostility. ... [a]mongst your own co-workers. ... "Well if this person didn't have so much family leave all the time," you know, that type of situation. ... You call in and say, "I'm sick, I'm taking a family leave day." But the end result of that is that it creates hostility in the workplace. They're not supportive because the employer doesn't replace the person. [1006]

This particular workplace practice deflects blame for the extra workload away from the employer because it frames workload problems as a conflict among workers rather than between workers and the employer. Although the FMLA now provides for leave, this workplace continues to be structured around the always-ready, always-present worker, and the employer lacks any contingency plan or substitute staff to cover workers who are on leave.

An alternative explanation for the slacker image might be employers' and coworkers' concerns about abuse of sick leave. Curiously, however, the slacker discourse seemed to apply even when there was no question that the worker's use of leave was legitimate. For example, one respondent reported that coworkers harassed a worker for taking leave, even though they were aware that her leave was for a documented brain tumor. Similarly, several respondents who had provided medical certification of their need for leave still found their absences interpreted as shirking. Thus, it seemed to be only an extended absence, even if medical documentation was provided, that triggered the slacker discourse. It bears mentioning that what has come to be understood as "abusive" use of sick leave is defined against institutionalized workplace policies that typically allow only a small number of sick days per year regardless of the medical needs of the employee. That is, workplace norms reflect and reinforce a power structure between employers and workers in which employers tightly control time in the service of profits, and not necessarily the health or welfare of their workers when those needs conflict with production goals.

The slacker discourse suggests that systems of meaning other than law can create resistance to rights and can discourage workers from using leave. By drawing upon the cultural image of the slacker, employers and coworkers reinterpret mandatory leave rights as a form of shirking. The slacker judgment is not a spontaneous local norm; its roots lie in the historical construction of the institution of work. The slacker image reflects assumptions that work and disability are mutually exclusive and therefore one cannot legitimately claim to be both a worker and disabled. The label "slacker" references deeply held beliefs that being really disabled means not being able to work at all. Accordingly, leave takers find themselves straddling the cultural line between disability and work, and disrupting the implicit reciprocal relationship between the two. The slacker discourse reflects and polices this line by penalizing workers who claim a disability, however temporary that disability may be.

Workers can draw on law as a symbolic discourse, however, to reconstruct the meaning of taking leave, as this respondent discovered.

> [W]hat I've done because of this situation and because I've heard all these things, is I've been meeting with groups of employees and telling them that you don't need to go there. People are entitled to this [leave]. If it was you or your family member you would want this leave too. And you sure wouldn't want to come back to work and find out that your own coworkers are being ugly about it. And if they don't replace you, it's not the employees' fault. It actually has to do with the employer. And trying to appease people. I talk to them and explain to them what the rules are and explain to them that the person who is the sick person, is entitled to this time. And you're just making it worse by doing this to them.
>
> Interviewer: And how has this been received?
>
> Actually pretty good. I've been trying to get them not to fuss with each other. ... [1006]

This respondent draws on legal rights to undermine the slacker discourse and to reveal how that discourse deflects attention from the employer's decision to increase the workload on the remaining workers rather than find a replacement for the worker on leave. First, she explains "what the rules are": that leave is an entitlement, and therefore not subject to qualification or discussion. Second, she references legal norms of equal treatment by pointing out that all workers can benefit from the FMLA's protections. She also undercuts the employer's "slacker" interpretation by pointing out that management, not the absent worker, controls workload distribution. This legal counterdiscourse reveals how the slacker label obscures the employer's responsibility for the increased workload and undermines the norm that good workers work even when they are sick.

This example illustrates how workers can draw on law as a symbolic resource to challenge institutionalized practices and norms in workplace negotiations over leave. In these microinteractions, legal discourse can disrupt existing cultural frameworks for understanding leave and can reveal alternative ways of organizing work life. To the extent that larger social structures are created and recreated through microinteractions such as these (Sewell 1992), law as a counterdiscourse provides one mechanism for bringing about social change.

Managerial Norms and Needs

FMLA rights clash with one more institutionalized work practice: employers' unilateral control over the schedule of work. Legal reforms can have difficulty penetrating these kinds of institutionalized relationships because they continue to shape how managers respond to the law. For example, Edelman et al. (1993) show how organizational-conflict managers reinterpret civil rights objectives in terms of managerial norms. Two-thirds of the respondents in this study reported a similar pattern in which employers used informal workplace practices to regain control over time off.

Some management strategies for taking back control reflected staffing concerns. For example, the employer of one respondent told him about his rights to parental leave, but then asked him not to use them because the employer was short staffed. Another strategy was to limit informally the number of workers who took leave at any one time.

[My supervisor] said well "So and so's on family leave and this one's on family leave and they haven't complained." Yeah they're not working it the same way with them. And then … she was telling me that they had family leave but that we couldn't discuss it. And then she says, "Oh someone else is applying for family leave, but we tried to keep [the number of people on leave] down to one a line." … And I'm saying "Hey, that's not what the law says."

Interviewer: And what did she say when you said that?

"Well, that's just what we try to do." [1003]

Another respondent's employer also managed leave requests in a way that would minimize staffing problems.

[D]epending upon your job position you were treated differently.

Interviewer: Oh really? And how was that, I mean which jobs were treated better and which were treated worse?

Well, I was treated worse. And I was a hostess. And the server that had had the same experience, she was treated better because I think there was more room for her to be accommodated in the schedule because there's 30 servers but there's only three hosts.… They just … it's again, whatever's convenient for them. It's not about the law with them. [1015]

Note that these employers did not completely ignore the law. They complied at least partially by telling workers about their rights, or by allowing some workers to take leave. Nevertheless, they implemented the law in a way that emphasized managerial norms about work schedules and staffing rather than the legal entitlement to leave. These informal workplace practices did not produce "order without law," but instead subtly transformed leave rights in the workplace so that they were consistent with managerial needs.

Managerial practices can affect workers' choices about leave in more subtle ways as well. For example, one respondent described how a management scheme that rewarded workers for meeting production targets undermined leave rights.

[I]t was bad because we were self directed, there was a lot of talk about you know, how will [the new law] affect us, as far as covering production numbers and all that when people take and make use of this Act. ... [T]hey diffuse everything because they get this self-directed, you're your own boss team oriented thing.... In order of importance its production, safety and whatever after that. Who knows. Production and safety is all we had to worry about. Fly like a bat out of hell, get it out the door, but don't hurt yourself. [1002]

As Burawoy (1979) notes, by setting workplace rules and production standards, and then allowing workers to run the production process, employers can manufacture consent to production norms and rules.

[J]ust as playing a game generates consent to its rules, so participating in the choices capitalism forces us to make also generates consent to its rules, its norms. It is by constituting our lives a series of games, a set of limited choices, that capitalist relations not only become objects of consent but are taken as given and immutable. We do not collectively decide what the rules of making out will be: rather, we are compelled to play the game, and we then proceed to defend the rules. (Burawoy 1979: 93)

By setting goals solely in terms of production and safety, and then rewarding self-directed workers for meeting those goals, employers can create rules of the game that undermine collective support for leave. In this workplace, workers enforce time standards against each other to ensure that they meet their production goals, and in the process reinforce and legitimize work practices that devalue leave. Other possible and desirable goals, such as balancing production needs against a worker's need for leave, are not considered. To the extent the workers buy into managerial norms, these norms can diffuse worker resistance by providing ready justifications for resisting leave.

The point here, of course, is not that managerial needs are not pressing or real in some sense, any less than workers' needs for leave are pressing and real. The law, however, changes the balance of power between employers and workers by removing employers' unilateral control over scheduling and by giving workers an entitlement to leave. Previously, employers could solve their managerial requirements by overriding the needs of workers; now the FMLA requires employers to solve their staffing requirements in other ways. These data suggest, however, that employers, rather than developing new organizational strategies to address staffing concerns, can subtly reassert their control over the timing and schedule of work in ways that resist and transform legal mandates to the contrary. To be sure, some respondents recognized and resisted this transformation, mobilizing legal discourse to challenge taken-for-granted ideas that managerial needs always take precedence over the personal needs of workers. In these instances, workers challenged power through overt resistance to dominant workplace norms, and stories of their resistance passed throughout the workplace may help undermine managerial norms (Ewick & Silbey 2003). Nevertheless, other workers may have accepted their employers' reinterpretation of their rights and, as a result, lost the opportunity to take leave when they needed it. Employers' ability to reformulate rights in this way can help them regain control over work schedules without appearing to refuse to comply with the law.

Conclusion

Because law is an authoritative institution, legal rights seem to be an obvious solution to workplace conflict over family and medical leave. The analysis in this chapter cautions, however, that workers negotiate for leave not only in the shadow of the law, but also in the shadow of other social institutions. Workplace rights mobilization remains embedded within existing practices, deeply held beliefs, and taken-for-granted expectations about work, gender, and disability, all of which can create subtle but persistent resistance to these new rights. This social context has important implications for civil rights laws, which are primarily enforced through an individual, private right of action that workers negotiate within these conflicting meanings. Nevertheless, the institutional context of civil rights also creates opportunities to build new coalitions and shape new meanings for family and medical leave. Thus, institutional embeddedness can be seen as both a constraint on and an opportunity for social change.

These findings go beyond the familiar conclusion that local norms can compete with the law. They show that local practices and norms can have roots in larger social structures, including the very social institutions the law was intended to change. For example, workplace rights negotiations are embedded within unequal relations of power that are inherent in the employment relationship and are tied to the historical development of work as an institution. Formally, rights appear to be nonnegotiable entitlements enforceable by law. In practice, however, legal conflict over leave rights may never arise because workers fear shift changes, bad relationships with managers, or the stigma of termination if their employer retaliates. In addition, employers can shape how workers understand and respond to conflict over leave simply by exercising their control over the workplace to limit information about rights.

Power goes deeper than its unequal distribution in the structure of employment, however. It also resides in institutionalized norms about work and its implicit relationship to gender and disability. By enacting the FMLA, Congress did not eradicate deeply entrenched beliefs about work that shape perceptions that leave takers are shirkers, or that women do not need their jobs because they can be supported by their husbands. Cultural ideologies and material practices can also work together to resist rights. Workplace structure may determine, for example, which cultural frame is most likely to be deployed, as employers' strategies for controlling information suggest. Conversely, cultural meanings like the slacker narrative can obscure the way employers exercise power over work rules, such as production goals or staffing levels. In the workplaces in this study, these factors combine to reinforce existing conceptions of work that disadvantage women and people with disabilities.

Thus, rights not only face resistance from local norms, but also from ideological frames like the family wage ideal or the slacker image that arise from the very institutions that legal rights attempt to change. This finding contradicts the arguments of some that "rights talk" in our society displaces other cultural norms (Glendon 1991). Instead, new civil rights become one of many competing cultural frameworks for interpreting social interactions, and do not always dominate in these interactions. In fact, because these rights must be individually mobilized in the context of these entrenched and competing meanings, alternative ideologies may continue to control informal workplace practices despite the formal mandates of the law.

These data confirm new institutionalist insights about the way institutions shape agency, undermining interpretations that treat mobilization decisions as rational choices based on preexisting idiosyncratic preferences. Indeed, these findings suggest that institutions shape perceptions, preferences, and choices into patterns largely consistent with those institutions. Treating these larger social forces as atomized, individual preferences obscures the way institutions constrain choices about mobilization. For example, family, friends, and coworkers all act as agents of transformation by drawing on legal and nonlegal cultural discourses to interpret the meaning of leave, helping shape what workers believed to be possible and appropriate responses to their situations. Conversely, when agents of transformation articulate cultural schemas that conflict with legal entitlements, they can create uncertainty in the minds of workers about what they should do. The institutional context of civil rights constrains not only which options are available as a practical matter, but also which options seem legitimate and appropriate as a normative matter. This is in part because preferences about mobilization emerge from an interactive social process shaped by existing institutions, sometimes in ways that undermine civil rights goals.

Ironically, formal rights may obscure how institutions and power shape agency because rights appear to provide a legal remedy when employers resist leave. For example, when women quit their jobs without asserting

their rights, it may confirm deeply held beliefs that most women prefer caring for children to working because those who preferred to work
could have sued. But relying on objective behavior alone to interpret
preferences overlooks the ways that power and legal norms influenced
these respondents. It also ignores how unequal power can help prevent
legal disputes from arising in the first place, even when workers recognize their legal rights. For this reason, qualitative studies that reveal the
subjective interplay of these factors are particularly important.

What are the implications of these data for rights and social change?
One must exercise caution in answering this question in light of the
powerful critique of rights that has been developed by law and society scholars in recent years. Nevertheless, while acknowledging rights'
limitations, it is also important to explore in what ways and in what
contexts rights might, in fact, make a difference. In a system in which
important social values are enforced almost exclusively through private rights of action, the utility of rights must be evaluated in comparison to the alternative – no rights at all (Matsuda 1989; Minow 1987;
Williams 1991).

The findings reported here challenge one claim about rights – that
they inherently create a consciousness among actors that frames grievances as individual problems, thereby undermining collective action.
Respondents in this study indicated that the existence of legal rights
prompted them to talk with others about their experiences in the workplace, to discuss whether their employers' actions were legitimate, and,
in some instances, to band together to resist their employer's reinterpretation of family and medical leave. Moreover, even in the absence
of overt collective action, sharing alternative interpretations of workplace conflict over leave reveals both the source and the vulnerability of
employers' power (Ewick & Silbey 2003). In this sense, informal rights
mobilization can be understood as a social, rather than individual, process of meaning construction as well as action. This process may give
rise to symbolic frameworks that undermine taken-for-granted practices, such as firing workers who need family or medical leave, and in

this way help change deeply entrenched beliefs about work, gender, and disability.

One must be cautious, of course, not to overstate this point, particularly given that these findings indicate that social institutions can constrain social change by displacing law or transforming it to be consistent with existing practices and norms. Nevertheless, respondents' experiences also suggest that rights can operate as a powerful cultural discourse in informal negotiations over leave. Indeed, one cannot dismiss the symbolic importance of rights claims in the workplace and the gains that workers sometimes achieve simply by pointing out the illegality of an employer's actions. Respondents reported feeling empowered by learning about their rights, and, in some instances, obtained tangible results by confronting their employer with the law. Thus, rights can still matter even when a worker lacks the resources to hire an attorney and pursue a formal legal claim.

Moreover, to the extent that the powerful as well as the powerless buy into the legitimacy of legal claims, rights discourse has a deep cultural resonance for workers and their employers, and so gives workers the agency to make their grievances heard. As Sewell (1992: 20) points out, by deploying alternative schema, agents are "capable of exerting some degree of control over the social relations in which [they are] enmeshed, which in turn implies the ability to transform those social relations to some degree." Without legal rights, these workers would not have access to the symbolic counterdiscourse of law to resist dominant discourses about work, gender, and disability. Indeed, if one takes seriously the social constructivist claim that institutions do not exist apart from the social interactions that recreate them, then the ability to disrupt and transform meaning by invoking rights becomes a significant mechanism of social change.

The fact that rights mobilization is embedded within institutions creates both constraints on change and opportunities for change. Although legal rights may not always be the dominant interpretive frame for workplace conflicts over leave, legal entitlements help make the contradictions in workers' circumstances more visible. They reveal cracks in the hegemonic institution of work, and allow workers to question the idea that penalties for leave are natural and normal. Certainly pervasive practices and expectations can constrain social change by resisting rights, but norms can also change in response to legal reforms. The FMLA provides an alternative interpretive framework through which work can be restructured, reinterpreted, and reimagined, and in this way may help bring about social change.

5   Mobilizing Rights in the Courts

The Paradox of Losing by Winning

WE HAVE SEEN THAT WHEN WORKERS MOBILIZE FMLA rights in the workplace, social institutions shape the meaning of these rights in ways that recreate inequality. Although informal mobilization of rights can challenge deeply entrenched social practices, change through these microlevel interactions can be slow and difficult, because each individual must negotiate the meaning of rights within this institutional context. At least in theory, rights formally mobilized in court are less likely to be displaced or transformed because courts enforce legal principles, not cultural norms. In addition, formal rights claims can force courts to articulate publicly the legitimacy and significance of rights, unlike informal claims that remain largely hidden from public attention (see, e.g., Zemans 1983). In this way, formal rights mobilization produces its own cultural framework for understanding social action in a more visible and authoritative manner than informal workplace negotiations. Thus, from this perspective, adjudication offers a means of shaping public policy and of changing cultural meanings that individuals can access without the need for political clout or a social movement. This claim about formal mobilization raises an important empirical question, however: Do individuals who mobilize FMLA rights in the courts generate legal decisions that affirm the legitimacy of taking leave, and in this way change expectations about work and leave?

Whether a formal rights claim produces a judicial declaration of the public values embodied in a statute depends in part on the institutional rules that determine how courts consider and resolve cases. In particular, procedural turning points at which either party may request a judicial decision create opportunities for judicial declarations interpreting rights. Whether the decision maker is a judge or a jury also matters; judicial decisions often create precedential opinions but jury determinations do not. For purposes of this study, key institutional questions are the following: How do these formal rules shape policy outcomes? How do the procedural rules through which courts consider cases shape opportunities to create judicial decisions that validate leave rights? To what extent do the courts' institutional rules facilitate or limit the capacity of formal rights claims to bring about social change?

The procedural rules of legal institutions reflect commitments to the efficient resolution of disputes, to the formation of precedent, and to *stare decisis*. These rules determine what is heard and when. They implicitly determine the costs of going forward with rights claims, relative to other options. They affect how individual disputes are resolved and affect future disputes by determining which cases set precedents and which do not. That is, when courts decide cases, they not only resolve the current dispute, they also interpret and give meaning to the law that will govern future disputes. In a common law system, these judicial opinions provide a mechanism for gathering individual rights claims into broader social policy.

Courts' procedural rules are designed to produce an orderly and efficient resolution of disputes within the bounds of fairness. As we shall see, however, despite its appearance of formal neutrality, the procedural framework for processing employment disputes tilts the content of adjudication toward interpretations that narrow the scope and meaning of rights. As a result, although rights litigation may produce many tangible benefits for workers who undertake FMLA claims, it offers little promise for changing the broader symbolic meaning of work and leave.

Why Do Ordinary Court Cases Matter for Social Change?

Most accounts of social reform through court litigation focus on impact or "test-case" litigation that aims to produce binding precedent with policy implications (Chayes 1976; Kluger 1976; Rosenberg 1991; Tushnet 1994). But even ordinary individual rights claims can produce wide-ranging effects with significant policy implications. Courts can produce broad-based change by resolving garden-variety disputes, remedying rights violations, and punishing wrongdoers. In a common law system, substantive policy is said to emerge as courts aggregate outcomes and reasoning from individual claims (Zemans 1984). For example, courts' formal institutional rules, such as respect for precedent and the doctrine of *stare decisis*, require them to decide claims based on principles established by earlier decisions, particularly decisions in cases that presented similar facts or similar legal questions. Consequently, decisions in individual cases have the potential to influence all subsequent similar actions.

Individual litigation can also affect social behavior even outside of courts. Court decisions can deter future rights violations and encourage compliance with the law (Galanter 1983). Because the court's opinions communicate the likely outcome of similar disputes if they were litigated, these opinions also bolster or weaken the claims of parties who negotiate disputes in the shadow of the law (Mnookin & Kornhauser 1979). In this way, litigated claims

> may have powerful mobilizational or demobilizational effects. [They] may encourage claimants and lawyers to invest in claims of a given type. [They] may provide symbols for rallying a group, broadcasting awareness of grievance, and dramatizing challenge to the *status quo*. On the other hand, grievances may lose legitimacy, claims may be discouraged, and organizational capacity dissipated. (Galanter 1983: 125–26)

This mobilization or demobilization process can have feedback effects. Courts are passive institutions; their agendas are created by individuals

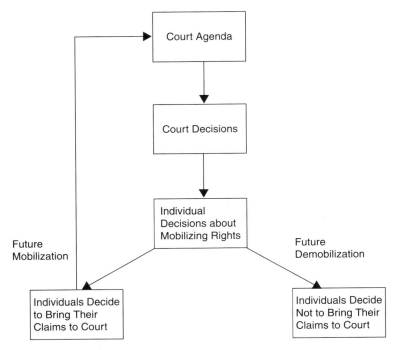

Figure 5.1. *The relationship between court decisions and legal mobilization.*

bringing their claims to court (Black 1973). As a result, current court decisions affect future rights mobilization, and this in turn determines the content of future decisions (Figure 5.1).

Of course courts are not the only social context in which the meaning of law is constructed; it is also constituted within everyday locations such as the neighborhood or workplace. But adjudication has unique symbolic and cultural power. When courts find liability, their decisions name wrongs and lay blame. Conversely, when they find no violation, their decisions validate and legitimize a defendant's conduct. Legal rulings shape social categories and relationships by marking certain people as legal actors or by defining certain actions as illegitimate, and in the process, change the way people think about their everyday lives.

It follows that individual litigation potentially affects much more than the specific litigants before the court. Decisions rendered in individual cases can induce or reduce compliance, affect bargaining outside the court system, and encourage or discourage mobilization of future claims. These decisions shape the meaning of rights and communicate judgments about what is fair or right. In other words, when courts adjudicate a dispute, they perform two important functions: They resolve the underlying conflict in the individual case, and they communicate authoritative rules about legitimate conduct to the broader society.

Most of the social effects of litigated rights claims, however, depend upon the rule-making function of courts. Individuals' decisions to mobilize rights claims influence social life more broadly only to the extent that the outcomes of these claims are communicated effectively. Litigants and judges rely on published judicial opinions that are distributed through electronic archives and in official reports as resources in future disputes, not on dispositions that go unpublished. Given this system of published precedent, procedural rules are important because they determine when rule-making opportunities occur, and thus shape when and how courts construct and communicate the meaning of rights.

Although the substantive content of rights may favor one party or the other, the framework through which legal mobilization takes place is theoretically neutral and impartial. However, the procedural requirements of courts interact with the context-specific features of employment litigation to limit plaintiffs' access to rule-making opportunities. As a result, some successful instances of rights mobilization are never publicly communicated, and unsuccessful attempts to mobilize rights are overrepresented in published authority. In short, the procedural institutions of courts affect how they aggregate and communicate the outcomes of rights claims, and, to the extent that adjudicated outcomes shape the meaning of rights, these systematic effects undermine the potential of rights to produce social change.

The Litigation Process and the Evolution of Rights

What forces shape the disputes that become the basis for judicial interpretations of rights? Published judicial opinions capture only a small part of what goes on regarding a new law; not every statutory violation results in a written judicial opinion interpreting that law. Courts do not automatically detect legal violations; they depend on wronged parties to mobilize the law and bring disputes to a legal forum (Black 1973). Of course, unrecognized violations never reach a legal forum (Felstiner et al. 1981). Even individuals who recognize a harm sometimes decline to sue, instead doing nothing or exiting from their relationship with the wrongdoer (Bumiller 1988; Galanter 1974; Hirschman 1970; Miller & Sarat 1981). Some disputants mobilize the law outside the view of courts by negotiating solutions "in the shadow of the law," with an eye toward the likely adjudicated outcome should the dispute ever reach a legal forum (Mnookin & Kornhauser 1979). Others resolve their legally actionable differences through normative systems other than law (Ellickson 1986, 1991; Macaulay 1963), and the results of these negotiations do not appear in published judicial interpretations of the law.

What is less obvious is that even violations that reach a legal forum do not necessarily result in judicial interpretations of rights. It is well known, although often overlooked, that courts adjudicate only a small fraction of disputes that become formal legal claims (Maccoby & Mnookin 1990; Trubek et al. 1983), and adjudicated disputes are not a representative sample of all the disputes that arise under a statute like the FMLA. Understanding how disputes are selected to become the basis of the judicial interpretations of rights provides some insight into whether the law reflects inequalities between the parties, and whether there are any biases present in the litigation process itself. The following sections explore two factors that influence the evolution of judicial interpretations of employment rights: strategic settlement by employers and the institutionalized distribution of rule-making opportunities in the litigation process.

Settlement and Selection Bias

Because employment rights typically involve an individual employee's claim against an organizational defendant (the employer), employment claims implicate questions of relative power between the parties. Galanter (1974) addresses these questions of power by showing how the characteristics of parties influence the development of legal rules. He argues that some large, often institutional parties appear in court again and again on similar claims. These "repeat players" shape legal development by "playing for the rules": settling cases likely to produce precedent adverse to them and litigating cases likely to produce rules that promote their interests (Galanter 1974). By controlling the cases on which courts create the law, repeat players secure legal interpretations that favor their interests.

This argument suggests that the decisions of parties to settle sometimes encompass factors beyond the circumstances of individual disputes. Several factors may influence this choice, including assessments of the likelihood of success, the costs of going forward, and the resources of the parties. Repeat players, however, have strategic interests beyond the monetary stakes of a particular dispute. Because they expect to experience similar disputes in the future, generally have low stakes in the outcome of any one case, and often have the resources to pursue long-run interests, they

> may be willing to trade off tangible gain in any one case for rule gain (or to minimize rule loss). We assume that the institutional facilities for litigation [are] overloaded and settlements [are] prevalent. We would then expect RPs [repeat players] to "settle" cases where they expected unfavorable rule outcomes. Since they expect to litigate again, RPs can select to adjudicate (or appeal) those cases which they regard as most likely to produce favorable rules. (Galanter 1974: 101)

Parties who do not expect to litigate again are more likely to make the opposite trade-off – trading the potential to make good law for tangible gain as they do not value a favorable legal opinion for future disputes.

This process creates a selection bias in the sample of disputes presented for adjudication. Cases that settle drop out of the caseload on which judges interpret the law, therefore shaping the circumstances under which legal questions arise. Strategic settlement influences the selection of cases presented for adjudication by tending to select cases in which the repeat player is more likely to win. Consequently, Galanter concludes, "we would expect the body of 'precedent' cases – that is, cases capable of influencing the outcome of future cases – to be relatively skewed toward those favorable to [repeat players]" (Galanter 1974: 102). This insight suggests how the unequal resources and incentives of parties allow repeat players to control the content of law and create precedent favorable to their interests.

Some economic models investigating the effect of selective litigation on the efficiency of rules support the repeat-player thesis. These models indicate that where parties have asymmetrical future stakes, the choice for litigation over settlement will occur only where the odds for success favor the party with the greater future stakes, that is, the repeat player (Landes & Posner 1979). Not only is litigation more likely in these circumstances, but the litigant with the greater future stakes will invest more resources into the litigation, and consequently is more likely to win (Cooter 1996; Cooter & Kornhauser 1980; Landes & Posner 1979). Thus, even if the collective benefit of the opposite rule is greater, rules favoring repeat players will survive because a one-shot opponent has no incentive to consider the collective benefit to other one-shot players, and thus has no incentive to represent others' interests by refusing to settle (Cooter 1996:1693).

Similarly, several empirical studies of these various combinations support the repeat-player thesis (Galanter 1975). Studies of courts of general jurisdiction have found that organizations are more successful than individuals in litigation, both as plaintiffs and defendants (Galanter 1975; Wanner 1975). In addition, both individual and organizational plaintiffs are more successful opposing individuals than opposing organizations (Galanter 1975; Kritzer & Silbey 2003; Wanner 1975; Wheeler et al. 1987).

Employment civil rights litigation presents a classic instance of one-shot player versus repeat-player litigation. Employment rights statutes typically provide individuals with a private right of action against their employers. Repeat-player employers consider not only the one-time costs of the outcome of a dispute, but also the future costs of an unfavorable rule. Employers have ongoing relationships with many employees. They anticipate being sued in the future, and even if they are never sued again, they still must comply with employment laws. Adverse legal developments may increase employers' costs of complying with the law. Consequently, employers have a future stake in the interpretation of substantive provisions of employment laws.

Workers, however, are unlikely to consider the future benefits of favorable rules because these benefits are collective, not individual. Few workers bring more than one employment-related lawsuit. Although they might benefit long term from a ruling protecting employees, they are unlikely to turn down an attractive settlement offer for the uncertain chance of preserving this nebulous benefit. Individual workers have little incentive to represent the collective interest of all employees in a favorable ruling because they cannot reap the collective benefit of a ruling friendly to all employees who would be affected by the law. Thus, individual litigants are likely to forego rule gain for monetary gain in settlement negotiations.

Of course, not all employers will have the characteristics of repeat players. Employers vary in size and legal sophistication. Larger and more sophisticated employers may have more experience with litigation and may retain more experienced counsel, but smaller employers may be less experienced and more like one-shot players. Similarly, not all workers will necessarily behave as one-shot players. Some workers may value vindication in court more than the prospect of a monetary settlement, and thus be less likely to forego a judicial determination of their disputes. In addition, those workers who belong to unions may have more bargaining power and may receive legal assistance from their unions. When a public-interest organization or government entity represents the worker, these types of suits are more like repeat-player versus repeat-player litigation, although these situations are rare.

Public-interest representation of plaintiffs in these actions, although infrequent, warrants further discussion. Public-interest organizations sometimes act strategically, engaging in carefully chosen litigation to further social change and occasionally settling a case to avoid a setback to social change through rule loss. In addition, public-interest representation may be more common in disputes arising under remedial statutes. For example, government agencies such as the Equal Employment Opportunity Commission and the Department of Labor occasionally undertake employment litigation on behalf of workers. Some private, nonprofit organizations also represent workers in employment rights actions. Changing the characteristics of one-shot players to make them more like repeat players may reduce the advantages of repeat players by offsetting the motivational and power imbalances between repeat players and one-shot players (Galanter 1974). Thus, public-interest organizations may better represent the collective interests of one-shot worker litigants and be less likely to trade rule gain for monetary compensation.

Public-interest representation has limitations, however. Government agencies that undertake civil rights litigation sometimes settle cases for less than they are worth (Handler et al. 1978). These "sweetheart" settlements trade away both rule gain and monetary gain. In addition, plaintiffs represented by public-interest organizations still control their own cases, and when a plaintiff wants to trade rule gain for monetary compensation but the public-interest organization does not, a conflict of interest arises between the client and the public-interest attorney. In these circumstances, repeat-player employers can defeat the social change objectives of the public-interest organization by offering the plaintiff a substantial sum for damages, while refusing to pay legal fees.[1] This kind of offer induces settlement while simultaneously damaging the public-interest organization's ability to undertake future litigation because public-interest organizations often depend on the fees generated from successful litigation to continue their activities.

Despite these qualifications, an employer is more likely than an individual worker to have the characteristics of a repeat player, particularly in litigation under the FMLA. To begin with, only employers with fifty or more employees are covered under the FMLA, so smaller employers are not defendants in the type of cases discussed here. Employers of this size are organizations; workers generally are not, except in rare cases of union or public-interest representation. Only about 16 percent of workers are covered by collective bargaining agreements, and unions do not usually undertake representation in statutory employment claims, as opposed to disputes arising under collective bargaining agreements.[2] Accordingly, in employment disputes, one would expect that employers generally have the characteristics of repeat players, while workers generally do not.

---

[1] *See* Evans v. Jeff D., 475 U.S. 717 (1985). In *Jeff D.*, Idaho Legal Aid represented a class of children with emotional and mental handicaps seeking injunctive relief to cure deficiencies in both the educational programs and health care services provided to such children who are under state care. The state offered to settle the case by agreeing to all the injunctive relief requested by the plaintiffs, but refusing to pay any costs or fees associated with bringing the lawsuit. This offer created a conflict of interest between Idaho Legal Aid and its clients. The attorney in question felt ethically bound to protect the interests of the clients by accepting the offer, but made the waiver of costs and fees conditional upon approval by the District Court. *Id*. at 722. The Court of Appeals invalidated the fee waiver and the case came before the Supreme Court, where Idaho Legal Aid argued that this type of settlement offer "exploits the ethical obligation of plaintiffs' counsel to recommend settlement in order to avoid defendant's statutory liability for its opponents' fees and costs." *Id*. at 729. The Court upheld the fee waiver, noting that "a general proscription against negotiated waiver of attorney's fees in exchange for settlement on the merits would itself impede vindication of civil rights ... by reducing the attractiveness of settlement." *Id*. at 732.

[2] Bureau of the Census, Statistical Abstract of the United States (1997), Table 688. Approximately 43 percent of public sector workers are covered by union contracts, but only 11 percent of private sector workers are covered by union contracts. *Id*.

In employment cases, employers have other incentives beyond avoiding rule loss to settle cases they expect to lose, for example, because a public victory might encourage their other disgruntled employees to sue. By settling, employers can control the timing, terms, and conditions of the resolution of the dispute. Employers can also avoid the risk of unpredictable damage awards by a jury, and control dissemination of information about the settlement through confidentiality agreements, which typically state that the employer denies liability and which prohibit disclosing the amount of the settlement, particularly to the employer's other employees. Some agreements also prohibit the plaintiff from publicly announcing the settlement or from discussing the factual allegations underlying the dispute. These restrictions sometimes extend to attorneys representing the plaintiff.

Settlement prior to an adjudicated loss also serves the interests of another repeat player in employment litigation, counsel for the employer. Employers often retain one firm to represent them in employment disputes and advise them on compliance matters. Settling a losing case avoids a clear-cut defeat that might damage that firm's relationship with the client or that might prompt the client to find different representation in the future. Also, the employer may have to pay more for settlement after a judge rules in the worker's favor on liability, an outcome defense counsel may want to avoid.

What does this suggest about using litigation to develop expansive interpretations of employment rights? Although employment rights statutes give the rule advantage to workers, employers may still settle cases they expect to lose, and litigate those they expect to win, ensuring that judicial interpretations of the statute occur in cases with the odds in their favor. If employers engage in this strategic behavior, the repeat-player thesis predicts that judicial opinions will develop a pattern in which employers consistently win. Public-interest representation of workers may mitigate this pattern, but on balance one would expect that, over time, published judicial opinions interpreting the scope and meaning of employment rights will come to favor employers.

Empirical research about outcomes in the employment civil rights context has generated mixed results. Burstein has studied outcomes in federal actions under federal equal employment opportunity statutes, and finds mixed success for plaintiffs in these actions (Burstein 1991; Burstein & Monaghan 1986); however, he also finds some support for the idea that public-interest representation of the plaintiff improves chances of success (Burstein 1991). Other studies of outcomes in actions brought pursuant to the Americans with Disabilities Act indicate that employers are almost always successful (ABA Commission on Mental and Physical Disability Law 1998; Colker 1999). These differences are likely attributable to methodological differences. Burstein studied only appellate actions and used a relatively broad standard of plaintiff success, while the ADA study looked at trial and appellate outcomes in only those cases for which the final outcome could be determined. These variations in methodology suggest that litigation procedure may be an important determinant of outcome in published opinions, and that the rule-making opportunities determined by procedure may be related to outcomes.

Rule-Making Opportunities in the Litigation Process

Models of legal evolution typically describe the development of law as a result of a binary decision to settle or go to trial (Landes & Posner 1979; Priest & Klein 1984). However, these models are problematic because they are quite reductionist and undertheorize the complexity of the litigation process. Strategic settlement alone does not capture how the litigation process influences the evolution of law. Very few cases go to trial; many more resolve at some point before trial, often after some kind of court decision or action (Kritzer 1986). Thus, legal evolution depends in part on when in the litigation process a case settles and how it is resolved if it does not. Modeling litigation as the choice between settlement and trial overlooks how the formal institutional rules that guide the litigation process create rule-making opportunities and selection bias in the evolution of legal doctrine.

Litigation is not a one-time choice between trial and settlement. It is a process with rule-making and settlement opportunities along the way. *Rule-making opportunities* are points in the litigation process that may produce published judicial opinions containing substantive interpretations of the law. Judges create and shape legal rules through published judicial opinions interpreting the scope of a statute, and both judges and litigants rely on those published opinions in future litigation.

Settlement and rule-making opportunities are not mutually exclusive. Rule-making opportunities occur at different points in the life of a litigated case. Some written judicial opinions set forth interpretations of a remedial statute without resolving all the issues in the case. For example, when deciding summary judgment motions, courts sometimes interpret the legal requirements of a claim without resolving the underlying dispute. Even if the case settles as a result of this ruling, settlement does not remove the judicial interpretation of the law from the public record.

Choosing to litigate, however, does not ensure that a rule-making opportunity will occur. For example, jury verdicts usually do not produce judicial opinions, and therefore do not become part of the judicial authority interpreting the requirements of a statute. Thus, not only settlement behavior but also the formal institutional rules that define rule-making opportunities in litigation must be examined to understand how law evolves.

Figure 5.2 shows how litigation proceeds in a typical employment claim through a series of steps defined by the rules of civil procedure. Many of these procedural steps – such as motions to dismiss or motions for summary judgment – present rule-making opportunities. An employment lawsuit in federal court typically begins with a complaint. Motions to dismiss for failure to state a claim upon which relief may be granted often are the next step in litigation, followed by an answer. Following these initial steps, the parties typically engage in a period of discovery regarding the underlying facts of the case. Toward the end of discovery, one or both parties may bring a motion for summary judgment to narrow

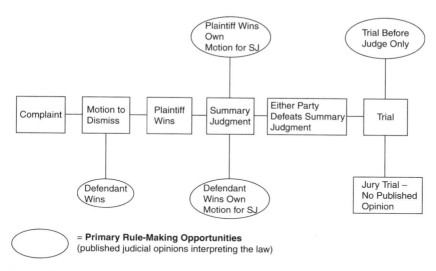

Figure 5.2. *Rule-making opportunities in the litigation process.*

the issues for trial or to dispose of the case entirely. Should part or all of the action survive summary judgment, the case may proceed to trial, typically a jury trial in employment disputes. During or after trial, the parties may bring a variety of trial-related motions. Once the parties receive a final judgment, the case may, but does not always, proceed to appeal (Figure 5.2).

The rules of civil procedure help determine which points in the litigation process present opportunities for a substantive interpretation of the statute underlying the worker's cause of action. The most common rule-making opportunities in employment disputes are motions to dismiss for failure to state a claim, and motions for summary judgment. These motions may produce written judicial opinions that interpret a statute's substantive legal requirements in a particular factual context. Although courts commonly address a variety of discovery disputes, these rarely involve substantive interpretations of the underlying statute.

Some points in the litigation process generally do not produce written judicial opinions. For example, the parties may settle at any point in the litigation process, but settlement generally does not produce a judicial opinion interpreting the law and thus is not a rule-making opportunity. Generally, jury trials also are not rule-making opportunities, as they do not produce published judicial applications of law. Decisions on some trial-related motions, such as motions for a directed verdict, may be the exception.

Appellate decisions are perhaps the most important rule-making opportunities. Published appellate opinions bind trial courts within their jurisdiction, and trial courts in other federal jurisdictions tend to find them authoritative and persuasive. Although appellate courts often issue written opinions, they do not publish every written opinion, and many restrict citation of unpublished opinions in matters before the court.

Formal rules create rule-making opportunities that arise at different stages in the litigation process, and each rule-making opportunity carries a distinct procedural posture with a corresponding standard of decision. Some rule-making opportunities may be invoked by either party, others by only one. In addition, the frequency of each type of rule-making opportunity varies; appeals are rare compared to the more plentiful summary judgment motions. A single case may provide several rule-making opportunities. The distribution of outcomes and procedural postures among published opinions influences the parties' decisions to settle or go forward, and also influences the outcome of future rule-making opportunities. These, in turn, shape the judicial interpretation of rights.

The following sections address the types of rule-making opportunities and their likely influence on the body of published judicial interpretations of employment rights such as the FMLA. For simplicity, this discussion assumes that the employer will be the defendant and the worker the plaintiff in employment litigation, while recognizing possible exceptions to that assumption.

Motions to Dismiss for Failure to State a Claim

The rules of procedure create a legal standard for motions to dismiss for failure to state a claim on which relief may be granted that favors the plaintiffs. These motions test the legal sufficiency of the claim. At the time the cases discussed in this chapter were decided, the court evaluated whether the alleged facts, if true, would entitle the plaintiff to a legal remedy.[3] Under this standard, courts construe the complaint in the light most favorable to the plaintiff, accept the factual allegations of the plaintiff as true, and grant the motion only if the plaintiff could prove no set of facts that would support a claim for relief.[4] Courts generally do not consider factual materials outside the pleadings on motions to dismiss for failure to state a claim; if either party includes factual materials, the court may convert the motion to one for summary judgment.[5]

This plaintiff-friendly standard suggests that workers should win most motions to dismiss in employment cases. However, defendant employers have incentives to avoid bringing these motions when they are unlikely to prevail. Bringing an unsuccessful motion to dismiss may waste resources, or may antagonize the court if the court concludes the defendant brought the motion for purposes of harassment or delay. In addition, an employee who survives a motion to dismiss may increase his or her settlement demands. Finally, motions to dismiss on easily corrected defects in the complaint seldom result in final judgments, because courts generally permit parties to amend the pleadings.[6] Consequently, such a motion may simply alert the plaintiff to the need to develop further evidence without disposing of the case. Because motions to dismiss arise early in a dispute, employers may wait to dispose of the worker's claim on summary judgment. All of these factors suggest that employers may bring motions to dismiss primarily in weak cases suffering from legal defects that cannot be cured.

---

[3] Conley v. Gibson, 355 U.S. 41, 45–6 (1957). In Bell Atlantic Corp. v. Twombly, 550 U.S. 544 (2007), the Supreme Court abrogated the standard set forth in *Conley*, a standard that had applied to federal pleadings for fifty years. In its place, the Court articulated a "plausibility" standard that is apparently stricter than the liberal *Conley* rule. How this new standard for pleading will affect the dynamics discussed here remains to be seen, but it seems at least possible that motions to dismiss will become more common going forward as parties test what the new standard will mean.

[4] Cahill v. Liberty Mutual Insurance Company, 80 F.3d 336, 337–38 (9th Cir. 1996).

[5] Fed. R. Civ. P. 12(b).

[6] Fed. R. Civ. P. 15; Foman v. Davis, 371 U.S. 178, 182 (1962).

Judges' decisions about publishing their opinions also affect how the law develops. Judges may be more inclined to publish their opinions when they grant motions to dismiss than when they deny them because they believe that granting a motion to dismiss carries more precedential value than a routine denial. This is not because judges are somehow biased against plaintiffs, but because granting the motion disposes of the plaintiff's claims, whereas denying the motion does not change the course of the litigation.

Although many federal court opinions are widely available on electronic databases or in official reporters, not every judicial opinion appears in these sources (Olson 1992; Siegelman & Donohue 1990; Songer, Smith, & Sheehan 1989). Indeed, the Judicial Conference of the United States has suggested that federal appellate and district court judges should only authorize publication of opinions that are of general precedential value (Olson 1992). If judges, publishers, or litigants tend to select for publication those cases in which judges grant motions to dismiss, the law available to litigants and courts will contain more authority for granting employers' motions at this procedural point in the litigation process.

Given these factors, one would predict that rulings on motions to dismiss would be some of the first published opinions regarding a new law, that there is a tendency for defendants to prevail in those published opinions, and that there are fewer motions to dismiss than motions for summary judgment in the published body of case law interpreting a new statute.

Summary Judgment Motions

The rules of procedure allow courts to resolve cases without the expense of trial where the undisputed facts show one party is entitled to judgment through a mechanism called "summary judgment." Summary judgment permits piecemeal resolution of the case, such as establishing liability without determining damages, but may also dispose of the case entirely, thus becoming a final judgment that can be appealed. Parties often bring summary judgment motions in federal employment cases to narrow the issues for trial or to avoid trial altogether. Even an unsuccessful motion tends to point out the weaknesses in the opposing party's case by highlighting a lack of admissible evidence on key issues, and in this way prompts that party to settle rather than risk trial. Summary judgment motions can inform the judge about the facts and issues in the case, and establishing liability through summary judgment may produce settlement by narrowing the dispute to a reckoning of damages. Summary judgment motions typically occur later in the litigation process than motions to dismiss, but before trial.

Unlike motions to dismiss, motions for summary judgment can be brought by either party, and the legal standard is weighted against the party who brings the motion. Nevertheless, it is much more difficult for a plaintiff than for a defendant to obtain summary judgment because the plaintiff generally bears the burden of proof. To prevail on this motion, a defendant must show undisputed facts in its favor on only one essential element of the plaintiff's claim, thereby negating the plaintiff's ability to prove his or her case. In contrast, a plaintiff must show that the facts establishing each element of his or her claim are undisputed – a difficult burden to carry. Moreover, because summary judgment presents a rule-making opportunity, the plaintiff with undisputed facts supporting every element of the claims is unlikely to reach this stage; as discussed earlier, such clear-cut winners settle.

Simply defeating a defendant's summary judgment motion constitutes a success for a plaintiff because it preserves the case for trial and often produces settlement. Nevertheless, judicial decisions regarding which opinions to publish may limit the availability of this type of precedent for future cases. Judges may be more inclined to publish opinions granting summary judgment to either party than opinions denying summary judgment, again because they believe a decision that resolves the dispute is a more significant and thus precedent-worthy decision. Because it is more difficult to prevail on summary judgment as a plaintiff than as a defendant, however, one would expect the universe of published opinions granting summary judgment to contain more defendant victories than plaintiff victories.

This discussion suggests that summary judgment will be the most common rule-making opportunity in federal employment rights cases. In addition, because plaintiffs bear the burden of proof, one would expect to see more defendants than plaintiffs prevail when they are the moving party on summary judgment. Consequently, it is likely that the early weight of authority addressing a new law will involve summary judgment motions, and most published judicial opinions will involve successful motions for summary judgment brought by employers.

Jury Trial and Trial-Related Motions

Jury trials are rare. The Federal Judicial Center estimates that only about 7 percent of cases brought under federal employment statutes reach trial (Administrative Office of the United States Courts 1995). Some of these settle during trial, leaving an even smaller number of cases on which courts may issue trial-related opinions. Although trial-related opinions such as directed verdicts are possible, those cases resolved by jury verdicts generally do not require a judicial opinion. Some bench trials may result in a published judicial opinion, although in employment cases most plaintiffs prefer a jury trial. Therefore, an employment case resolved by trial may affect the development of law no more than a case that settles.

Jury verdicts still may be disseminated even without a published judicial opinion, however. Some practitioner publications provide information about jury verdicts; in addition, lawyers may share information through informal networks, unless prevented from doing so by confidential settlements, and workers who win at trial may receive media attention. Yet, even when a jury verdict is publicized, it does not change the judicial interpretation of the law or hold precedential value for the cases that follow. Without a published judicial opinion, the results of trials are invisible to the developing body of precedent.

Trials present rule-making opportunities through trial-related motions, such as motions for directed verdict. Because jury trials themselves are relatively rare, however, opinions addressing trial-related motions and appeals of jury verdicts will be rare among judicial interpretations of a statute. Because they follow trials, these kinds of rule-making opportunities also occur later in the litigation process than motions to dismiss and motions for summary judgment.

Appeals

Of all the rule-making opportunities in the litigation process, appeals are the most important because published appellate decisions bind lower courts within the appellate court's jurisdiction. Appeals are taken from final dispositions in the trial courts, so each appeal arises with a particular procedural posture that is based on the point in the litigation process at the trial level that produced the final disposition of the case. The distribution of procedural postures among appellate decisions will reflect the distribution of procedural postures of dispositive decisions in the trial courts. Appellate outcomes depend in part on the procedural posture presented on review because the nature of the final judgment under appeal determines whether the court applies a deferential or nondeferential standard of review. For example, appellate courts review motions for summary judgment *de novo*, revisiting the question as if it had not been heard before and as if no decision had been previously rendered. The standard of review for a jury verdict in a civil case, however, involves a fair degree of deference to the jury's decision. Reversal of a jury verdict requires an appellant to show that the verdict is not supported by substantial evidence, a difficult standard to meet.

Appeals are not automatic. They must be actively mobilized and only losing parties may do so. This provides another opportunity for strategic behavior to influence the development of law. Employers may choose to appeal only those cases in which they believe they are likely to succeed and to forego less promising appeals that may reinforce unfavorable decisions. Employers may also settle a one-shot player's appeal if the appeal appears likely to succeed. In some instances, repeat players may condition settlement of their own appeal on vacating the unfavorable lower court ruling, removing its effect on future litigation (Purcell 1997; Slavitt 1995). Although in employment cases the repeat player is likely to be the employer, public-interest organizations engage in this strategic behavior as well, litigating test cases likely to create precedents favorable to their interests.

For these reasons, the largest category of appealable trial court decisions is likely to be orders granting summary judgment, and, because summary judgment occurs relatively early in the litigation process, the earliest appeals under a new statute are likely to be appeals of orders granting summary judgment. Appeals take time, and the appeal process alone will delay the appearance of appellate opinions interpreting the new law. Thus, one might predict that appellate opinions will not appear until some time after enactment of a new law, and that district court opinions form the primary legal authority in the initial years of a new remedial statute.

The Winnowing Process

One way to think about the winnowing process from initial dispute to law-making opportunity is to conceptualize a distribution of possible cases, ranging from weak to strong from the perspective of the plaintiff, and then consider how prelitigation processes may screen out particular cases. Determining the quality of a given legal claim is an inexact and subjective process. Most models of the litigation process, however, assume that both lawyer and litigants engage in a rational decision-making process to decide whether to proceed with litigation (see, e.g., Priest & Klein 1984). In the following analysis, the quality of a claim is evaluated from the plaintiff's perspective, much the same way that court would evaluate a legal case, so that "strong" claims are those in which the plaintiff is more likely to prevail, and "weak" claims are those in which the defendant has the advantage.

One might expect that the cases at either end of the distribution would be weeded out early in the process. For example, plaintiffs' lawyers typically screen potential cases before agreeing to represent new clients. Consequently, potential plaintiffs with very weak cases may find it difficult to obtain legal representation, and be unwilling or unable to pursue their claims without an attorney. Cases can be weak for a variety of reasons. They may suffer from a fatal defect such as the running of the statute of limitations, or the evidence of wrongdoing may not be strong. A few cases are dropped or dismissed for lack of prosecution even after they reach federal court, suggesting that plaintiffs may abandon weak claims after filing (Siegelman & Donohue 1990).

A similar process screens particularly strong cases. Potential plaintiffs with strong cases may be able to negotiate settlement with their employers even without the assistance of legal counsel. Many attorneys routinely send demand letters to potential defendants before filing an action, and strong cases may settle at this stage. In employment actions, plaintiffs often must pursue administrative remedies as a prerequisite to filing suit, and some disputes are resolved through this process. Plaintiffs with strong cases that proceed to litigation may also, with the aid of preliminary discovery, establish early in the process undisputed facts showing they are likely to prevail. At this point, defendants are likely to settle to avoid additional costs of litigation or future damaging revelations in discovery.

The remaining cases are less clear-cut. Cases that fall in this middle range tend to involve disputed questions of fact or uncertain interpretations of law, so that the outcome is difficult to predict. In those cases closer to the strong end of the spectrum, the facts and the law will favor the plaintiff slightly. In these cases, defendants may be less likely to file a motion to dismiss. The repeat-player thesis predicts that defendants would settle these cases to avoid creating a negative ruling at a lawmaking point such as summary judgment, because defendants have a long-term interest in preventing precedent unfavorable to them.

Some cases in the middle of the spectrum will be equally uncertain for plaintiff and defendant. If uncertainty results from disputed facts, the case is likely to go to trial or to settle shortly before trial. Disputed facts will preclude summary judgment, regardless of the party who brings that motion, and the court is unlikely to publish an opinion on this nondispositive ruling. If uncertainty results from unsettled law, the repeat-player thesis suggests that defendants may settle before reaching a law-making point in the process to avoid creating precedent unfavorable to them.

Cases closer to the weak end of the spectrum are those in which the facts and the law favor the defendants slightly. The repeat-player thesis suggests that defendants will proceed in these cases because they think they are likely to win. Defendants may win cases suffering from legal defects on a motion to dismiss, or may bring a summary judgment motion before attempting to settle because success on summary judgment is likely and the judge is unlikely to publish an opinion in an unsuccessful motion. All this suggests that most law-making opportunities will occur on summary judgment motions in relatively weak cases.

Data and Method

Although the FMLA essentially creates an employment benefit, like the protections of most other employment statutes, those benefits are structured as an individual right, enforceable through either a private right of action or an action brought by the Secretary of Labor.[7] Aggrieved workers may file a complaint with the Department of Labor, or they may proceed directly to court.[8] The Department of Labor files relatively few enforcement actions, and therefore most federal FMLA cases involve individual workers mobilizing their rights by suing their employers.

[7] 29 U.S.C. § 2617.
[8] 29 U.S.C. § 2617.

The FMLA provides an opportunity to examine how procedural rules and the characteristics of parties affect the mobilization of employment rights. Because it creates a federal cause of action, FMLA suits can be evaluated nationally through both trial-level and appellate opinions. Unlike state-trial court opinions, many federal-trial court opinions are published in official reporters or are accessible through electronic databases. This allows closer examination of how the litigation process at the trial level produces law through published opinions, as well as how the distribution of trial-level outcomes and procedural postures influences the nature of appeals.[9] Moreover, the FMLA provides an opportunity to examine who wins in published judicial opinions interpreting an individually mobilized right. Do employment rights give the rule advantage to workers seeking to enforce that right? Does the litigation process affect the outcomes reflected in published judicial opinions in the early life of this new law?

The data analyzed in this chapter are drawn from published judicial opinions interpreting the FMLA in the first five years after the statute was enacted. An electronic database search for FMLA cases decided by federal courts from 1993 through 1997 produced an initial list of 288 trial-level opinions and 58 appellate opinions.[10] Of these, 64 trial-level opinions and 25 appellate-level opinions involved cases in which the plaintiff did not bring a FMLA cause of action; these opinions were excluded from the data set.[11] The remaining 221 trial-level opinions and 36 appellate opinions were coded on a number of factors, including their

[9] Although both state and federal courts have jurisdiction over FMLA claims, even FMLA claims originally brought in state court will likely end up in federal court through the process of removal.

[10] These opinions include opinions published only in a electronic database and opinions published in the *Federal Reporter* or *Federal Supplement*. The FMLA was enacted in 1993 and no published opinions were found for that year.

[11] Often judges mentioned the Family and Medical Leave Act in passing in circumstances in which the plaintiff had taken a leave while at the employer but did not include a FMLA cause of action in her complaint. Some irrelevant cases came up because the acronym "FMLA" also refers to the Federal Maritime Lien Act.

procedural posture, the gender of the plaintiff, whether the opinion was published in official reporters, the prevailing party, the date of the opinion, *amicus curiae* participation in the matter, and public-interest group or government representation of the plaintiff.

It is important to note that the unit of analysis here is the published opinion, not the lawsuit itself. A single lawsuit can, and in some instances does, result in more than one written opinion. Because this chapter addresses how judicial interpretations of employment rights evolve, however, it is appropriate to include all the published opinions interpreting the FMLA, even where the underlying lawsuit may be included more than once.

Some cautions are in order regarding the use of published opinions in law and society research. Not all judicial determinations are published, either in electronic databases such as Westlaw and Lexis, or in the official reports such as the *Federal Supplement* (Olson 1992; Siegelman & Donohue 1990; Songer et al. 1989). Some court opinions are filed only in the case file at the courthouse. Opinions published in official reporters generally may be cited to any other federal court, and both parties and courts have access to these opinions through a variety of indexing systems. Online electronic databases contain all opinions that appear in the official reporters, and collect some additional cases not designated for publication in official reporters. These additional cases may come from judges or involved parties, or sometimes are sought out by the database service itself (Olson 1992). Although courts and litigants can access opinions that are published electronically but not in the official reporters, some courts do not allow litigants to cite officially unpublished opinions in their legal papers. There is no comprehensive and systematic way for litigants and courts to access opinions that are not published in some manner.

Songer et al. (1989: 969) found that almost 40 percent of all cases filed in the Eleventh Circuit in 1986 went unpublished. Siegelman and Donohue found that roughly 80 percent of the 4,310 employment discrimination cases they studied did not produce a published opinion (Siegelman & Donohue 1990: 1137). As Siegelman and Donohue (1990: 1139) note, the simple fact that only a small proportion of cases produced published opinions renders the representativeness of published opinions suspect, as "[o]ther things equal, published cases are more likely to be representative of unpublished cases if the ratio of published to unpublished is 1:2 than if it is 1:10". Siegelman and Donohue also point out that judges are more likely to publish opinions with dispositive rulings, and therefore settlement tends to reduce the likelihood that any given case will generate a published legal opinion. Indeed, Siegelman and Donohue (1990: 1155) found that the level of settlement in cases without published opinions – 68 percent – was much higher than settlement in cases with published opinions – 35 percent.

The following section examines how formal rules of procedure in federal courts affect the content of published opinions, focusing on procedural rule-making opportunities. Formally neutral procedural rules governing motions to dismiss, summary judgment, and the like, together with judges' tendency to publish opinions that are dispositive, skew publication toward opinions that favor employers. The effect of this process is to limit the capacity of a right to bring about social change.

Results and Discussion

Distribution of Procedural Posture in Early Opinions

Figure 5.3 shows the procedural posture of FMLA cases at the district court level that were published in the first five years after the statute was enacted. As expected, the most frequent procedural posture was summary judgment, which constituted about half of the published opinions. Motions to dismiss were the next most common published opinions. Approximately 21 percent of these published opinions were motions to dismiss for failure to state a claim under Federal Rule of Civil Procedure 12(b)(6). Another 4.5 percent were motions to dismiss for other reasons, such as lack of jurisdiction. There were only four bench trials recorded in these published opinions. In addition, eleven opinions were trial-related,

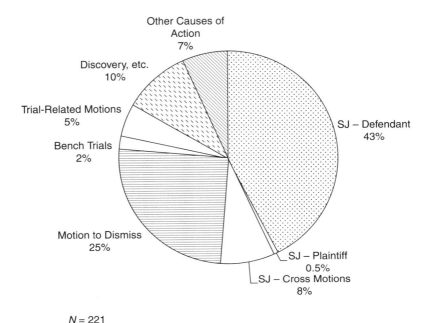

$N = 221$

Figure 5.3. *Distribution of procedural posture district court FMLA opinions.*

such as motions to exclude evidence or motions regarding fees. Finally, twenty-two of these opinions were nondispositive discovery disputes or other types of motions, including motions regarding other legal claims in the lawsuit and motions to compel arbitration.

Figure 5.3 shows that the weight of authority interpreting the FMLA arose from motions for summary judgment and motions to dismiss, both of which increased in number over time. The vast majority of early published judicial interpretations of the FMLA were based on these two rule-making opportunities in the litigation process.

Distribution of Outcomes by Procedural Posture in Early Cases

Figure 5.4 shows the distribution of outcomes for trial-level published opinions in the primary rule-making opportunities in the litigation process – motions to dismiss for failure to state a claim, motions for summary judgment, and bench trials. The practical meaning of an outcome clearly depends upon the procedural posture of the opinion; an employee who survives the employer's summary judgment motion does not win the case but preserves his or her claim and may present it to the trier of fact. An employee who prevails on his or her own motion, however, wins part or all of the case outright. A few outcomes coded "other" are omitted from Figure 5.4; these were situations in which neither party prevailed (such as a denial of both motions on cross motions for summary judgment), or in which the outcome was too mixed to declare one party the victor. Although plaintiffs may have sued under several different but related employment statutes, "wins" and "losses" are coded with regard only to the worker's FMLA cause of action.

As predicted, in the published opinions, employers prevailed much more often than workers when the employer was the only moving party on summary judgment; employers won 76 percent of their own motions for summary judgment. Where both parties brought motions for summary judgment, however, employers prevailed only 50 percent of the time. This may be because those cases in which workers brought their own summary judgment motions were stronger claims. Workers did better in these cases, with 28 percent winning on their own motion and 22 percent defeating the employer's motion. Nevertheless, there were far more published opinions in which only the employer moved for summary judgment ($N = 94$) than those in which the court addressed cross motions for summary judgment ($N = 18$). By far the largest category of published opinions were grants of the employer's motions for summary judgment ($N = 80$).

Published opinions on employers' motions to dismiss for failure to state a claim show a similar pattern. Employers prevailed two to one over workers in these opinions. Once again, "prevailing" is coded only on the FMLA cause of action. Despite the dominance of employer success, given the theory that employers would tend to bring motions to dismiss primarily when they were likely to win, it is somewhat surprising

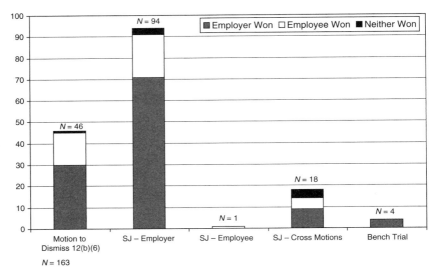

Figure 5.4. *Outcomes by procedural posture district court FMLA opinions.*

that so many workers defeated motions to dismiss. Closer examination revealed that in many cases, the employer's motion to dismiss encompassed not only the worker's FMLA claim but also other causes of actions in the lawsuit. Employers may have evaluated the chances of success of the motions to dismiss with reference to other causes of action, and simply added the FMLA claim because they were bringing the motion anyway.

Workers lost the few bench trials reported. This may be a small sample effect given the small number of bench trials reported in these published opinions ($N = 4$). It may also reflect unequal skill levels in representation of the parties. (Bench trials in employment cases are unusual, as generally plaintiffs' attorneys request a jury trial, believing that a jury will be more sympathetic and hoping for a large compensatory damage award.) The likelihood of prevailing did not differ significantly by gender of the plaintiff. Finally, there was no significant difference in outcome between opinions published in the electronic database and those published in the *Federal Reporter* or *Federal Supplement*.

Appeals

As predicted, appeals were relatively rare and took time to work their way through the courts. Only 36 of these 257 published opinions were appeals, of which 30 were decided in 1997, five in 1996 and only one in 1995. In addition, appeals reflect the influence of the litigation process at the trial level. Sixty-seven percent of published opinions were appeals of a decision granting summary judgment to the employer, reflecting the large numbers of these types of final judgments. The remaining opinions were scattered among various other types of final judgments, including judgments on claims other than the worker's FMLA cause of action. Only one appeal involved the grant of a motion to dismiss (see Table 5.1). This is not surprising, as a plaintiff generally may amend a complaint after losing a motion to dismiss, so that a decision on a motion to dismiss is rarely a final judgment.

Table 5.1. *Procedural posture on appeal*

	Number	Employer Won	Employee Won
Grant of summary judgment to employer	24	19	5
Grant of motion to dismiss	1	1	–
Judgment for employer following bench trial	2	2	–
Trial-related motion	2	2	–
Non-FMLA cause of action	2	2	–
Other	5	5	–
Total	36	31	5

In general, appellate courts tend to uphold trial-level decisions. For example, data from the Administrative Office of the United States Courts (1995: Table B5) indicate that of appeals terminated on the merits in the twelve-month period ending September 30, 1995, more than 80 percent were affirmed or enforced. Published employment opinions in this study followed this pattern. Workers were the appellants in every published appellate opinion except two, and workers seldom succeeded on appeal. Employers prevailed in approximately 86 percent of published appellate opinions.

These data suggest some trends in the published judicial determination of rights early in the life of this employment statute. First, employers' motions for summary judgment or motions to dismiss were by far the largest categories of published opinions, supporting the hypothesis that motions to dismiss and motions for summary judgment are the most common rule-making opportunities in the litigation process. Appeals reflected the distribution of procedural posture at the trial level, and seldom overturned the outcome at the trial level.

Second, among these published opinions, employers win by a significant margin. Employers prevailed two to one against workers on motions to dismiss, nearly three to one against workers on motions for summary judgment, and four to one in appellate opinions, which have the greatest precedential value. Consequently, judges and practitioners evaluating the strength of a given case will find that the available case law suggests that workers seldom prevail.

These results are consistent with the prediction that repeat players will play for the rules; that is, employers are likely to settle cases they expect to lose, and litigate cases they are likely to win. Indeed, the incentive to engage in this behavior may be greater at the beginning of the life of a statute where almost every dispute raises a question of first impression. In addition, these data reflect the influence of the procedural posture of the rule-making opportunities in the litigation process. The most common rule-making opportunities involved motions for which dispositive outcomes occur primarily when employers win.

Perhaps the most important insight, however, is what is not represented in published judicial interpretations of the law – settlement and jury verdicts. The fact that employers win in most published opinions does not necessarily mean that they prevail in most cases, despite the protections of the remedial statute. The outcomes in FMLA opinions may simply reflect the combined influence of strategic settlement and the characteristics of rule-making opportunities in the litigation process. Employers may settle strong cases likely to produce adverse decisions, ensuring that these cases never become the basis for a published judicial opinion. Employers may dispose of weak cases, on the other hand, through motions to dismiss or for summary judgment, which often do become part of the judicial interpretation of the law. Cases somewhere in between are likely to involve disputed material facts, and consequently proceed to trial. Judges are unlikely to publish denials of motions to dismiss or motions for summary judgment that occur in these cases along the way, however, because these are not dispositive decisions. Many cases that proceed this far settle on the eve of trial. To the extent that the rest are decided by jury, they usually do not produce a published judicial opinion.

Although these data only include lawsuits raising FMLA claims, they are consistent with a recent study by the Commission on Mental and Physical Disability Law regarding another recent remedial statute, the Americans with Disabilities Act (ABA Commission on Mental and Physical Disability Law 1998). In a study examining outcomes in trial and appellate cases brought under the ADA, the commission found that employers prevailed in 92 percent of the 760 opinions in which it could be determined which party prevailed. Consistent with the strategic settlement argument, one employee advocate who was asked to comment on the study noted that "[c]ases that are clearly in our favor usually settle before they are decided" (Flaherty & Heller 1998). Those cases that would have reflected employee wins may have never reached a rule-making opportunity in the litigation process. In addition, the study excluded 440 cases in which the final outcome could not be determined. At least some of these may have been cases in which plaintiffs survived a motion to dismiss or a motion for summary judgment, and then negotiated a settlement, leaving no record of the final outcome of the case. In other words, summary judgment often leaves a clear published record of who won, while settlement and trial generally do not.

What do we know about cases that did not produce published opinions, including those that settled or went to trial? In their study of employment litigation in the federal courts, Siegelman and Donohue (1990: 1137) found that only about 20 percent of cases produced a published opinion. Although predicting the outcome of settled cases had they proceeded to adjudication is impossible, indirect evidence may shed some light on the subject. For example, Siegelman and Donohue (1990: 1155) found that settlement was nearly twice as likely among cases that did not produce published opinions than among those that did. Although cases may settle for many reasons, the larger proportion of settlements in unpublished cases suggests that these cases may have been more likely to survive a dispositive pretrial motion than those that produced published opinions. Indeed, Siegelman and Donohue report that more cases were resolved by defendants winning 12(b)(6) motions, summary judgment motions, and trials in cases with published opinions than in those without (Siegelman & Donohue 1990: 1155). These findings suggest that the common sense notion that stronger cases settle is not off the mark.

As for trial, few cases proceed that far. Analysis of data collected by the United States Administrative Office of the Courts indicate that 77 percent of employment cases terminate before reaching a pretrial conference, some without any court action (Administrative Office of the United States Courts 1995: Table C4). This analysis also indicates that approximately 7 percent of district court cases brought under federal employment statutes reach jury trial, apparently resolved by verdict or settlement thereafter. Some studies based on data collected from different sources suggest that plaintiffs with employment claims who make it to trial may often be successful (Gross & Syverud 1991); other studies suggest that these plaintiffs may win at trial only about one-third of the time (Siegelman & Donohue 1990).

What does this analysis suggest about litigation as a strategy to produce expansive interpretations of employment rights? The combined effects of strategic settlement and institutionalized rule-making opportunities in litigation suggest that, over time, the published opinions interpreting an employment statute will reflect more adjudicated wins for employers than for workers. Advocates seeking authority to support their respective positions will find substantially more published opinions in which courts granted summary judgment for the employer than for the worker. As one court has noted:

> In the normal and traditional operation of the American justice system, each party walks to the courthouse with a compilation of opinions in its favor under one arm and a collection of opposing views under the other.... In many instances, particularly in litigation involving institutional litigators, understandably enamored with the majority approach, one or both parties may state that "the weight of authority" supports their view. A string of citations follows. Courts may then, for understandable reasons, accept the majority view as the view tending toward more stability and predictability in the law and toward fewer accusations of renegade activism.[12]

Because the norms of the rule of law traditionally require law to be generally and consistently applied, rules articulated in case law have implications for the resolution of future disputes. Judges decide cases and generate opinions by synthesizing existing law and applying it to the case at hand. If most published opinions – as opposed to litigation outcomes – favor employers, the synthesized law will come to favor employers' interests. Common law systems of law are flexible; judges may revise

---

[12] Benevides v. Jackson Nat'l Life Ins. Co., 820 F. Supp. 1284, 1289 (D. Colo. 1993).

and distinguish rules when faced with counterfactual cases in which the outcomes suggested by the rules seem unjust. Significantly, however, the strategic settlement argument suggests that the counterfactual case will rarely, if ever, be considered, because it will settle before reaching a rule-making opportunity.

Public Interest and Government Participation

Can public-interest representation or participation of *amicus curiae* representing the interests of employees ameliorate the advantage employers enjoy in shaping the law? Public-interest representation was very rare in this group of cases; the worker was represented by a public-interest organization or the Department of Labor in only seven published opinions. *Amicus curiae* participation also was rare, and, as expected, occurred only at the appellate level where a binding interpretation of the law was at stake.[13] Although the numbers are too small to draw any meaningful conclusions, on balance public-interest and *amicus curiae* participation appeared to improve workers' chances of prevailing. Of the eight underlying cases with either public-interest representation or *amicus curiae* participation, plaintiffs definitively lost in only two.

The relative dearth of public-interest participation in published judicial opinions may reflect public-interest activities outside the judicial forum. For example, the Department of Labor accepts and resolves complaints regarding violations of the FMLA. As of June 1998, the Department had received 12,633 complaints from workers, and found violations of the Act in 7,499, or nearly 60 percent of them (Bureau of National Affairs 1998).[14] The Department of Labor successfully resolved

---

[13] *Amici* participated in three appellate cases, Bauer v. Varity Dayton-Walther Corp., 118 F.3d 1109 (6th Cir. 1997), Manuel v. Westlake Polymers Corp., 66 F.3d 758 (5th Cir. 1995), and Victorelli v. Shadyside Hosp., 128 F.3d 184 (3rd Cir. 1997).

[14] The Department found no violation in many instances because either the employer was not covered by the FMLA or the worker was not eligible for leave.

88 percent of complaints in which it found a violation of the Act, obtaining $11,772,607 in damages from employers.

A few results are striking about this analysis of the Department of Labor complaint data. First, the figures reported by the Department of Labor suggest that many more disputes arise regarding the FMLA than the limited number that reach the federal courts would indicate.[15] Indeed, many may not reach court because the Department resolves them.[16] Second, the Department of Labor found violations in 60 percent of cases, compared to the plaintiff success rate of approximately 22 percent in published opinions,[17] suggesting that workers may mobilize the law and win at least some remedy more often than these opinions suggest. Third, the average damage award for the 88 percent of violations that the Department resolved is approximately $1,800, suggesting that administrative complaints address disputes over small damages, although aggregate figures include disputes that vary in value.[18] Thus, the role of the Department of Labor in resolving violations may be to facilitate settlement of low-damage disputes without resort to the courts. Although this may help overcome the advantages of repeat-player employers over workers with small claims, once again these employee successes will not be reflected in the judicial determination of rights.

[15] Of course, this may reflect a lag time between the violation and the appearance of the dispute in court, as the FMLA has a two-year statute of limitation. In addition, it is unclear how many FMLA lawsuits actually reach court and then settle without any judicial action.

[16] It is important to note, however, that Department of Labor administrative proceedings and participation in a federal court action are not mutually exclusive alternatives. In addition, unlike many other federal employment statutes, the FMLA does not require exhaustion of administrative remedies before filing in federal court.

[17] This success rate includes success (either winning the plaintiff's own motion or defeating the defendant's motion) on all motions with published opinions, including discovery motions, even if the underlying dispute remained unresolved.

[18] There are alternative explanations. The Department of Labor may resolve disputes before much back pay accrues. It also may be reluctant to be particularly punitive with employers because the law is new. Alternatively, it may cut "sweetheart" deals with the employers, settling cases for much less than they are worth.

A two-fold conclusion emerges. First, outcomes in published judicial interpretations of this employment right favor employers. Employers win far more often than workers in these published opinions. This trend may result, in part, from the relative power of the parties, given that the limited data regarding workers with public-interest representation suggest that these workers – who are more like repeat players – do better. However, the trend toward legal interpretations favoring employers may also result from how institutional rules shape the litigation process: the fact that the most common rule-making opportunities arise when defendant employers prevail on certain motions. The overwhelming trend in favor of employers is the result of not only victories in individual cases, but also the concentration of published judicial interpretations of the law in motions to dismiss and motions for summary judgment.

This leads to a second conclusion: that published judicial interpretations of the statute favor employers because published opinions may not reflect much of what a statutory right accomplishes. For example, unproblematic compliance with the remedial statute is nowhere represented in these judicial opinions because it does not create a dispute (Hadfield 1992). In addition, the common ways to succeed in an employment dispute after surviving dispositive motions – settlement and trial – usually do not produce published opinions. Also, some cases settle before reaching any rule-making opportunity or even before reaching court. Thus, by "winning" – either by obtaining a settlement or by winning a jury trial – workers render their own experiences invisible to the judicial determination of rights. This may eventually erode the power of the remedial statute.

Early Opinions and the Interpretive Path of the Law

Although the data presented here do not directly address this point, it is important to consider how courts' institutional rules, by determining rule-making opportunities in litigation, may also shape the meaning of rights. The norms of the rule of law form an institutional coordination structure through which judges examine each other's positions and coordinate the development of law (Rubin & Feeley 1996).[19] *Stare decisis* and the norm of consistency may amplify the general tenor of early published opinions interpreting a remedial statute if judges seek interpretations that are consistent with the published decisions of their colleagues. Initially, the earliest published opinions may be the only interpretive guidance about a new right. Judges may then rely on these few cases to decide the next wave of disputes arising under that statute. Consequently, early published opinions addressing unsettled areas of law potentially set the direction of the interpretation of a statute. If early published interpretations favor employers, later judicial interpretations applying these early authorities may also favor employers.

Settlement and the timing of rule-making opportunities in the litigation process suggest that employers will win in the first law-making opportunities under a new employment statute. Employers can avoid early negative rulings by settling cases they are likely to lose. In addition, most early rule-making opportunities are likely to involve motions for which dispositive outcomes occur when employers win – motions to dismiss and motions for summary judgment – because these dispositive rulings occur before trials or appeals in the litigation process. Moreover, because early appeals will be drawn from cases with adjudicated, not settled, outcomes, they are likely to involve these relatively weak cases in which courts granted employers' motions to dismiss or motions for summary judgment.[20]

---

[19] There is a body of literature regarding judicial decision making that disputes this proposition (Segal & Spaeth 1996; Spaeth & Segal 1999). Most studies of judicial decision making that find that judges follow their preferences rather than precedent, however, examine this process at the level of the Supreme Court. There is reason to believe that trial judges will be more likely to follow precedent for fear of being reversed. Some research shows that precedent affects the decisions of appellate judges as well (Songer, Segal, & Cameron 1994).

[20] That is, appeals are likely to be appeals from grants of summary judgment to the employer in cases that the employer chose not to settle because it believed it could win. Employers are unlikely to appeal grants of summary judgment to an employee, as these tend to be very strong cases. Employers are also unlikely to appeal after

Parties evaluate the strength of their positions by taking into account published interpretations of the law. Once a sufficient body of authority supporting an employer-friendly interpretation of the law develops, even workers with strong cases may have difficulty overcoming the weight of authority against them. Interpretations unfavorable to employees may cause lawyers to decline to take these cases, and cause plaintiffs to settle their cases for less. If these circumstances arise, the scope of rights created by remedial statute may be slowly limited.

An empirical exploration of this hypothesis regarding early judicial interpretations of a statute is beyond the scope of this project, and this study makes no claims that the data presented here prove the validity of this argument. However, there are intuitive reasons to believe that early interpretive paths shape the eventual scope and meaning of a new statutory right. Particularly in federal court, where courts publish many trial-level opinions, early published opinions interpreting a new law provide paths of least resistance as well as frames of interpretation for judges grappling with new statutes. Because initially there are few published interpretations of a new law, they do not compete with as many other authorities for recognition or attention, and the first published interpretations offer alternatives to starting from scratch for judges wrestling with similar problems.

Other institutional norms come into play here as well. Judges mindful that legitimacy of the rule of law rests in part on consistency may be inclined to follow the lead of their colleagues on the bench. Although the earliest published interpretations of new rights will be trial-level opinions and therefore not binding on other courts, judges often look to their colleagues, even those in other jurisdictions, for persuasive or at least instructive resolutions of undecided questions (Walsh 1997). Once an interpretive path emerges, a judge may find it hard to reject without contrary authority to support an alternative approach. This may be

an employee wins a jury verdict, as appellate courts are reluctant to overturn jury verdicts.

particularly true in federal court, where the underlying law often remains the same across jurisdictions and cannot easily be distinguished. In addition, attorneys may be reluctant to make legal arguments contrary to existing authority without some contrary authority to cite.

This is not to say that judges blindly follow the path set by the first to reach a particular question. For example, although many judges interpreting the FMLA have borrowed the burden-shifting analysis applied in antidiscrimination cases, not all have chosen this interpretive path. A well-respected judge, Judge Easterbrook of the Seventh Circuit, broke ranks with this approach and criticized judges for adopting standards from other employment laws without considering their jurisprudential utility.[21] As this example suggests, however, other judges faced with unsettled issues of law may have concluded that relying on existing authority from any source offers some assurance of reaching the right, or at least a defensible, outcome. Judges may also be more likely to find a party's arguments persuasive if at least some authority supports them.

In addition to shaping judicial interpretations of rights, the weight of authority among early published opinions may also affect whether employees mobilize their rights. Existing authority affects the party's estimate of likely success, and thus the decision to settle or to proceed. A published opinion is a valuable resource for the party whose position it supports, both in negotiation and in arguing his or her position before the judge. Although cases can always be factually distinguished, it may be difficult for a party to overcome the weight of negative authority with little contrary authority to cite. Thus, if early authorities favor employers and gain increasing acceptance, employees may confront a less hospitable legal landscape, notwithstanding the FMLA's protections.

---

[21] *See* Diaz v. Fort Wayne Foundry Corp., 131 F.3d 711 (7th Cir. 1997). Although looking to existing interpretive paths is common, judges with greater status (or confidence) may be more likely to reject early interpretive paths they find unconvincing.

The Paradox of Losing by Winning

The analysis above points out an ambiguity in the concepts of "winning" or "losing" when rights mobilization occurs largely outside the context of formal adjudication. Studies addressing who wins often define winning as victory in published judicial opinions (ABA Commission on Mental and Physical Disability Law 1998; Burstein 1991; Burstein & Monaghan 1986; Galanter 1975; Wheeler et al. 1987). Focusing on adjudicated disputes, however, overlooks other ways of winning. Most cases eventually settle, and, as the analysis in Chapter 4 suggests, employees often negotiate a settlement in the shadow of the law even before their disputes reach court. Indeed, workers who settle may find a favorable settlement to be as much a victory as a jury verdict after trial. Many workers also may win in some sense because their employers comply with the law, or because rights subtly change their everyday social relationships. Workers may even bargain for more than the remedial statute requires, using rights legislation as leverage in negotiations (McCann 1994). All reflect tangible benefits enjoyed as a result of statutory rights.

For workers who claim their employment rights as plaintiffs, however, the paradox of losing by winning is that, even if rights mobilization creates change for individual litigants, the coordinating power of rights adjudication is not equally available to both parties. Simply put, workers and employers do not have the same procedural opportunities to win published authorities through litigation. Consequently, workers who mobilize their rights risk benefiting from the dispute-resolution power of courts while foregoing courts' law-making role.

Courts depend upon the private mobilization of rights to generate their caseloads and rule-making opportunities (Black 1973). Consequently, when employers settle cases they are likely to lose, judicial determinations of employment rights are based on a selective group of weaker cases. Courts' published opinions do not reflect disputes that eventually settle or that result in jury verdicts, nor do they show the benefit of rights in everyday life. Contrary to claims that court interpretations bolster and strengthen rights, the rule-making opportunities in the litigation process concentrate published opinions around dispositive outcomes on motions to dismiss and summary judgment motions – motions for which dispositive outcomes typically occur when employers win.

Judicial decisions are important signposts about the meaning of rights; they do more than resolve the disputes of parties. Through adjudication, courts communicate the scope and moral force of employment rights. By deciding disputes, courts specify what constitutes compliance with the law and induce compliance from parties and organizations that may never appear in court (Galanter 1983). If the FMLA claims reported in judicial opinions rarely succeed, employers may make fewer efforts to comply with the law. In addition, published opinions in which employers consistently win create an employer-friendly standard for compliance with the law.

Published judicial opinions also affect private ordering through negotiation of rights. Legal rules establish each party's bargaining endowments in negotiations by indicating the likely outcome should negotiations fail (Mnookin & Kornhauser 1979). The institutional features of the litigation process, however, create more legal authority to support employers' position and arguments. In contrast, little information exists about the average settlements or jury awards in similar cases, short of an attorney's own experience, because these outcomes are difficult to track (Erlanger et al. 1987). Consequently, even workers with strong claims may be forced to lower their settlement demands because they cannot point to any objective authority showing the success of a similar claimant.

The influence of institutional rules on published outcomes also affects mobilization of rights in the future. Published opinions showing successful claims may encourage wronged individuals to "name" their injury and claim a remedy, or may give rise to broader social movements (Black 1973; Felstiner, Abel, & Sarat 1981; McCann 1994). Conversely, published opinions documenting unsuccessful claims may cause wronged individuals to conclude success is unlikely and forego their claims. Published opinions in losing cases also may curtail access to legal representation because attorneys, particularly those who take cases on contingency, decide these claims are too financially risky to undertake. Consequently, the invisibility of successful claims may diminish the mobilization of employment civil rights.

A steady parade of rulings against workers may also undermine the moral authority of the right itself, because laws have constitutive as well as instrumental influence in society (Sarat & Kearns 1993). Judicial interpretations enter a dynamic exchange in which law shapes everyday life, and in turn is informed and transformed by everyday categories and routines (Ewick & Silbey 1992, 1998; Yngvesson 1988). Without being specifically invoked or even explicitly considered, law may shape everyday thoughts and actions (Engel & Munger 1996); it may change the way social interactions take place and are perceived without any explicit awareness of the legal underpinnings of this change. In addition, legal recognition and validation of rights communicate normative judgments about the underlying rights themselves and those who claim them (Williams 1991).

When the public face of rights litigation primarily shows adjudicated wins for defendants, judges and citizens may come to believe that most claims lack merit. Citizens may conclude that the underlying problem the statute addresses no longer exists, or never existed to begin with. This erosion of the moral force of the statute may, in turn, erode individuals' willingness to mobilize its protections because they risk social disapproval by bringing such a claim.

Of course a significant body of sociolegal research indicates that even when favorable authority is available, it does not necessarily translate to change on the ground. Thus, one might reasonably ask whether these negative findings matter if judicial authority has little impact in the workplace. Most studies that show that law can be displaced or transformed in particular social settings, however, indicate that actors at least grapple with the meaning of law in some manner. Even if law is sometimes transformed in particular social settings, statutes and judicial interpretations are the starting point in this process of negotiation, and it still is desirable to start from a favorable position in terms of statutory and judicial authority. In addition, the effect of law can be measured many ways – negative conclusions are likely if outcomes are compared to an idealized world in which rights were fully realized, but more positive evaluations are likely if rights are compared to the likely state of affairs given weaken legal authority or no legal rights at all. Thus, favorable authority may be a necessary but not sufficient condition for change, yet the findings presented here indicate even this preliminary step may be difficult to achieve and sustain.

This discussion suggests how published judicial opinions influence mobilization through feedback effects. If institutional features of the litigation process systematically exclude successful claims from the judicial determination of rights, successful rights mobilization has little opportunity to affect future mobilization, compliance, or negotiation. Over time, this dynamic produces narrow interpretations of rights that tend to favor employers. Once this process restricts the scope and meaning of the FMLA, the law's capacity to produce social change may become similarly confined. In his article *Against Settlement*, Owen Fiss argues that:

> the duty of the courts is not to maximize the ends of private parties, nor simply to secure the peace, but to explicate and give force to the values embodied in authoritative text such as the Constitution and statutes: to interpret those values and bring reality into accord with them. This duty is not discharged when parties settle. (Fiss 1984: 1085)

Fiss treats the common law as a public good, socially owned, and with profound social meaning. He takes one position in the larger debate about whether courts are dispute-resolution institutions for private conflict, or whether their opinions serve wider public and social functions (Chayes 1976). If dispute resolution were the only objective, however, a simple declaration of winner and loser by the courts would suffice.

Courts go beyond this to produce opinions because their opinions justify their decision and also reinforce their legitimacy and authority
(Bourdieu 1987).

Rights litigation presents a particularly salient example of courts'
rule-making function, because statutory rights reflect public norms
and goals (Silbey & Sarat 1989). Rights litigation shapes society by har-
nessing the legitimacy and authority of law to constrain the powerful.
Indeed, social change through rights litigation seems possible because
of the ideal of the rule of law: a society governed not by the arbitrary
exercise of power but by a rational system of rules that claim legitimacy
and authority (Mills 1946). Rights litigation provides democratic access
to the power to make law and the instrumental and constitutive effects
of legitimate authority (Zemans 1983).

Scholars have recognized the significance of landmark rights litigation for broader social change (Chayes 1976). But even in an ordinary
case, more is at stake than resolution of an individual dispute. Individual
disputes form the building blocks of a system of common law precedent
through which courts explain and interpret the law. Settlement and trial,
even in ordinary cases, remove a dispute from courts' interpretation of
the law, and separate the dispute-resolution function of courts from their
law-making role.

Adjudicated outcomes may be particularly important for statutory
rights that express public norms. The paradox of losing by winning, however, suggests that the litigation process hamstrings law's capacity for
social change by focusing published adjudication on the weaker claims.
The institutional characteristics of the legal system then extend these
published decisions through the system of interpretation and precedent,
while allowing settlement and unpublished dispositions to drop from
sight. The invisibility of many successful claims affects the content of
the law and consequently all those who order their relationships according to that law.

Perceptions of fairness and the ultimate legitimacy of the rule of law
flow in part from courts' procedural protections and process (Friedman

1975; Tyler 1990). But the procedural characteristics of the rule of law that seem to constitute a fair and impartial system of justice are safeguards against historical forms of the arbitrary exercise of power, such as the whim of the king, not the more subtle, evolutionary influences that may undermine the impartiality of the law. Litigation procedures may provide individuals with equal access to courts to enforce the laws and to resolve disputes; not all litigants, however, have equal access to courts as institutions of law creation. Even when the courts remain neutral as to outcome, the rule-making opportunities in the litigation process may nevertheless produce interpretations of rights that favor employers. Procedural protections locate justice and fairness in the equal ability of parties to present their positions and influence the outcomes of their cases, in short, the opportunity to be heard. The paradox of losing by winning is that, for workers claiming employment rights, success often means silence in the historical record of the common law.

Conclusion

THE STORY OF THE FMLA IS A FAMILIAR ONE IN MANY WAYS. New rights promise to change society in fundamental ways that will help eradicate inequality. In reality, however, individuals fail to mobilize these rights, or when they do, their claims are seldom successful. Organizational priorities, power differentials, the influence of family and friends, the inherent conservatism of courts, and the clash between rights and other normative systems all create obstacles to social change. As a result, these new rights fail to live up to their potential. This facile summary, however, does not capture the structural and institutional mechanisms in play in the mobilization process, mechanisms that this study seeks to illuminate. Examining these mechanisms is a way to begin to make theoretical sense of the myriad obstacles to rights mobilization identified in previous research, and to begin to consider systematically the conditions under which these obstacles might be overcome.

The FMLA responds to complex problems that arise from significant institutional change. Longstanding historical relationships among work, gender, and disability have begun to shift with changes in the labor market, in family structure, in women's workforce participation, and in the social understanding of what disability is and what it means. Yet the FMLA is often portrayed as a straightforward regulation of workplace practices, and resistance to this new law could easily be dismissed as merely the continuing influence of persistent stereotypes about the abilities of women, mothers, and people with disabilities. This interpretation locates the dynamics of resistance within individual consciousness and animus, much as current legal doctrine does. But this approach fails to take into account the institutional structures that have grown up around these stereotypical assumptions and that reproduce social patterns compatible with them long after the social foundations of those institutions have shifted.

The concept of *institutional inequality* introduced in this study shifts the theoretical focus from individual intent to social structure, and in this way begins to address the influence of institutions. This concept draws on social constructivist theories that social categories such as gender and disability are shifting and are historically contingent, rather than static and natural. It is also consistent with poststructural theories that power resides in social processes and institutional structures, rather than with particular individuals or groups (Bourdieu 1977; Digeser 1992; Foucault 1979). For purposes of this study, institutional inequality represents contemporary structural and normative conditions that reflect the historical construction of the relationships among work, gender, and disability, but do not necessarily result from historical discriminatory animus toward women or people with disabilities. Institutional inequality represents not individualized bias, or even social bias, but instead institutionalized practices and beliefs that cross organizational boundaries and that reproduce outmoded conceptions of identity and social relations.

By examining mobilization in both the courts and the workplace, this study reveals common interpretive frames that shape how workers, courts, and employers understand FMLA rights to be consistent with institutional inequality. Unlike doctrinal approaches to understanding inequality, which focus on individual workplaces and discriminatory animus, this institutional analysis focuses on societal-level institutions that give rise to interpretive frames that operate across organizational boundaries and at different levels of rights mobilization. These frames developed, along with institutionalized work practices, from the historical struggle for control over work time. Resistance to mobilization of the FMLA reflects this history. Obstacles to mobilizing FMLA rights are more than organizational objectives to preserve efficiency here, local norms against time off there, and familial preferences to avoid conflict in another instance. Instead, taken together, these obstacles reflect and recreate the established but taken-for-granted relationships among work, gender, and disability that the law attempts to change. More generally, resistance to rights is more than the persistence of stereotypes and discriminatory animus in the minds of some individuals; it is a much larger structural phenomenon in which "patterns of relations [are] reproduced, even when actors engaging in the relations are unaware of the patterns or do not desire their reproduction" (Sewell, 1992: 3).

The institutional framework used here to study rights mobilization focuses on how these societal-level institutions shape the meaning of rights and affect their potential for bringing about change, regardless of the conscious intent of workplace decision makers or judicial actors. In this view, rights are not just tools for social change (whether instrumental sanction or constitutive discourse) that can be wielded or understood separately from the social institutions within which they reside. Nor is the meaning of a right established permanently by a newly enacted law. Instead, legal meaning is constructed through an interactive and fragmented process of judicial interpretation and everyday negotiations over rights. In both these contexts, existing institutional frameworks influence how courts, employers, and workers understand FMLA rights, the legitimacy of taking leave, and their alternatives for action when the choice whether to mobilize rights must be made.

What does this institution-oriented study of rights mobilization tell us about the conditions under which mobilization might be successful, even when the institutional context is hostile to their exercise? First, this study's analysis of formal court processes teaches that although courts may engage in the symbolic and expressive transmission of meaning through their opinions, those opinions must be understood as institutional products, and rare ones at that. The procedural gauntlet for generating authoritative judicial statements regarding the values of the FMLA is formidable; reaching a procedural opportunity for a precedential ruling is very difficult, even when leaving aside the well-established constraints on courts' abilities to enact sweeping change or enforce their judgments. The institutional processes that give rise to formal judicial interpretations of FMLA rights shape the substance of those interpretations to be favorable to employers. Although occasional employee-friendly interpretations of FMLA rights are certainly possible, the argument here is probabilistic – expansive interpretations of rights and authority favorable to employees will be scarce – not categorical. Identifying these procedural obstacles alters our understanding of the utility of litigation as a social change strategy by showing how relationships of power permeate the mundane institutional features of the litigation process. These findings challenge celebratory views of litigation's potential to bring about change, and raise sobering questions about the impact of institutional design on rights mobilization and equality. At the very least, this analysis reveals structural constraints that limit precedents favorable to workers and that cannot be easily overcome by shoring up parties, as Galanter (1974) suggests, or by increasing enforcement activities in the courts. This understanding of the litigation process raises important questions about whether additional mechanisms for generating interpretive authority – such as regulatory change, interpretive guidance, or more explicit examples in legislative history – can be mobilized to counteract the limitations of litigation as a means for generating balanced interpretations of rights.

Second, this study indicates that the specific form a right takes matters because the more ambiguous the right, the more interpretive room is created for institutions to take hold and shape the meaning of rights. Organizational studies have shown this phenomenon at the organizational level, noting how ambiguous rights can be reframed and co-opted within organizational borders to be consistent with core organizational objectives. Often these organizational constraints are contrasted with a somewhat idealized view that court proceedings, with the trappings of due process and procedure, would not be subject to the same co-optation. The findings reported here, however, which come from a multilevel analysis of mobilization, suggest that regardless of whether the context is work organizations or the courts, ambiguous prohibitions against discrimination or vague requirements for fair treatment facilitate resorting to taken-for-granted cognitive frames to determine what constitutes discrimination or which actions are fair and appropriate. Moreover, internal managerial objectives are not the only threat to ambiguous workplace rights, either in the workplace itself or when these rights are formally mobilized in court. Resistance to rights is also related to much broader social structures that permeate organizational boundaries and implicate nonworkplace aspects of social life as well. These broader social institutions create obstacles to change in a myriad of large and small ways that tend to reproduce long-standing relationships of power and inequality.

These findings suggest that legal reforms that directly challenge the institutions that perpetuate inequality, rather than simply prohibiting discrimination and leaving it to the courts to decide what actions constitute discrimination, have a better chance at interrupting the social processes that recreate institutionalized inequality. For example, in the context of work and family policy, identities such as gender and disability are contingent, in part, on the workplace institutions that construct them, including time standards. As a result, strategies that focus on equal treatment within the existing structure of work do little to change workplace institutions that were historically built around outmoded conceptions of those identities. Strategies that attempt to force work to accommodate protected identities tend to mark women and people with disabilities as different from (and inferior to) all other workers, who become normalized in the process. And, as the analysis in Chapter 3 indicates, these strategies encourage judicial interpretations that focus on the meaning of identities such as disabled or on whether actions such as firing workers who miss work are discrimination or "common sense" business decisions. Thus, questions of equal treatment for protected groups invite courts to focus on intent and identity, while accepting institutional arrangements that give meaning to those identities as natural and normal. This strategy leaves workplace practices such as time standards intact, and locates the problems that arise from these practices in the identities of workers that are different from the norm, such as women and people with disabilities. In contrast, rights strategies that target institutional arrangements directly not only seem to produce better outcomes, but also avoid reifying gender and disability as naturalized social categories.

The ways in which institutions shape judicial interpretation of anti-discrimination statutes have significant implications for social change because court decisions carry cultural legitimacy and authority. When courts accept time norms as justifications for terminating workers, they not only fail to protect women and people with disabilities from workplace penalties, they also shore up exclusionary work practices and reinforce the social inequality that is constituted by these practices. Ironically, courts recreate institutional inequality through their interpretations of the very statutes designed to eradicate it. When courts require substantive change to work, however, their decisions also have an authoritative effect. When courts reject employers' arguments about the need for control over workers or the necessity of time norms, they undermine the structural arrangements that support inequality in the workplace.

Courts may be more willing to challenge institutionalized time norms in FMLA actions because the FMLA advances a legal theory of reform based on minimum workplace standards, rather than prohibitions against discrimination. The FMLA's mandatory rights reflect a normative judgment that time off for family or medical purposes is as socially valuable as time off for jury duty or military service, which are similarly protected. By targeting time standards directly, rather than leaving to judicial interpretation whether changes to workplace practices are required for equal treatment, the FMLA draws on a different yet familiar set of cultural frameworks associated with minimum employment standards, such as the minimum wage and workplace safety requirements. In this way, the FMLA's substantive standards enjoy some cultural legitimacy while avoiding the pitfalls of attempting to change work through the identity categories that constitute it: gender and disability.

Third, as this study shows, law can still matter in significant ways even when alternative normative systems threaten to displace or transform it. Prior studies tended to emphasize the finding that in particular social settings, there was "order without law" such that legal regulation had little impact on everyday social relations. The conclusion of these studies, much to the consternation of traditional legal scholars, was that legislation and court decisions had little effect on social relations on the ground. Instead, alternative systems of order or values – such as organizational objectives, norms against conflict in business relations, and economic efficiency – tended to dominate (Edelman et al. 1993; Ellickson 1991; Macaulay 1963). These are enormously important insights that raise significant questions about the origins of and mechanisms for reproducing the alternative normative conditions that compete with law. Nevertheless, the focus on the surprising displacement of law left somewhat under-theorized the conditions under which law and rights continue to have some meaning and influence in everyday settings, and perhaps even interact with these other normative systems to bring about change.

This study of the FMLA indicates that the relative influence of law and other normative systems in particular social settings may best be understood as a dialog, rather than a winner-take-all contest for dominance among competing frameworks. Each opportunity for claiming rights, for labeling events as legal wrongs, or for interpreting workplace experiences, creates a new situation for deploying these frameworks. As actors navigate their social relationships, these frameworks become resources for giving meaning to social events and for contesting the taken-for-granted operation of the workplace. For example, the family wage ideal, the slacker discourse, and managerial objectives all create cognitive frameworks that conflict with workers' statutory entitlement to leave. But not every cognitive framework is created equal, and, as this study shows, several factors influence which frame becomes dominant in any given situation. Caution in making even tentative conclusions on this point is warranted, and this limited study can only begin to consider systematically which factors might matter. Nevertheless, in the data reported here, social networks, power relations, and the cultural resonance of frames all emerged as important themes in this process.

Social networks transmit information about rights, frame the meaning of social events, and encourage resistance and collective action. Social networks help workers make meaning of workplace conflict over leave, suggesting that workers who receive positive messages from social contacts about standing up for leave rights will be more likely to mobilize rights than workers who hear from those around them that losing a job when you have a baby is "just how it is." This finding is consistent with Ewick and Silbey's (2003) theory that stories about resistance can lay the groundwork for future mobilization and collective action, although workers' experiences with FMLA rights also raise the cautionary point that stories about retaliation, passed through social networks, may have the opposite effect. More generally, the findings reported here indicate that with regard to the conditions under which workplace rights matter, strong social networks and solidarity among workers can facilitate sharing of information, frame workplace experiences in terms of rights, and even encourage collective action.

The findings reported here also challenge the idea that individual rights inherently undermine collective action by conceptualizing difficulties as individual problems rather than collective concerns. In fact, substantive rights may *generate* social networks as workers talk with one another to find information about rights, to hear about others' experiences mobilizing rights, and to evaluate what actions are fair, appropriate, and legal. The social process of rights mobilization can build solidarity among individuals who share common grievances, and can give rise to a framing process that may eventually lead to collective action. This finding raises an important question for future comparative study: whether formal prohibitions against discrimination, which are much less specific about legal benefits, have the same network-generating effects.

Relations of power also affect both mobilization and which framework becomes dominant when conflict over rights arises. To the extent that employers control the dissemination of information about leave rights in the workplace, they can dampen workers' willingness to claim rights or even ask about time off. Lack of information about rights also limits the cognitive impact of rights as a new framework for understanding workplace events. As a policy matter, this finding about control of information highlights the importance of seemingly minor legal provisions requiring posting of information about rights and of notification to employees of the right to take leave. It also suggests that additional mechanisms for providing information about rights, especially mechanisms that are not controlled by or connected to a worker's employer, would facilitate rights mobilization. From a more theoretical perspective, this finding complicates claims that, as a general matter, law will have little influence on the ground in work organizations, suggesting instead that structural and institutional mechanisms in the workplace, including employer power over workers, affect the degree to which legal rules penetrate established workplace practices and norms.

Finally, the research reported here suggests the importance of cultural resonance in making interpretive frames salient and powerful. The literature on framing and social movements increasingly has examined how issues are framed discursively, the cultural resonance of those frames, and how power relationships shape dominant discourses (Ferree 2003; Oliver & Johnston 2000) – all issues that are relevant to individual rights mobilization as well. The genealogical analysis in this study unpacks the deep cultural roots of resistance to rights in the workplace, showing how workplace resistance to FMLA rights resonates with broader social structures and ideologies that reinforce inequality. Workers' experiences with the law reveal that cultural resonant frames that reinforce outmoded conceptions of gender and disability shape responses to FMLA rights and decisions about mobilization. These frames lend instant recognition and credence to claims that leave takers are slackers, that employers need not accommodate pregnancy, and that true disability requires the complete inability to work. Moreover, the meaning of leave rights varies along dimensions of gender inequality, tracking cultural assumptions about women as caretakers and men as breadwinners. At the same time, workers' experiences indicate that law is an interpretive frame that also carries legitimacy and authority. Despite the skepticism of law and society scholars that formal law has any meaningful impact on the ground, the respondents in this study reported that references to law were often successful in overcoming employers' resistance and in convincing coworkers that leave was legitimate. This informal success-ful mobilization of law, however, is largely invisible except to fine-grain qualitative studies such as this one. Although locating a systematic sam-ple of informal disputes is notoriously difficult methodologically, fur-ther comparative study is needed to understand more about the factors that affect both mobilization and outcome when these kinds of informal rights claims are made.

More generally, the findings reported here indicate that workplace rights cannot be dismissed as irrelevant because they can be too easily brushed aside or ignored in the workplace. In fact, employers in this study seemed to avoid blanket resistance to law, perhaps because they feared it would be perceived as illegitimate. Instead, they found more indirect ways to evade or compromise on rights, such as letting only one person take leave at a time, limiting information about leave, or asking workers to "voluntarily" take less leave than they legally could. Although these strategies diminished the effectiveness of FMLA rights, they did not block these rights altogether. Workers reported that law continued to have important symbolic authority and legitimacy in infor-mal negotiations over leave. In these negotiations, law mattered not just in terms of occupying the moral high ground, but also in terms of mate-rial benefits and remedies employees obtained by referencing law to negotiate time off successfully. One area for future study is whether this symbolic authority is more potent when the right confers a substan-tive benefit, such as a specific amount of time off, rather than a vague requirement of fair treatment that workers may find harder to define and assert.

Rights Mobilization and the Potential for Social Change

Like most antidiscrimination statutes, the FMLA creates a private right of action mobilized by individual workers, a method of enforcement that is consistent with the core values of liberalism. One of the classic debates in law and society literature is whether this decentralized system of rights offers significant potential to bring about social change. Positive views emphasize that rights give individual holders autonomy over enforcement, that social movements can use rights litigation to gain access to policy making without having to muster the resources or coalition building efforts demanded by political action (Zemans 1983), and that individual judicial victories communicate the public values embodied in rights (Fiss 1984). In addition, individuals can mobilize rights as cultural discourses or interpretive frames to reveal contradictions, inequalities, and relations of power even in informal settings (Ewick & Silbey 2003; McCann 1994). More negative perspectives note that even in a formally neutral legal system, repeat players retain the upper hand (Galanter 1974), that courts are constrained by institutional norms against expansive policy declarations and lack the ability to enforce their decisions (Rosenberg 1993), that the social meaning of rights can inhibit mobilization by labeling claimants as victims, poor sports, or complainers (Bumiller 1987, 1988; Marshall 2003, 2005; Quinn 2000), and that organizations can transform the meaning of rights when they implement the law internally (Edelman 1999; Edelman et al. 1993; Heimer 1999).

What does this institution-focused study of rights mobilization contribute to this debate about rights and social change? This study's central theme has been that decentralized enforcement through individual rights mobilization creates structural opportunities for institutions to construct the meaning of rights. Autonomy over enforcement may insulate formal rights enforcement from state discretion and control, but that autonomy is tempered by institutions that shape how courts, employers, and workers respond to FMLA rights. Although private rights of action and private ordering may fit well with the American tradition of liberalism and limited government, decentralized rights enforcement requires each individual to negotiate the meaning and scope of rights in the fragmented process of judicial interpretation and everyday interactions. This constant process of negotiation creates opportunities to interpret leave rights to fit the existing institutional regime of entrenched social practices, traditional conceptions of status based on gender and disability, and power. Celebratory views of rights tend to assume that decentralized enforcement preserves a neutral place for claiming legal protection, but this study indicates that institutions – culturally determined and widely shared beliefs, values, norms, and practices – occupy that putatively neutral space. Thus, despite democratic aspirations that individual rights promote autonomy and equality, decentralized rights enforcement allows institutions to inhibit social change by constructing rights to be consistent with existing social structures and relations of power.

Nevertheless, despite this powerful critique of private rights enforcement, the comparative institutional perspective must also be considered. Social policy is often enforced through private rights of action because private enforcement offers advantages over the alternatives. Private rights of action avoid the need for a large governmental enforcement apparatus funded through taxpayer dollars, which would likely be expensive and politically unpopular (Burke 2002). In addition, private rights insulate enforcement from political pressure and capture by established interests, preventing – or at least mitigating – enforcement efforts from fluctuating with the ideology of changing administrations (Burke 2002; Coffee 1983; Thompson 2000; Zemans 1984). Private enforcement also promotes efficient detection of violations by individuals on the ground (Gilles 2000; Rubenstein 2004). Thus, despite the vulnerability of private rights to co-optation and transformation by institutions, alternative enforcement systems are also limited, perhaps even more so, in their ability to bring about social change. Accordingly, this critique should not be read as a call to do away with private rights of action, but instead as a plea to study carefully the nuances of this process.

The utility of FMLA rights must also be evaluated against the absence of any family leave policy at all. Without this statute, power and inequality, and the institutionalized practices that reflect them, would determine access to leave to an even greater degree. Historically determined work arrangements would remain unchallenged, and the implicit contradictions among work, gender, and disability would be less visible. Without overarching legal reforms, change would require workers to challenge family leave practices workplace by workplace, an approach that imposes enormous coordination burdens. Thus, it is misleading to assess the utility of FMLA rights by measuring the experiences of workers against an idealized standard in which leave rights are universally acknowledged and easily exercised.

Institutional analysis connects microlevel alternative systems of ordering to macrolevel social structures and systems of meaning that shape social behavior. It highlights the diffuse, depersonalize operation of power and suggests how that power might be overcome. For example, this study documents how alternative normative systems that compete with FMLA rights are not merely contingent, local customs, but instead are manifestations of larger social processes that help reproduce and maintain existing relations of power and control. Although this theory makes opposition to rights seem more formidable, it also offers a mechanism through which rights might facilitate social change. Social transformation can occur when actors draw on available cultural schema to reinterpret meanings and to enact social practices in new ways. The same institutional processes that recreate inequality are also vulnerable to new cognitive frameworks for understanding leave, and, as the respondents in this study note, law is an authoritative institution for articulating and promulgating such a framework. This is not to say that law is determinative or dominant in any given situation. Legal discourse is only one of many possible frames or schemas for understanding and constructing the social world. Yet institutions are subject to displacement, disruption, and change when new cultural frameworks are brought to bear in interpreting the social practices and meanings of which they are made. Legal rights provide a culturally authoritative alternative framework for interpreting time off from work for family and medical needs, and thus a resource for bringing about social change.

I conclude with the observation that the fact that rights remain embedded within existing institutional arrangements creates both constraints *and* opportunities for change. Opportunities for change arise because institutions do not exist apart from the actions and beliefs that recreate them; they are socially constructed when our behavior and expectations conform to their taken-for-granted characteristics. To the extent that law provides a counter-hegemonic discourse potentially backed by legal sanction, it can disrupt conventional understandings of the relationships among work, gender, and disability. Legal rights are powerful in this sense, because rights have a deep cultural resonance for both the powerless and the powerful. As the respondents in this study noted, the cultural legitimacy of law gives credence and authority to legal interpretations, even when those claims seem antithetical to the way things have always been done. Rights are only one of many possible interpretive frames, it is true, but by deploying rights, workers may exercise some influence and control over the social relations within which they are embedded, and perhaps change those social relations to some extent (Sewell 1992: 20). Without legal rights, workers would not only lack legal remedies, but would also have fewer discursive options for legitimating their claims to leave. With legal rights, workers gain a new interpretive schema for reinterpreting and changing social institutions that define our choices.

Along these lines, the findings of this study are neither fully consistent with the pessimistic myth-of-rights view, nor fully consistent with the more optimistic symbolic/strategic view of law. Certainly law can be displaced or transformed by other institutions. But law also makes and remakes meaning in ways that can challenge longstanding social practices. Law names legitimate and illegitimate conduct, creates new roles and practices, and, perhaps most importantly, enables individuals to view social relationships in new ways. Legal rights helped some workers in this study explicitly challenge long-entrenched work practices and expectations. It may be that in this way – in interrupting and rechanneling the reproduction of social structure through both everyday interactions and judicial interpretations – that legal rights have the greatest potential for bringing about social change.

Appendix A

I located respondents for the qualitative component of this research through a state-wide legal information line in California that gave legal advice and assistance to workers. The information line is a free service provided by a private, nonprofit, public-interest law organization. I contacted those individuals who accessed the line within a one-year period from 1998 to 1999 with questions about family or medical leave. Appendix A provides more detailed information about the characteristics of those respondents.

My research benefited from the diverse population that exists in California. My respondents were fairly racially diverse, and spanned a range of ages and household incomes (see Table A.1). They also came from a variety of workplaces and occupations (see Table A.1). There were more women than men among my respondents, however. Perhaps this is because many of these women took maternity leaves, which tend to be longer in duration and therefore perhaps more contentious in the workplace (Commission on Leave 1996). Also, some scholars suggest that women may experience disproportionate conflict in the workplace over leave to meet family responsibilities (Gwartney-Gibbs 1994).

Again, I emphasize that I make no claim that my respondents are representative of leave takers in general; indeed, one might expect that those who experience conflict over leave would differ from leave takers in general. I did, however, compare my respondents to data

Table A.1. *Characteristics of Respondents*

ID	Gender	Ethnicity	Age Range	Marital Status	Education	Income	Leave Reason[a]	Job Title	Job Tenure (Years)
1001	Female	White	50–64	Married	College grad	30–50k	Multiple-pg	Admin. Assistant	26
1002	Male	White	35–49	Divorced	High school grad	<20k	Own condition	Production associate	4
1003	Female	White	50–64	Widowed	Some college	30–50k	Own condition	Station agent	5
1004	Female	White	25–34	Married	Some college	50–75k	Multiple-pg	Customer service rep	8
1005	Female	White	65+	Divorced	Some college	50–75k	Sick child	Case manager	10
1006	Female	Hispanic	35–49	Married	College grad	75k+	Own condition	Medical assistant	16
1007	Female	White	50–64	Married	College grad	75k+	Own condition	Comptroller	3
1008	Female	White	25–34	Live w/partner	Some college	30–50k	Own condition	Manager	3
1009	Female	Hispanic	35–49	Married	Some college	75k+	Multiple-pg	Reservation manager	16

ID	Gender	Race	Age	Marital status	Education	Income	Reason	Occupation	
1010	Male	Asian	25–34	Married	Some college	75k+	New child	X-ray technician	10
1011	Female	White	18–24	Separated	Some college	<20k	Pregnancy	Electronic component merchandiser	7 months
1012	Male	Hispanic	35–49	Married	High school grad	<20k	Spouse	Laborer	5
1013	Female	Hispanic	25–34	Married	Some college	<20k	Multiple-pg	Human resources assistant	2
1014	Female	Black	25–34	Live w/ partner	Some college	50–75k	Multiple-pg	Deli clerk	8
1015	Female	White	18–24	Married	Some college	30–50k	Multiple-pg	Hostess	2
1016	Male	Hispanic	25–34	Married	Some college	75k+	New child	Car washer	1
1017	Female	Black	25–34	Widowed	Some college	50–75k	Pregnancy	Courtesy clerk	1.5
1018	Female	White	35–49	Separated	Some college	50–75k	Sick child	File manager	7

(continued)

Table A.1. *(continued)*

ID	Gender	Ethnicity	Age Range	Marital Status	Education	Income	Leave Reason[a]	Job Title	Job Tenure (Years)
1019	Female	White	35–49	Live w/partner	Some college	30–50k	Own condition	Account clerk	3
1020	Female	White	35–49	Married	Graduate school	75k+	Multiple-pg	Account supervisor	4
1021	Female	Other	25–34	Live w/ partner	Some college	20–30k	Own condition	Service representative	2.5
1022	Male	White	25–34	Married	Graduate school	75k+	Spouse	Pilot	2
1023	Female	Asian	25–34	Married	Some college	30–50k	Multiple-pg	Key associate	8
1024	Female	White	35–49	Married	Some college	50–75k	Multiple-pg	Bakery clerk	10

[a] "Multiple-pg" designates a leave taken for pregnancy and other reasons, such as recovering from a pregnancy-related illness after childbirth, or parental leave after childbirth.

Table A.2. *Comparison with national sample of leave takers*

Respondent Characteristics	Respondents (Percent)	National Sample (Percent)
Gender		
Female	79.2	58.2
Male	20.8	41.8
Race		
Black	8.3	10.5
Hispanic	20.8	8.8
White	58.3	75.5
Asian	8.3	N/A
Other[a]	4.2	1.9
Age		
18–24	8.3	11.5
25–34	41.7	29.6
35–49	33.3	40.8
50–64	12.5	15.3
65+	4.2	2.9
Marital status		
Married or living with a partner	75.0	70.7
Separated, widowed, divorced	25.0	16.5
Single	–	12.5
Education		
Less than high school	–	10.4
High school graduate	8.3	26.7
Some college	70.8	30.0
College graduate or more	20.8	32.6
Income[b]		
<20,000	12.5	17.5
20,000–30,000	4.2	15.8
30,000–50,000	29.2	25.3
50,000–75,000	25.0	11.8
75,000+	29.2	10.1

Source: A Workable Balance: Report to Congress on Family and Medical Leave Policies from the Commission on Family and Medical Leave, Table 5.A.

[a] "Other" in the national sample appears to include Asians.

[b] Income percentages for the national survey do not add to 100 percent because 25 percent of respondents did not answer that question.

drawn from a national sample of workers who took FMLA leave in the two years following enactment of the law (see Table A.2). This telephone survey of workers randomly sampled the household population of the conterminous United States, age eighteen years and older, who had been employed for pay at any time between January 1, 1994, and the time of the interview. The interview field period was from June to August 1995. Research based on these survey data indicates that 20 percent of workers perceived a need for FMLA leave, and of these, about 80 percent actually took leave (Commission on Leave 1996; Gerstel & McGonagle 1999).[1] The survey identified both "leave needers," or persons who did not take a leave but needed to take one in the identified time period for FMLA-covered reasons, and "leave takers," or persons who did take a leave in the identified time period for FMLA-covered reasons (Commission on Leave 1996). As most of my respondents did, in fact, take some leave, I report comparison data for "leave takers."

Compared to this national sample of leave takers, my respondents were more likely to be Hispanic (reflecting the larger Hispanic population of California relative to other states), more likely to be women, and tended to have more education. My respondents were comparable to the national sample in terms of age and marital status, but I had no respondents who were single and had never been married. Although my respondents tended to have higher family incomes, this may be because average family income in the Bay Area is higher than average family income nationally, and the income figures from the national survey have not been adjusted for inflation.[2] Also, it should be noted that my percentages were computed from a very small group of twenty-four respondents,

---

[1] For a detailed discussion of patterns of leave taking in general based on these data, see Gerstel and McGonagle (1999).

[2] The national data were collected in 1995, whereas my interviews were conducted in 1998 and 1999.

so that small fluctuations in numbers could change these percentages significantly. Nevertheless, these data allow some comparison between my respondents, who experienced workplace conflict over leave, and a representative national sample of leave takers in general.

Appendix B

To direct my interviews, I used open-ended qualitative interview questions. I followed the same progression of questions in each interview, and attempted to maintain as much consistency as possible in terms of how the interviews progressed. In many instances, however, I asked spontaneous follow-up questions as appropriate to inquire in more detail into respondents' experiences. At times, respondents would answer questions before I asked them, and as a result the continuity and flow of the interviews sometimes varied. I also used standard probes such as "anything else?," "tell me more about that" and "can you think of an example of that?" as appropriate. In addition, I sometimes repeated back respondents' comments and made noncommittal response such as "I understand" or "um hmm" to encourage more detailed answers. Accordingly, the following outline describes the skeleton for the qualitative component of these interviews, but does not capture every question that I asked.

Outline of Open-Ended, Qualitative Interview Questions

1. Please describe for me the situation that made you contact the information line.
2. How did you decide what to do in your situation?
   What did you do first?

What happened?

What did you do next?

3. What was your reaction to this situation? How did you feel about what was happening?

4. Were you concerned that taking time off would affect your position at work?

[yes] What kinds of things were you worried about?

[no] What about the situation caused you not to be concerned?

5. Did anything happen at work because you [asked for/took] leave?

[yes]What kinds of things happened?

6. Were you concerned about being able to take care of your [health/baby/family responsibilities, as appropriate]?

[yes] What kinds of things were you worried about?

[no] What about the situation caused you not to be concerned?

7. Is there anything that you would have liked to have done [concerning your health/baby/family responsibilities, as appropriate] that you couldn't do in your situation?

What was that? What about the situation prevented you from doing that?

8. Do you know anything about the experiences of other people who took leave at your employer?

[if yes] What have you heard? Can you give me an example?

Did that influence what you did in your situation? How?

9. Did anyone ask you about your experience taking leave?

Who? Can you give me an example?

10. Did you talk with others about your situation? Who did you talk with about your situation when you were deciding what to do?

What kinds of things did you talk about?

What did [person] think you should do?

Did that influence what you did in your situation? How?

[probe for certain contacts where appropriate – employer, union, coworkers, family, friends, doctor, lawyers; ask "anyone else?"]

11. How important was what other people told you in terms of what you decided to do in your situation?

12. How did you first approach your employer about taking leave? Can you describe that interaction for me?

13. Did you file any formal grievances or complaints about your situation?

14. A lot of people in a situation like this would just not stand up for their rights. What made you decide to do something in this situation?

15. Some people will sue no matter what. What made you decide not to do anything more in this situation?

16. Has the FMLA changed the way you think about taking leave from work for family or medical reasons?
    [if yes] How?

17. Do you think the way your employer handled your situation was fair or unfair?
    What about it makes it [fair/unfair]?

18. In practice, are all people at your employer treated the same, or are some people treated differently than others with regard to leave?
    [if differently] How are some people treated differently? Can you give me an example?

19. Do you think your employer would give employees family or medical leave even if the law did not require it? What makes you think that?

20. Are you satisfied or unsatisfied with the way things turned out in your situation?
    [if satisfied] What about the way things turned out makes you satisfied?
    [if unsatisfied] What about the way things turned out makes you unsatisfied?

21. Is there anything that would have made you more satisfied with the way things turned out?

22. Did you get everything you wanted in this situation, or was there something you wanted that you did not get?

What was it that you most wanted?

What did you want that you did not get?

23. Would you say it was easy, difficult, or neither easy nor difficult to get what you wanted in this situation?

    What made it [easy/difficult]?

    What about the situation made it [easy/difficult]?

24. Do you think things would have turned out differently for you if the FMLA did not exist? How?

25. Would you have asked for the same amount of time off if the FMLA did not exist?

26. How did you first hear about the FMLA?

27. Tell me all the sources of information you used to get information about taking leave.

28. How did these sources of information influence what you did in your situation, if at all?

29. How did you hear about the information line?

30. What kind of help were you looking for when you contacted the line?

31. Did you find the information line helpful?

    What about it was helpful?

32. Is there anything that would have made the information line assistance more helpful?

33. Do you think the help you received from the information line changed the outcome in your situation in any way?

    How did it change the outcome?

34. [Most interviewees were also asked to respond to the following vignettes. For each, the interviewee was asked what would be a fair way to resolve the situation, and what about their proposed solution made it seem fair to them.]

A father who works full time and who has been with his employer for two years wants three months unpaid time off because he has a newborn baby. His employer wants the father to take his accrued paid vacation time instead, which is about three weeks.

An employer hires a woman who discovers, shortly after she begins working, that she is pregnant. She misses a few days of work because of morning sickness. Because the company has policy of denying any sick leave to employees during their first year with the company, the employer wants to fire the woman.

An employee misses about 25 days of work in one year because she has a chronic illness. Her employer wants to fire her for absenteeism, and she wants to keep her job.

35. [In addition to these qualitative questions, I also used close-ended questions to code standard demographic information and other information about occupation, job title, and details about the leave and the respondent's perception of the leave, much of which had already come out through the open-ended questions.]

References

ABA Commission on Mental and Physical Disability Law. 1998. Study Finds Employers Win Most ADA Title I Judicial and Administrative Complaints. *Mental and Physical Disabilities Law Reporter* 22:403–7.

Abrams K. 1989. Gender Discrimination and the Transformation of Workplace Norms. *Vanderbilt Law Review* 42:1183–248.

Acker J. 1990. Hierarchies, Jobs, Bodies: A Theory of Gendered Organizations. *Gender and Society* 4:139–58.

Administrative Office of the United States Courts. 1995. Judicial Business of the United States Courts: 1995 Report of the Director, Administrative Office of the United States Courts, Washington, D.C.

Albiston C. 2007. Institutional Perspectives on Law, Work, and Family. *Annual Review of Law and Social Science* 3:397–426.

Albiston CR. 2005. Anti-Essentialism and the Work/Family Dilemma. *Berkeley Journal of Gender, Law & Justice* 20:30–49.

Albiston CR, Nielsen LB. 2007. The Procedural Attack on Civil Rights: The Empirical Reality of Buckhannon for the Private Attorney General. *UCLA Law Review* 54:1087–134.

Allen TD, Russell JEA. 1999. Parental Leave of Absence: Some Not So Family-Friendly Implications. *Journal of Applied Social Psychology* 29:166–91.

Anderson DJ, Binder M, Krause K. 2003. The Motherhood Wage Penalty Revisited: Experience, Heterogeneity, Work Effort and Work-Schedule Flexibility. *Industrial and Labor Relations Review* 56:273–94.

Armenia A, Gerstel N. 2006. Family Leaves, the FMLA and Gender Neutrality: The Intersection of Race and Gender. *Social Science Research* 35:871–91.

Bagenstos SR. 2006. The Structural Turn and the Limits of Antidiscrimination Law. *California Law Review* 94:1–47.

Baum CL. 2003. The Effect of State Maternity Leave Legislation and the 1993 Family and Medical Leave Act on Employment and Wages. *Labor Economics* 10:573–96.

Berg M. 1985. *The Age of Manufacturers*. London: Fontana Press.

Berger PL, Luckman T. 1967. *The Social Construction of Reality*. New York: Anchor Books.

Berkowitz L, Walker N. 1967. Law and Moral Judgments. *Sociometry* 30:410–22.

Black D. 1973. The Mobilization of Law. *The Journal of Legal Studies* 2:125–49.

Blair-Loy M, Wharton AS. 2002. Employees' Use of Work-Family Policies and the Workplace Social Context. *Social Forces* 80:813–45.

Bond JT, Galinsky E, Lord M, Staines GL, Brown KR. 1991. Beyond the Parental Leave Debate: The Impact of Laws in Four States, Families and Work Institute, New York.

Boris E. 1993. The Power of Motherhood: Black and White Activist Women Redefine the "Political." In *Mothers of a New World: Maternalist Politics and the Origins of the Welfare State*, ed. S Koven, S Michel. New York: Routledge, pp. 213–45.

Borsay A. 1998. Returning Patients to the Community: Disability, Medicine and Economic Rationality before the Industrial Revolution. *Disability and Society* 13:645–63.

Bourdieu P. 1977. *Outline of a Theory of Practice*. Cambridge: Cambridge University Press.

Boydston J. 1990. *Home and Work: Housework, Wages, and the Ideology of Labor in the Early Republic*. New York: Oxford University Press.

Budig MJ, England P. 2001. The Wage Penalty for Motherhood. *American Sociological Review* 66:204–25.

Bumiller K. 1987. Victims in the Shadow of the Law: A Critique of the Model of Legal Protection. *Signs* 12:421–39.

Bumiller K. 1988. *The Civil Rights Society*. Baltimore: Johns Hopkins University Press, 161 pp.

Bureau of National Affairs. 1998. DOL Summary of Outreach, Compliance Activity under the 1993 Family and Medical Leave Act. *Daily Labor Report*:E-1.

Bureau of the Census. 2000. *Statistical Abstract of the United States.* Department of Commerce, Washington, D.C.

Bureau of Labor Statistics 2007. Employment Characteristics of Families in 2006, United States Department of Labor, Washington, D.C.

Burke TF. 2002. *Lawyers, Lawsuits and Legal Rights.* Berkeley: University of California Press.

Burstein P. 1991. Legal Mobilization as a Social Movement Tactic: The Struggle for Equal Employment Opportunity. *American Journal of Sociology* 96:1201–25.

Burstein P, Monaghan K. 1986. Equal Employment Opportunity and the Mobilization of Law. *Law and Society Review* 20:355–88.

Cantor D, Waldfogel J, Kerwin J, Wright MM, Levin K, et al. 2001. Balancing the Needs of Families and Employers: The Family and Medical Leave Surveys, U.S. Department of Labor, Washington, D.C.

Chayes A. 1976. The Role of the Judge in Public Law Litigation. *Harvard Law Review* 89:1281–316.

Coffee JC. 1983. Rescuing the Private Attorney General: Why the Model of the Lawyer as Bounty Hunter Is Not Working. *Maryland Law Review* 42:215.

Cohen PN, Bianchi SM. 1999. Marriage, Children, and Women's Employment: What Do We Know? *Monthly Labor Review* 112:22–31.

Colker R. 1999. The Americans with Disabilities Act: A Windfall for Defendants. *Harvard Civil Rights-Civil Liberties Law Review* 34:99–162.

Collins PH. 1991. *Black Feminist Thought: Knowledge, Consciousness, and the Politics of Empowerment.* New York: Routledge.

Commerce US Dept of. 1997. Statistical Abstract of the United States, Washington, D.C.

Commission on Leave. 1996. A Workable Balance: Report to Congress on Family and Medical Leave Policies, Commission on Family and Medical Leave, Washington D.C.

Cooter R, Kornhauser L. 1980. Can Litigation Improve the Law Without the Help of Judges? *Journal of Legal Studies* 9:139–63.

Cooter RD. 1996. Decentralized Law for a Complex Economy: The Structural Approach to Adjudicating the New Law Merchant. *University of Pennsylvania Law Review* 144:1643–96.

Correll SJ, Benard S, Paik I. 2007. Getting a Job: Is There a Motherhood Penalty? *American Journal of Sociology* 112:1297–338.

Cott NF. 1977. *The Bonds of Womanhood: "Woman's Sphere" in New England, 1780–1835.* New Haven: Yale University Press.

Cuddy AJC, Fiske ST, Glick P. 2004. When Professionals Become Mothers, Warmth Doesn't Cut the Ice. *Journal of Social Issues* 60:701–18.

Davis AE, Kalleberg AL. 2006. Family-Friendly Organizations? Work and Family Programs in the 1990s. *Work and Occupations* 33:191–223.

Deacon D. 1985. Political Arithmetic: The Nineteenth-Century Australian Census and the Construction of the Dependent Woman. *Journal of Women in Culture and Society* 11:27–47.

Digeser P. 1992. The Fourth Face of Power. *The Journal of Politics* 54:977–1007.

DiMaggio PJ, Powell WW. 1991. Introduction. In *The New Institutionalism in Organizational Analysis*, ed. WW Powell, PJ DiMaggio, Chicago: University of Chicago Press, pp. 1–38.

Donohue JJ, Siegelman P. 1991. The Changing Nature of Employment Discrimination. *Stanford Law Review* 43:983.

Dowd NE. 1989. Work and Family: The Gender Paradox and the Limitations of Discrimination Analysis in Restructuring the Workplace. *Harvard Civil Rights-Civil Liberties Law Review* 24:79–172.

Dreyfus HL, Rabinow P. 1983. *Michel Foucault: Beyond Structuralism and Hermeneutics.* Chicago: University of Chicago Press, 271 pp.

Drimmer JC. 1993. Cripples, Overcomers, and Civil Rights: Tracing the Evolution of Federal Legislation and Social Policy for People with Disabilities. *UCLA Law Review* 40:1341–410.

Edelman LB. 1992. Legal Ambiguity and Symbolic Structures: Organizational Mediation of Civil Rights Law. *American Journal of Sociology* 97:1531.

Edelman LB. 1999. When the "Haves" Hold Court: Speculations on the Organizational Internalization of Law. *Law and Society Review* 22:941–92.

Edelman LB, Erlanger HS, Lande J. 1993. Internal Dispute Resolution: The Transformation of Civil Rights in the Workplace. *Law and Society Review* 27:497–534.

Edwards R. 1979. *Contested Terrain: The Transformation of the Workplace in the Twentieth Century.* New York: Basic Books, Inc.

Ellickson RC. 1986. Of Coase and Cattle: Dispute Resolution Among Neighbors in Shasta County. *Stanford Law Review* 38:623.

Ellickson RC. 1991. *Order Without Law: How Neighbors Settle Disputes.* Cambridge: Harvard University Press.

Engel D, Munger F. 2003. *Rights of Inclusion: Law and Identity in the Life Story of Americans with Disabilities.* Chicago: University of Chicago Press.

Engel DM. 1993. Law in the Domains of Everyday Life: The Construction of Community and Difference. In *Law and Everyday Life*, ed. A Sarat, TR Kearns, Ann Arbor: University of Michigan Press, pp. 123–70.

Engel DM, Munger FW. 1996. Rights, Remembrance, and the Reconciliation of Difference. *Law and Society Review* 30:7–53.

Epstein CF, Kalleberg AL, eds. 2004. *Fighting for Time: Shifting Boundaries and Work and Social Life*. New York: Russell Sage Foundation.

Epstein CF, Seron C, Oglensky B, Saute R. 1998. *The Part-Time Paradox: Time Norms, Professional Life, Family and Gender*. New York: Routledge.

Erlanger HS, Chambliss E, Melli MS. 1987. Participation and Flexibility in Informal Processes: Cautions from the Divorce Context. *Law and Society Review* 21:585–604.

Ewick P, Silbey S. 1992. Conformity, Contestation, and Resistance: An Account of Legal Consciousness. *New England Law Review* 26:731–49.

Ewick P, Silbey S. 2003. Narrating Social Structure: Stories of Resistance to Legal Authority. *American Journal of Sociology* 108:1328–72.

Ewick P, Silbey SS. 1995. Subversive Stories and Hegemonic Tales: Toward a Sociology of Narrative. *Law and Society Review* 29:197–226.

Ewick P, Silbey SS. 1998. *The Common Place of Law: Stories from Everyday Life*. Chicago: University of Chicago Press.

Felstiner WLF, Abel RL, Sarat A. 1981. The Emergence and Transformation of Disputes: Naming, Blaming, Claiming … *Law and Society Review* 15:631–54.

Ferber MA, Waldfogel J. May 1998. The long-term consequences of nontraditional employment. *Monthly Labor Review* 121(5): 3–12.

Ferree MM. 2003. Resonance and Radicalism: Feminist Framing in the Abortion Debates of the United States and Germany. *American Journal of Sociology* 109:304–44.

Ferree MM, Hess BB. 1994. *Controversy & Coalition: The New Feminist Movement across Three Decades of Change*. New York: Twayne Publishers.

Fields J, Casper LM. 2001. America's Families and Living Arrangements: Population Characteristics. *Rep. P20–537*, U.S. Census Bureau.

Fineman M. 1994. *The Neutered Mother, the Sexual Family, and Other Twentieth Century Tragedies*. New York: Routledge, 239 pp.

Finkelstein V. 1980. *Attitudes and Disabled People*. New York: World Rehabilitation Fund, Inc.

Finley LM. 1986. Transcending Equality Theory: A Way Out of the Maternity and the Workplace Debate. *Columbia Law Review* 86: 1118–1182.

Fiss OM. 1984. Against Settlement. *Yale Law Journal* 93:1073–90.

Flaherty K, Heller E. 1998. Workers Face Tough Odds in Disability Suits, ABA Study Finds. *Fulton County Daily Report* (June 30).

Folbre N. 1991. The Unproductive Housewife: Her Evolution in Nineteenth-Century Economic Thought. *Signs* 16:463–84.

Foucault M. 1979. *Discipline and Punish*. New York: Vintage Books.

Frank M, Lipner R. 1988. History of Maternity Leave in Europe and the United States. In *The Parental Leave Crisis: Toward a National Policy*, ed. EF Zigler, M Frank. New Haven: Yale University Press, pp. 3–22.

Fraser N, Gordon L. 1994. A Genealogy of *Dependency*: Tracing a Keyword of the U.S. Welfare State. *Signs* 19:309–36.

Freeman A. 1998. Antidiscrimination Law from 1954 to 1989: Uncertainty, Contradiction, Rationalization, Denial. In *The Politics of Law: A Progressive Critique*, ed. D Kairys. New York: Basic Books, pp. 285–311.

Freeman AD. 1982. Antidiscrimination Law: A Critical Review. In *The Politics of Law*, ed. D Kairys. New York: Pantheon Books, pp. 96–116.

Fried M. 1998. *Taking Time: Parental Leave Policy and Corporate Culture*. Philadelphia: Temple University Press.

Friedman LM. 1975. *The Legal System: A Social Science Perspective*. New York: Russell Sage.

Fuegen K, Biernat M, Haines E, Deaux K. 2004. Mothers and Fathers in the Workplace: How Gender and Parental Status Influence Judgments of Job-Related Competence. *Journal of Social Issues* 60:737–54.

Fullerton HNJ. 1999. Labor Force Participation: 75 Years of Change, 1950–98 and 1998–2025. *Monthly Labor Review* 122(12): 3–12.

Galanter M. 1974. Why the Haves Come Out Ahead: Speculations on the Limits of Legal Change. *Law and Society Review* 9:95–160.

Galanter M. 1975. Afterword: Explaining Litigation. *Law and Society Review* 9:347–68.

Galanter M. 1983. The radiating effects of courts. In *Empirical Theories About Courts*, ed. K. Boyum, L. Mather, New York: Longman, pp. 117–42.

Gerstel N, McGonagle K. 1999. Job Leaves and the Limits of the Family and Medical Leave Act: The Effects of Gender, Race and Family. *Work and Occupations* 26:510–34.

Giddens A. 1984. *The Constitution of Society*. Berkeley: University of California Press.

Gilles ME. 2000. Reinventing Structural Reform Litigation: Deputizing Private Citizens in the Enforcement of Civil Rights. *Columbia Law Review* 100:1384–1453.

Glass J. 2004. Blessing or Curse? Work-Family Policies and Mothers' Wage Growth over Time. *Work and Occupations* 31:367–94.

Glass J, Fujimoto T. 1995. Employer Characteristics and the Provision of Family Responsive Policies. *Work and Occupations* 22:380–411.

Gleeson BJ. 1997. Disability Studies: A Historical Materialist View. *Disability & Society* 12:179–202.

Goodstein JD. 1994. Institutional Pressures and Strategic Responsiveness: Employer Involvement in Work-Family Issues. *Academy of Management Journal* 37:350–82.

Gordon DM, Edwards R, Reich M. 1982. *Segmented Work, Divided Workers: The Historical Transformation of Labor in the United States.* Cambridge: Cambridge University Press.

Gordon L. 1990. The New Feminist Scholarship on the Welfare State. In *Women, the State, and Welfare,* ed. L Gordon, Madison: University of Wisconsin Press, pp. 9–35.

Gornick JC, Meyers MK. 2003. *Families that Work: Policies for Reconciling Parenthood and Employment.* New York: Russell Sage Foundation.

Green T. 2003. Discrimination in Workplace Dynamics: Toward a Structural Account of Disparate Treatment Theory. *Harvard Civil Rights-Civil Liberties Law Review* 38:91–157.

Gross SR, Syverud KD. 1991. Getting to No: A Study of Settlement Negotiations and the Selection of Cases for Trial. *Michigan Law Review* 90:319–93.

Guthrie D, Roth LM. 1999. The State, Courts, and Maternity Policies in U.S. Organizations: Specifying Institutional Mechanisms. *American Sociological Review* 64:41–63.

Gwartney-Gibbs PA. 1994. Gender and Workplace Dispute Resolution: A Conceptual and Theoretical Model. *Law and Society Review* 28:265–96.

Haas L, Hwang P. 1995. Company Culture and Men's Usage of Family Leave Benefits in Sweden. *Family Relations* 44:28–36.

Hadfield GK. 1992. Bias in the Evolution of Legal Rules. *Georgetown Law Journal* 80:583–616.

Hahn H. 1997. Advertising the Acceptably Employable Image. In *The Disability Studies Reader,* ed. LJ Davis. New York: Routledge, pp. 172–86

Hale TW, Hayghe HV, McNeil JM. 1998. Persons with Disabilities: Labor Market Activity, 1994. *Monthly Labor Review* (9):3–12.

Han W-j, Waldfogel J. 2003. Parental Leave: The Impact of Recent Legislation on Parents' Leave Taking. *Demography* 40:101–200.

Handler JF. 1978. *Social Movements and the Legal System: A Theory of Law Reform and Social Change.* New York: Academic Press.

Handler JF, Hollingsworth EJ, Erlanger HS. 1978. *Lawyers and the Pursuit of Legal Rights.* New York: Academic Press.

Hareven TK. 1982. *Family Time and Industrial Time: The Relationship between the Family and Work in a New England Industrial Community.* Cambridge: Cambridge University Press.

Harlan SL, Robert PM. 1998. The Social Construction of Disability in Organizations. *Work and Occupations* 25:397–435.

Hayghe HV. 1990. Family Members in the Workforce. *Monthly Labor Review* (3):14–46.

Hayghe HV. 1997. Developments in Women's Labor Force Participation. *Monthly Labor Review* (9):41–46.

Heimer CA. 1999. Competing Institutions: Law, Medicine, and Family in Neonatal Intensive Care. *Law and Society Review* 33:17–66.

Hiley DR, Bohman JF, Schusterman R, eds. 1991. *The Interpretive Turn: Philosophy, Science, Culture.* Ithaca: Cornell University Press.

Hirschman AO. 1970. *Exit, Voice, and Loyalty: Responses to Decline in Firms, Organizations, and States.* Cambridge: Harvard University Press.

Hochschild A. 1989. *The Second Shift.* New York: Avon Books.

Hochschild A. 1997. *The Time Bind: When Work Becomes Home and Home Becomes Work.* New York: Metropolitan Books.

Horwitz MJ. 1977. *The Transformation of American Law 1780–1860.* Cambridge: Harvard University Press.

Hunnicutt BK. 1988. *Work Without End: Abandoning Shorter Hours for the Right to Work.* Philadelphia: Temple University Press.

Hunnicutt BK. 1996. *Kellogg's Six-Hour Day.* Philadelphia: Temple University Press.

Jacobs JA, Gerson K. 2004. *The Time Divide: Work, Family, and Gender Inequality.* Cambridge: Harvard University Press.

Jacobsen JP, Levin LM. 1995. Effects of intermittent labor force attachment on women's earnings. *Monthly Labor Review* 118(9):14–19.

Jacoby SM. 1985. *Employing Bureaucracy: Managers, Unions and the Transformation of Work in American Industry, 1900–1945.* New York: Columbia University Press.

Jepperson RL. 1991. Institutions, Institutional Effects, and Institutionalism. In *The New Institutionalism in Organizational Analysis*, ed. WW Powell, PL DiMaggio, Chicago: University of Chicago Press, pp. 143–63.

Jolls C. 2001. Antidiscrimination and Accommodation. *Harvard Law Review* 115:642–99.

Judiesch MK, Lyness KS. 1999. Left behind? The Impact of Leaves of Absence on Managers' Career Success. *Academy of Management Journal* 42:641–51.

Kalev A, Kelly E, Dobbin F. 2006. Best Practices or Guesses? Assessing the Efficacy of Corporate Affirmative Action. *American Sociological Review* 71:589–617.

Kalleberg AL. 1995. Part-Time Work and Workers in the United States: Correlates and Policy Issues. *Washington and Lee Law Review* 52:771–98.

Kalleberg AL, Reskin BF, Hudson K. 2000. Bad Jobs in America: Standard and Nonstandard Employment Relations and Job Quality in the United States. *American Sociological Review* 65:256–78.

Kamerman SB, Kahn AJ, Kingston P. 1983. *Maternity Policies and Working Women*. New York: Columbia University Press.

Kelly EL. 2005. Discrimination Against Caregivers? Gendered Family Responsibilities, Employer Practices, and Work Rewards. In *Handbook of Employment Discrimination Research: Rights and Realities*, ed. LB Nielsen, R Nelson, New York: Springer, pp. 353–374.

Kelly EL, Kalev A. 2006. Managing Flexible Work Arrangements in U.S. Organizations: Formalized Discretion or "a Right to Ask." *Socio-Economic Review* 4:379–416.

Kessler-Harris A. 1982. *Out to Work: A History of Wage-Earning Women in the United States*. Oxford: Oxford University Press.

Kessler-Harris A. 2001. *In Pursuit of Equity: Women, Men and the Quest for Economic Citizenship in 20th-Century America*. Oxford: Oxford University Press.

Kittay EF. 1995. Taking Dependency Seriously: The Family and Medical Leave Act Considered in Light of the Social Organization of Dependency Work and Gender Equality. *Hypatia* 10:8–29.

Kluger R. 1976. *Simple Justice*. New York: Knopf.

Knight J, Ensminger J. 1998. Conflict over Changing Social Norms: Bargaining, Ideology, and Enforcement. In *The New Institutionalism in Sociology*, ed. MC Brinton, V Nee, New York: Russell Sage Foundation, pp. 105–26.

Krieger L. 2000. Afterword: Socio-Legal Backlash. *Berkeley Journal of Employment and Labor Law* 21:475–519.

Krieger LJ, Cooney PN. 1983. The Miller-Wohl Controversy: Equal Treatment, Positive Action and the Meaning of Women's Equality. *Gold Gate University Law Review* 13:513.

Kritzer H, Silbey S, eds. 2003. *In Litigation: Do the Haves Still Come Out Ahead?* Stanford: Stanford University Press.

Kritzer HM. 1986. Adjudication to Settlement: Shading in the Gray. *Judicature* 70:161–5.

Kudlick CJ. 2003. Disability History: Why We Need Another "Other." *American Historical Review* 108:763–93.

Landes WM, Posner RA. 1979. Adjudication as a Private Good. *Journal of Legal Studies* 8:235–84.

Law S. 1983. Women, Work, Welfare and the Preservation of Patriarchy. *University of Pennsylvania Law Review* 131:1249–339.

Lawrence C. 1987. The Id, The Ego, and Equal Protection: Reckoning with Unconscious Racism. *Stanford Law Review* 39:317.

Lempert R. 1998. A Resource Theory of the Criminal Law: Exploring When it Matters. In *How Does Law Matter*, ed. BG Garth, A Sarat, Evanston, IL: Northwestern University Press, pp. 227–47.

Lerner G, ed. 1972. *Black Women in White America: A Documentary History*. New York: Vintage Books.

Lipschultz S. 1989. Social Feminism and Legal Discourse: 1908–1923. *Yale Journal of Law and Feminism* 2:131–60.

Lipset SM. 1996. *American Exceptionalism: A Double-Edged Sword*. New York: W.W. Norton & Co.

Liu G. 1999. Social Security and the Treatment of Marriage: Spousal Benefits, Earnings Sharing, and the Challenge of Reform. *Wisconsin Law Review* 1999:1–64.

Lopez IFH. 1999–2000. Institutional Racism: Judicial Conduct and a New Theory of Racial Discrimination. *Yale Law Journal* 109:1717–884.

Louis Harris and Associates I. 1986. The ICD Survey of Disabled Americans: Bringing Disabled Americans Into the Mainstream, Conducted for the ICD-International Center for the Disabled, New York.

Macaulay S. 1963. Non-contractual Relations in Business: A Preliminary Study. *American Sociological Review* 28:55–68.

Maccoby E, Mnookin R. 1990. *Dividing the Child*. Cambridge: Harvard University Press.

MacKinnon C. 1987. *Feminism Unmodified: Discourses on Life and Law.* Cambridge: Harvard University Press.

MacKinnon CA. 1989. *Toward a Feminist Theory of the State.* Cambridge: Harvard University Press.

Maine HS. 1986. *Ancient Law.* Tucson: University of Arizona Press.

Malin MH. 1993–94. Fathers and Parental Leave. *Texas Law Review* 72:1047–95.

Marshall A-M. 1998. Closing the Gaps: Plaintiffs in Pivotal Sexual Harassment Cases. *Law and Social Inquiry* 23:761–93.

Marshall A-M. 2003. Injustice Frames, Legality, and the Everyday Construction of Sexual Harassment. *Law and Social Inquiry* 28:659–89.

Marshall A-M. 2005. Idle Rights: Employees' Rights Consciousness and the Construction of Sexual Harassment Policies. *Law and Society Review* 39:83–124.

Marshall TH. 1965. *Class, Citizenship and Social Development.* Garden City, NY: Doubleday.

May M. 1987. The Historical Problem of the Family Wage: The Ford Motor Company and the Five Dollar Day. In *Families and Work*, ed. N Gerstel, HE Gross, Philadelphia: Temple University Press, pp. 111–31.

McCann M. 1986. *Taking Reform Seriously.* Ithaca: Cornell University Press.

McCann M. 1994. *Rights at Work: Pay Equity Reform and the Politics of Legal Mobilization.* Chicago: University of Chicago Press.

McCann M. 2006. On Legal Rights Consciousness: A Challenging Analytical Tradition. In *The New Civil Rights Research: A Constitutive Approach*, ed. B Fleury-Steiner, LB Nielsen, Burlington, VT: Ashgate Press, pp. ix–xxx.

McNeil JM. August 1997. Americans with Disabilities: 1994–95, Current Population Reports P70–61, U.S. Department of Commerce Economics and Statistics Administration.

Mettler S. 1998. *Dividing Citizens: Gender and Federalism in New Deal Public Policy.* Ithaca, NY: Cornell University Press.

Meyer JW, Rowan B. 1977. Institutionalized Organizations: Formal Structure as Myth and Ceremony. *American Journal of Sociology* 83:340–63.

Miller RE, Sarat A. 1981. Grievances, Claims and Disputes: Assessing the Adversary Culture. *Law and Society Review* 15:525–66.

Mills HHG, Wright, C. ed. 1946. *From Max Weber.* New York: Oxford University Press.

Minow M. 1987. Interpreting Rights: An Essay for Robert Cover. *Yale Law Journal* 96:1860–915.

Mnookin R, Kornhauser L. 1979. Bargaining in the Shadow of the Law: The Case of Divorce. *Yale Law Journal* 88:950–97.

Montgomery D. 1976. Workers' Control of Machine Production in the Nineteenth Century. *Labor History* 17:485–509.

Montgomery D. 1987. *The Fall of the House of Labor: The Workplace, The State and American Labor Activism, 1865–1925.* Cambridge: Cambridge University Press.

Morgan PA. 1999. Risking Relationships: Understanding the Litigation Choices of Sexually Harassed Women. *Law and Society Review* 33:67–91.

Nelson B. 1990. The Origins of the Two-Channel Welfare State: Workmen's Compensation and Mother's Aid. In *Women, the State, and Welfare*, ed. L Gordon. Madison: University of Wisconsin Press, pp. 123–151.

Nelson R, Bridges WP. 1999. *Legalizing Gender Inequality: Courts, Markets, and Unequal Pay for Women in America.* Cambridge, UK: Cambridge University Press.

Nielsen LB. 2000. Situating Legal Consciousness: Experiences and Attitudes of Ordinary Citizens about Law and Street Harassment. *Law and Society Review* 34:1055.

Nielsen LB. 2004. *License to Harass.* Princeton: Princeton University Press.

North DC. 1990. *Institutions, Institutional Change and Economic Performance (Political Economy of Institutions and Decisions)* Cambridge, UK: Cambridge University Press.

Okin SM. 1989. *Justice, Gender and the Family.* New York: Basic Books, Inc.

Oliver M. 1990. *The Politics of Disablement: A Sociological Approach.* New York: St. Martin's Press.

Oliver PE, Johnston H. 2000. What a Good Idea! Ideologies and Frames in Social Movement Research. *Mobilization* 4:37–54.

Olson SM. 1992. Studying Federal District Courts Through Published Cases: A Research Note. *Justice System Journal* 15:782–800.

Orloff A. 2002. Explaining U.S. Welfare Reform: Power, Gender, Race and the U.S. Policy Legacy. *Critical Social Policy* 22:96–118.

Orren K. 1991. *Belated Feudalism: Labor, the Law, and Liberal Development in the United States.* Cambridge: Cambridge University Press.

Osterman P. 1995. Work/Family Programs and the Employment Relationship. *Administrative Science Quarterly* 40:681–700.

Pateman C. 1988. *The Sexual Contract*. Stanford: Stanford University Press.

Pierson P. 2000. Increasing Returns, Path Dependence, and the Study of Politics. *American Political Science Review* 94:251–67.

Pleck JH. 1993. Are "Family-Supportive" Employer Policies Relevant to Men? In *Men, Work, and Family*, ed. JC Hood, London: SAGE Publications, pp. 217–37.

Powell WW. 2007. The New Institutionalism. In *The International Encyclopedia of Organizational Studies*. Thousand Oaks, CA: Sage, Volume 3, pp. 975–78.

Powell WW, DiMaggio PJ, eds. 1991. *The New Institutionalism in Organizational Analysis*. Chicago: University of Chicago Press.

Presser HB. 2003. *Working in a 24/7 Economy: Challenges for American Families*. New York: Russell Sage Foundation.

Priest GL, Klein B. 1984. The Selection of Disputes for Litigation. *Journal of Legal Studies* 13:1–55.

Purcell D. 1997. The Public Right to Precedent: A Theory and Rejection of Vacatur. *California Law Review* 85:867–917.

Quadagno JS. 1994. *The Color of Welfare: How Racism Undermined the War on Poverty*. New York: Oxford University Press.

Quindlen A. 1992. Public & Private: A (Rest) Room of One's Own. *The New York Times*:A25.

Quinn BA. 2000. The Paradox of Complaining: Law, Humor, and Harassment in the Everyday Work World. *Law and Social Inquiry* 25:1151–85.

Reich CA. 1964. The New Property. *Yale Law Journal* 73:733–87.

Reskin B, Padavic I. 1994. *Women and Men at Work*. Thousand Oaks, CA: Pine Forge Press.

Robert P. 2003. Disability Oppression in the Contemporary U.S. Capitalist Workplace. *Science & Society* 67:136–59.

Roediger D, Foner P. 1989. *Our Own Time: A History of American Labor and the Working Day*. New York: Westport.

Rosenberg G. 1993. Hollow Hopes and Other Aspirations: A Reply to Feely and McCann. *Law and Social Inquiry* 17:761–78.

Rosenberg GN. 1991. *The Hollow Hope: Can Courts Bring About Social Change?* Chicago: University of Chicago Press.

Rothman DJ. 1971. *The Discovery of the Asylum: Social Order and Disorder in the New Republic*. Boston: Little, Brown.

Rubenstein WB. 2004. On What a "Private Attorney General" Is – and Why It Matters. *Vanderbilt Law Review* 57:2129–2173.

Rubin E, Feeley M. 1996. Creating Legal Doctrine. *Southern California Law Review* 69:1989–2037.

Ruggie M. 1984. *The State and Working Women: A Comparative Study of Britain and Sweden.* Princeton, NJ: Princeton University Press.

Ruhm CJ. 1997. Policy Watch: The Family and Medical Leave Act. *Journal of Economic Perspectives* 11:175–86.

Ruhm CJ. 1998. The Economic Consequences of Parental Leave Mandates: Lessons from Europe. *Quarterly Journal of Economics* 113:285–317.

Russell M. 1998. *Beyond Ramps: Disability at the End of the Social Contract.* Monroe, ME: Common Courage Press.

Russell M. 2001. Disablement, Oppression, and the Political Economy. *Journal of Disability Policy Studies* 12:87–95.

Russell M. 2002. What Disability Civil Rights Cannot Do: Employment and Political Economy. *Disability & Society* 17:117–35.

Rutherglen G. 1987. Disparate Impact Under Title VII: An Objective Theory of Discrimination. *Virginia Law Review* 73:1297–1345.

Sarat A, Kearns TS. 1993. Beyond the Great Divide: Forms of Legal Scholarship and Everyday Life. In *Law in Everyday Life*, ed. A Sarat, TR Kearns. Ann Arbor, MI: University of Michigan Press, pp. 21–61.

Scheingold SA. 1974. *The Politics of Rights.* New Haven: Yale University Press, 224 pp.

Scheppele KL. 1994. Legal Theory and Social Theory. *Annual Review of Sociology* 20:383–406.

Schneiberg M, Soule SA. 2005. Institutionalization as a Contested Multilevel Process. In *Social Movements and Organization Theory*, ed. C. Davis et al. New York: Cambridge University Press, pp. 122–160.

Scotch RK. 1984. *From Good Will to Civil Rights: Transforming Federal Disability Policy.* Philadelphia: Temple University Press.

Scott WR. 1995. *Institutions and Organizations.* Thousand Oaks: Sage Publications.

Sellers C. 1992. *The Market Revolution: Jacksonian America, 1815–1846.* New York: Oxford University Press.

Selznick P. 1969. *Law, Society and Industrial Justice.* New Brunswick, NJ: Transaction.

Sewell WH. 1992. A Theory of Structure: Duality, Agency, and Transformation. *American Journal of Sociology* 98:1–29.

Shapiro JP. 1993. *No Mercy: People with Disabilities Forging a New Civil Rights Movement*. New York: Times Books.

Siegel R. 1985. Employment Equality under the Pregnancy Discrimination Act of 1978. *Yale Law Journal* 94:929–56.

Siegel R. 2000. Discrimination in the Eyes of the Law: How "Color Blindness" Discourse Disrupts and Rationalizes Social Stratification. *California Law Review* 88:77–118.

Siegel RB. 1994. Home As Work: The First Woman's Rights Claims Concerning Wives' Household Labor, 1850–1880. *Yale Law Journal* 103:1073–217.

Siegelman P, Donohue JJ. 1990. Studying the Iceberg From Its Tip: A Comparison of Published and Unpublished Employment Discrimination Cases. *Law and Society Review* 24:1133–70.

Silbey S, Sarat A. 1989. Dispute Processing in Law and Legal Scholarship: From Institutional Critique to the Reconstruction of the Juridical Subject. *Denver University Law Review* 66:437–98.

Skocpol T. 1992. *Protecting Soldiers and Mothers: The Political Origins of Social Policy in the United States*. Cambridge, MA: The Belknap Press of Harvard University Press.

Slavitt H. 1995. Selling the Integrity of the System of Precedent: Selective Publication, Depublication, and Vacatur. *Harvard Civil Rights-Civil Liberties Law Review* 30:109–42.

Smith-Rosenberg C. 1985. *Disorderly Conduct: Visions of Gender in Victorian America*. New York: Knopf.

Smith DE. 1987. Women's Inequality and the Family. In *Families and Work*, ed. N Gerstel, He Gross, Philadelphia: Temple University Press, pp. 23–54.

Snow DA, E. Burke Rochford J, Worden SK, Benford RD. 1986. Frame Alignment Processes, Micromobilization, and Movement Participation. *American Sociological Review* 51:464–81.

Songer DR, Smith D, Sheehan RS. 1989. Nonpublication in the Eleventh Circuit: An Empirical Analysis. *Florida State University Law Review* 16:963–84.

Steinfeld RJ. 1991. *The Invention of Free Labor: The Employment Relation in English and American Law and Culture, 1350–1870*. Chapel Hill: University of North Carolina Press.

Stone DA. 1984. *The Disabled State*. Philadelphia: Temple University Press.

Strauss DA. 1989. Discriminatory Intent and the Taming of *Brown*. *University of Chicago Law Review* 56:935–1015.

Sturm S. 2001. Second Generation Employment Discrimination: A Structural Approach. *Columbia Law Review* 101:458–568.

Suchman M. 1997. On Beyond Interest: Rational, Normative and Cognitive Perspectives in the Social Scientific Study of Law. *Wisconsin Law Review* 1997:475–501.

Suchman MC, Edelman LB. 1996. Legal Rational Myths: The New Institutionalism and the Law and Society Tradition. *Law and Social Inquiry* 21:903–41.

Sunstein CR. 1996. On the Expressive Function of Law. *University of Pennsylvania Law Review* 144:2021–53.

Swidler A. 1986. Culture in Action: Symbols and Strategies. *American Sociological Review* 51:273–86.

Taub N, Williams WW. 1985. Will Equality Require More Than Assimilation, Accommodation, or Separation from the Existing Social Structure? *Rutgers Law Review* 37:825–844.

Thomas C. 2002. Disability Theory: Key Ideas, Issues and Thinkers. In *Disability Studies Today*, ed. MO Colin Barnes, Len Barton. Cambridge: Polity Press, pp. 38–57.

Thompson BH. 2000. The Continuing Innovation of Citizen Enforcement. *University of Illinois Law Review* 2000:185–236.

Thompson EP. 1967. Time, Work-discipline, and Industrial Capitalism. *Past and Present* 38:56–97.

Tomlins CL. 1993. *Law, Labor and Ideology in the Early American Republic*. Cambridge, UK: Cambridge University Press.

Trubek DM, Sarat A, Felstiner WLF, Kritzer HM, Grossman JB. 1983. The Costs of Ordinary Litigation. *UCLA Law Review* 31:72–127.

Trzcinski E, Alpert WT. 1990. Leave Policies in Small Business: Findings from the U.S. Small Business Administration Employee Leave Survey, U.S. Small Business Administration, Office of Advocacy, Washington, D.C.

Tucker J. 1993. Everyday Forms of Employee Resistance. *Sociological Forum* 8:25–45.

Tushnet M. 1984. An Essay on Rights. *Texas Law Review* 62:1363–403.

Tushnet MV. 1994. *Making Civil Rights Law: Thrugood Marshall and the Supreme Court, 1936–1961*. New York: Oxford University Press.

Tyler T. 1990. *Why People Obey the Law*. New Haven: Yale University Press.

United States Commission on Civil Rights. September 1983. *Accommodating the Spectrum of Individual Abilities*: Clearinghouse Publication 81.

Valenze D. 1995. *The First Industrial Woman*. New York: Oxford University Press.

Waldfogel J. 1997. The Effect of Children on Women's Wages. *American Sociological Review* 62:209–17.

Waldfogel J. 1999a. Family leave coverage in the 1990s. *Monthly Labor Review* 122(10):13–21.

Waldfogel J. 1999b. The Impact of the Family and Medical Leave Act. *Journal of Policy Analysis and Management* 18:281–302.

Waldfogel J. 2001. Family and medical leave: evidence from the 2000 surveys. *Monthly Labor Review* 124(9):17–23.

Waldrop J, Stern SM. 2003. Disability Status: 2000. *Rep. C2KBR-17*, U.S. Census Bureau, Washington, D.C.

Walsh DJ. 1997. On the Meaning and Pattern of Legal Citations: Evidence from State Wrongful Discharge Precedent Cases. *Law and Society Review* 31:337–60.

Wanner C. 1975. The Public Ordering of Private Relations Part Two: Winning Civil Court Cases. *Law and Society Review* Winter 1975:293–306.

Wayne JH, Cordeiro BL. 2003. Who is a Good Organizational Citizen? Social Perception of Male and Female Employees Who Use Family Leave. *Sex Roles* 49:233–46.

Weber M. 1930. *The Protestant Ethic and the Spirit of Capitalism*. London: Unwin Hyman, 292 pp.

Welter B. 1966. The Cult of True Womanhood: 1820–1860. *American Quarterly* 18:151–74.

Whaples R. 1990. Winning the Eight-Hour Day, 1909–1919. *Journal of Economic History* 50:393–406.

Wheeler S, Cartwright B, Kagan RA, Friedman LM. 1987. Do the "Haves" Come Out Ahead? Winning and Losing in State Supreme Courts, 1870–1970. *Law and Society Review* 21:403–45.

Whipp R. 1987. "A Time to Every Purpose": An Essay on Time and Work. In *The Historical Meanings of Work*, ed. P Joyce, Cambridge, UK: Cambridge University Press, pp. 210–36.

Williams J. 2000. *Unbending Gender: Why Families and Work Conflict and What to Do About It*. Oxford: Oxford University Press.

Williams JC, Segal N. 2003. Beyond the Maternal Wall: Relief for Family Caregivers Who Are Discriminated Against on the Job. *Harvard Women's Law Journal* 26:77–162.

Williams P. 1991. *The Alchemy of Race and Rights.* Cambridge, MA: Harvard University Press.

Yngvesson B. 1988. Making Law at the Doorway: The Clerk, the Court, and the Construction of Community in a New England Town. *Law and Society Review* 22:409–48.

Zemans F. 1984. Fee Shifting and the Implementation of Public Policy. *Law and Contemporary Problems* 1984:187–210.

Zemans FK. 1983. Legal Mobilization: The Neglected Role of the Law in the Political System. *American Political Science Review* 77:690–703.

Zucker LG. 1991. Institutionalization and Cultural Persistence. In *The New Institutionalism in Organizational Analysis*, ed. WW Powell, PJ DiMaggio. Chicago: University of Chicago Press, pp. 83–107.

Index